.

LIBRARY OF NEW TESTAMENT STUDIES

442

formerly the Journal for the Study of the New Testament Supplement series

Editor

Mark Goodacre

ABUSE, POWER AND FEARFUL OBEDIENCE

Reconsidering 1 Peter's Commands to Wives

Jennifer G. Bird

t & t clark

Published by T&T Clark International
A Continuum imprint
The Tower Building, 11 York Road, London SE1 7NX
80 Maiden Lane, Suite 704, New York, NY 10038

www.continuumbooks.com

British Library Cataloguing-in-Publication Data
A catalogue record for this book is available from the British Library

ISBN: HB: 978-0-567-42750-2

Typeset by Pindar NZ, Auckland, New Zealand
Printed and bound in the United States of America

To all females whose trust in the Christian bible
has contributed to, instead of freed them from,
their experience of frightening things.

CONTENTS

ACKNOWLEDGEMENTS

This work would not have been possible, much less imaginable, without the work of the wo/men who have gone before me: speaking truth to power, hearing voices into speech, and creating spaces of new ways of being in the world.

I am deeply indebted to my advisor, Fernando F. Segovia, for his continually supportive and directive feedback in the process of writing my dissertation, upon which this manuscript depends heavily. His feedback showed me how to do this work and encouraged me to find my voice, which is singularly noteworthy given the typical experience in graduate studies in this field. Fernando's work ethos and enduring graciousness has continued to be an example for me, as a professor, a scholar, and a human being. Elisabeth Schüssler Fiorenza threw me a life-preserver as I was drowning in the sea of malestream scholarship and ethos of graduate studies, and has continued to believe in me ever since — a vote of confidence I feel I neither earned nor deserve, but embrace freely. I am even more so deeply indebted to her scholarship and am constantly thankful for the courageous work she has done and consistently continues to do. Robert Barsky gave me space to make the connections in writing that I was making in my mind, noteworthy for the respect he offered me in doing so. I am also keenly aware that I am able to speak of women claiming their own voices and lives because my parents, Marianne and Jennings, taught me to do likewise.

The main focus on the abusiveness of this passage would not have been as pointed or informed without Susan Hall, LMHC, and her explanations of the relevant issues of coercion, aggression, violence and abuse that come up within this passage of 1 Peter, and her recommended research on these matters.

There are numerous friends, family members and colleagues who have been voices of support and affirmation at crucial moments, often unbeknownst to them. Among the family members are Carol Purvis, Mark Bird, Patrick Bird, Lise Rowe, David and Karina Bird, Katie Freeman, the Israel Family: Pam, Jeff, Jeremy and Jessica, and of course my parents, Marianne and Jennings Bird. Many people at Greensboro College — both departmental and otherwise — have been supportive colleagues and examples of diligence in the realm of teaching without losing a passion for their scholarship. The support of my friends over the past few years is at times beyond my ability to express. My utmost gratitude and gratefulness go to Bridget Saladino, Emy and Dave

Hollander, Ebony Staton Weidmann, Hollis Gabriel, Sara Koenig, Brian Hughes, Juan Escarfuller, Anni Judkins, and Jennifer Fouse.

Joe Marchal's words of encouragement and challenge have been repeatedly precisely the words needed to get over the next hurdle. My deepest thanks, Joe. I am also grateful for the numerous brief yet supportive and inspiring encounters with professional colleagues, such as James Crossley, Melanie Johnson-DeBaufre, Denise Kimber Buell, Davina Lopez, Shelly Matthews, Stephen Moore, Todd Penner, Christina Petterson, Erin Runions and Caroline Vander Stichele, and for people I may never see again who heard the message of this manuscript and appreciated its value. Those votes of confidence and appreciation help keep me invested in and connected to this work.

Introduction

> The history of effects shows that texts have power and therefore cannot be separated from their consequences.[1]

The idea that new testament texts reflect and even embody the cultural milieu out of which they came is not a new or debated proposition. What does seem to be a matter of debate is how and to what extent we are to take these social, political, economic, gendered, and religious dynamics into consideration when trying to understand these writings. Since the texts of the early church had a wide range of implications within their original contexts, I think it is important that we bring as many of these contextual factors to bear on an understanding or interpretation of them.

This particular project is the result of a culmination of diverse experiences both within and outside Christian communities and churches. Growing up as both an active leader and a female within Christian communities, I eventually began to wrestle with theological and ideological questions concerning the texts, doctrines, theologies and traditions of my faith communities. Certainly these are complicated and multi-faceted issues, involving symbolic and political power and language, matters of authorship and pseudonymity, and canonization and tradition to name a few of the pieces of the puzzle. To be sure, though, this wrestling was and always has been a matter of "faith seeking understanding."

That first semester of my doctoral work is indelibly written into my memory. I was enrolled in a seminar on 1 Peter, which had me translating and "interpreting" this letter on a daily basis while listening to a disturbing evening ritual. A young couple, my upstairs neighbors, fought more nights of the week than not. These arguments started with verbal abuse, issued by both partners, and usually ended with the young woman being beaten or thrown around by her lover, who also was the father of her child. Another neighbor, who volunteered at a woman's shelter, warned me not to get involved, as this would most likely create more problems for the young woman. Needless to say, I was stunned and

---

1. Ulrich Luz, *Matthew in History: Interpretation, Influence, and Effects* (Minneapolis: Fortress, 1994), 33.

somewhat paralyzed by the seriousness of the situation, and wondered when I would see the abused woman carried out on a stretcher.

While others in the 1 Peter seminar took to their studies with admirable "objective" perspectives, I could not help but wonder if the woman I heard was scared into staying in part because of socio-religious beliefs that told her that her suffering made her Christ-like and she might "win over" her partner if she would patiently forgive him and bear the abuse: thoughts drawn directly from the second and third chapter of 1 Peter. Being in a culture highly influenced by evangelical and often fundamentalist Christianity, even if this young woman did not hold those specific theological beliefs, it was quite likely that she had bought into a social script that maintained similar expectations of her. No amount of parsing and translation kept me from making the connection between the content of the household code in 1 Peter and the modern-day multi-layered stigma surrounding the choice a woman makes between staying in or escaping an abusive situation.

Knowing that today there are many other factors beyond religious — such as matters of survival, political interests in traditional family units, lack of self-worth — that make deciding whether to stay or leave an abusive relationship quite difficult, I began to realize that just as those "non-religious" dynamics were playing out in the apartment above me, they were also a part of households in the first century, thus were implicitly present in the *Haustafel* of 1 Peter. Regardless of the fact that it was faith communities that were being addressed by this letter, economic, political, and cultural pressures and expectations were also present in the manifest problems and the language chosen for the proposed solution. I saw in 1 Peter an imitation of the kyriarchal domestic codes, a social construct regarding the management of households, which were discussed by various philosophers of ancient Greece because of their importance in maintaining social stability. I was clearly in need of a methodology that would allow me to sufficiently engage numerous dimensions of this or any other text.

Homi Bhabha's concepts of ambivalence, mimicry, and hybridity became useful vocabulary for creating a framework for discussing the ideological implications of the adaptation of various aspects of the surrounding culture within the Christian movement.[2] The extensive work of Elisabeth Schüssler Fiorenza is primary in forming my feminist voice in engaging biblical passages, most specifically noted in what she calls a "hermeneutics of suspicion"

2.   Homi Bhabha, *The Location of Culture* (New York: Routledge, 1994), Chapter 4 in particular. See also, Gayatri Spivak, *A Critique of Postcolonial Reason: Toward a History of the Vanishing Present* (Cambridge, Mass.: Harvard University, 1999) and Edward Said, *Orientalism* (New York: Vintage Books, 1994), and Said, *Culture and Imperialism* (New York: Vintage, 1994).

when engaging both "contemporary androcentric interpretations of the Bible and the biblical texts themselves."[3] Finally Rosemary Hennessy's materialist feminist work provided vocabulary for engaging and critiquing the subject(s) discursively constructed by this or any other biblical text.[4]

1 Peter has yet to be thoroughly analyzed through the matrix of gender role, socio-political and materialist discourses, with a view toward the implications such an analysis has for the church and its relation to Empire. Given these lacunae and the work that can be done simply focused upon the *Haustafel* in 1 Peter, I will offer a feminist, postcolonial, materialist method for engaging biblical texts and apply it to 1 Pet. 3.1-6 and its surrounding material. This project combines a suspicion of the patriarchal and kyriarchal context in which this letter was written, an awareness of the political influences of Roman occupation in Asia Minor on both the problem and the way it is addressed in this letter, and the experience of witnessing the socio-cultural expectations of the letter still at work in the world today.

The author of 1 Peter adapts aspects of a Greco-Roman socio-cultural expectation, that of the hierarchically ordered relations within households, and prescribes this adaptation for the behavior of certain members of the religious communities. Though the exhortations are related to behavior in their own homes, drawing upon household relationships in discussing faithful discipleship blurs the line between family households and the religious "family" gathered in households. As a result, the structure of the basic communal unit within burgeoning Christianity mimics the basic unit of the State.[5]

I argue that such a move has socio-political implications that lead to collusion with Empire, thus, 1 Peter is one of many texts in the Christian canon that perpetuate imperial ideology. It also constructs women's subjectivity and agency in terms of their silent Christ-like suffering, and circumscribes them within the household domain. The issue of "silencing" the wives addressed in the household code may be understandable given the sustainability of the movement that the author was trying to ensure. It is worth an extended discussion, however, given that there are several parallels between the tone and

---

3.   Elisabeth Schüssler Fiorenza, *Bread Not Stone: The Challenge of Feminist Biblical Interpretation* (Boston: Beacon, 1995), xii.

4.   Rosemary Hennessy, *Materialist Feminism and the Politics of Discourse* (New York: Routledge, 1993).

5.   There is a great deal of scholarship on the issue of the development in the Christian movement, in terms of its purpose and its leadership. I am granting a basic premise that letters written to communities in Asia Minor from a missionary or leader in Rome suggests a significantly different structure than what we see or have evidence for in the "grass roots" movement begun by Jesus. While I understand that my designation "grass roots" is not univocally agreed upon, it serves to highlight the significant swing from organic movement to what we begin to see in the structured and house-based gatherings.

positionality of the author to the wives, noted in this short segment of 1 Peter, and dynamics that often characterize abusive relationships.

While I fully agree with Musa Dube in her clarion call to feminist biblical scholars to be conscious of producing interpretations that "resist and reject kyriarchal oppression and allow the experiences and voices of colonized people to articulate a liberative interpretation,"[6] I am consciously not including such redemptive and resistant readings at this point. I am choosing to remain with the colonizing effect the texts have over females because the materialist aspect of my critique requires it, and because I think that this piece is often overlooked in the effort to get to redemptive interpretations. In order to address the symptoms, the problem must be aired and named for what it is.

6.	Musa W. Dube, *Postcolonial Feminist Interpretation of the Bible* (St. Louis: Chalice, 2000), 43.

1

LAYING THE FOUNDATION: A HISTORY OF THE SCHOLARSHIP

State of 1 Peter Studies

In the mid-1970s John Elliott sounded a clarion call to all who would listen, asking for a rehabilitation of the exegetical stepchild, the letter of 1 Peter.[1] Whatever aspect of 1 Peter that would be the focus of successive studies, this article would be noted as a significant piece of the renewed interest in this letter. One can only surmise the motivations behind Elliott's "rehabilitation" article. What we do know is that in part he was responding to the social climate in the way that biblical studies in general do. Though the response may take a decade or so, the issues that are raised in the public/social realm of the educated Western society eventually enter into the realm of biblical studies, bringing with them new questions to take to the texts. I will address the early scholarship and the "post-1981" scholarship separately in what follows.

Early Scholarship

Prior to this clarion call, there had been two main realms of scholarship on 1 Peter: one debating the letter's genre and the other its sources. At the end of the nineteenth century, Adolf von Harnack declared that the letter of 1 Peter was initially a sermon, to which the opening and closing pieces were added later for the sake of circulation.[2] Not 15 years later, Perdelwitz added that it was not just any sermon, but a baptismal homily in particular. He also had a hunch that it was crafted specifically with those "converting" from mystery cults in mind.[3] Though later scholars do not all agree on this mystery cult influence, several echoed the baptismal homily idea. Then Edward Selwyn, in the late

---

1. John Hall Elliott, "The Rehabilitation of an Exegetical Step-Child: 1 Peter in Recent Research," *JBL* 95/2 (1976): 243–54.
2. Adolf von Harnack, *Die Chronologie der altchristlichen Litteratur bis Irenaus* vol. 1 (2nd ed.; Leipzig: Hinrichs, 1897), 451–65.
3. Richard Perdelwitz, *Die Mysterienreligion und das Problem des I. Petrusbriefes: Ein literarischer und religionsgeschichtlicher Versuch* (Giessen: Töpelmann, 1911).

1940s suggested that 1 Peter was initially an encyclical letter.[4] Other scholars would chime in that the baptism aspect was not central to the entire letter, thus should not be noted as the overall purpose as some had suggested.[5]

The middle of the twentieth century saw discussions regarding the sources for this letter. Affirming the idea that 1 Peter was not a homily but was initially put together as a letter, Eduard Lohse noted that the aporias within the text, the strange jumps or breaks in it, are attributable to the author drawing upon various sources.[6] After him, Helmut Millauer also noted the two particular strands of thought, what he called the *Leidenstheologie*, regarding the author's depiction of suffering in the letter. There was suffering as a result of the judgment of the elect for their deeds in this world, something that built upon martyr traditions; and there was a strand of innocent suffering of the elect for the sake of identifying with the Christ.[7] Leonhard Goppelt picked up on this assessment of suffering in 1 Peter, emphasizing that the issue was not the suffering per se, but that the community was to persevere in following Christ in spite of the persecution.[8]

In the early 1980s John Elliott and David Balch each contributed volumes to the corpus on 1 Peter,[9] which changed the primary focus of malestream[10] Petrine scholarship from issues of authorship, dating, and the use of baptismal liturgy, to socio-critical concerns, specifically how to handle the implications

---

4.   Edward Gordon Selwyn, *The First Epistle of Saint Peter: The Greek Text with Introduction, Notes and Essays* (London: Macmillan, 1946).

5.   Francis Wright Beare, *The First Epistle of Peter: The Greek Text with Translation and Notes* (Oxford: B. Blackwell, 1947); Hans Windisch, *Die katholischen Briefe* (dritte Auflage von Herbert Preisker; Tübingen: J.C.B. Mohr, 1951), 49–82. David Hill, "On Suffering and Baptism in 1 Peter," *NovT* 18 (1976): 181–89.

6.   Eduard Lohse, *Märtyer und Gottesknecht; Untersuchungen zur urchristlichen Verkündigung vom Sühntod Jesu Christi* (Göttingen, Vandenhoeck & Ruprecht, 1955), 201.

7.   Helmut Millauer, *Leiden als Gnade: eine traditionsgeschichtliche Untersuchung zur Leidenstheologie des ersten Petrusbriefes* (Bern: Herbert Lang, 1976).

8.   Leonhard Goppelt, *A Commentary on 1 Peter* (John E. Alsup, trans.; Grand Rapids: Eerdmans, 1993; *Der erste Petrusbrief*, Göttingen: Vandenhoeck & Ruprecht, 1978).

9.   David Balch, *Let Wives be Submissive: The Domestic Code in 1 Peter* (SBLMS 26. Chico: Scholars Press, 1981), and John Elliott, *A Home for the Homeless: A Social-Scientific Criticism of 1 Peter, Its Situation and Strategy* (Philadelphia: Fortress, 1981).

10.   Elisabeth Schüssler Fiorenza explains that this play on words is not a pejorative but a descriptive term. The discourses that are usually referred to as "mainstream" are typically defined by and therefore benefit certain males. Because the main-/malestream we are discussing is that of Western biblical scholarship, I must also point out that these males are typically white, heterosexual, and elite, and contribute scholarly interpretations of biblical passages that are notably more positivistic than critical. Thus, in this discussion, the point is that any scholar — male, female or otherwise — can employ malestream language. It is quite common to see someone who is harmed by such language, knowledge, or power, taking it up as her/his own, simply because that is what she/he has been socialized, and now theologically grounded, to use; see Schüssler Fiorenza, *Rhetoric and Ethic: The Politics of Biblical Studies* (Minneapolis: Fortress, 1999), 1–14.

of the identity of the recipients as "aliens and exiles" (in 1.1 and 2.11, per Elliott) and how the presence of the "domestic code" affects interpretation (per Balch).[11] What both men were aiming for was a step beyond historical-critical studies, one that would take social, political and cultural dynamics into consideration.

Elliott applied his interest in social-scientific studies, noted by his book *What is Social-Scientific Criticism?*,[12] to the task of determining the make-up of the community. His primary question asks how we are to understand the use of terms such as *paroikoi, parepidēmos, eklektos*, and *hagioi*. He claims that the use of *parepidēmos* indicated that the people were actually transient, or were not native to that area, so they were already identifying with the socio-political labels of stranger or alien before they became a part of the Christian community. With this in mind, the author used *oikos* terminology to give these "homeless" people a new identity as the people of God in the household of God. While this interpretation has fantastic theological application today, in embracing all who are homeless, literally or figuratively, it does not address the social and relational implications of household dynamics that were simultaneously a part of these directives, much less the ramifications for the church when it maintains such hierarchies and inequalities.

Balch, as his title *Let Wives be Submissive: The Domestic Code in I Peter* implies, also applies an approach that takes seriously the context of the communities addressed in the letter, and the possible influence of popular and philosophical writings of the day on the content of 1 Peter. He concludes that the letter of 1 Peter was an apologetic and that the use of the household code was a move to encourage acculturation and assimilation. He also sees in the adaptation of the household code in new testament texts a subtle critique of Aristotelian patriarchal (kyriarchal) relations and a continuation of the "egalitarian" Jesus tradition. At times, slaves and women were held up as exemplary members and the household code is directed not simply toward the *paterfamilias* but to other specific household members. This is a new twist, to be sure.

In spite of Balch's noted criticism of the trajectory within the history of the church that has misinterpreted these passages in ways that take away freedoms from women and slaves, the problem remains that these texts are open to such "misinterpretation" because they do embody the kyriarchal socio-political ethos in which these texts were written. There are additional pieces of the

11. Torrey Seland suggests that the "aliens and exiles" terminology indicates that many of the members of these communities were proselytes. Torrey Seland, *Strangers in the Light: Philonic Perspectives on Christian Identity in 1 Peter* (Boston: Brill, 2005), 39–78.

12. John Hall Elliott, *What is Social-Scientific Criticism?* (Minneapolis: Fortress, 1993).

development that Balch could have critiqued, including the language used that defines some members of the assemblies as wives and slaves. This is a striking move in light of Paul's declaration in Galatians 3 that renders such defining characteristics inconsequential within these communities.[13]

While these two scholars and their respective contributions focus on two separate parts of 1 Peter, they each maintain the "correctness" of their own approach and the limitations of the other's for grasping the overall theme of the letter, which can be seen in a dialogue between the two in *Perspectives on First Peter*.[14] These two scholars exemplify that fascinating dynamic at work in most malestream scholarship, which is that "the" interpretation of a given passage must be determined and claimed, instead of, for instance, discussing if the letter itself is useful for liberative and life-sustaining work or whether this text needs to be questioned because of its potentially oppressive and dominating effects upon people. It is in the next phase of scholarship that we see these latter interests addressed.

Post-1981 Scholarship

In the work done after 1981, five foci can be identified: 1) discerning the precipitating circumstances for the letter and the make-up of the initial recipients, 2) addressing Christological content, 3) assessing the letter from a literary or rhetorical perspective, 4) analyzing its social and theological implications, and 5) naming the typically feminist concerns. The fifth category is relegated to the "Uniqueness of 1 Peter's *Haustafel*" section, given that the majority of the content for feminist concerns is all unique to 1 Peter.[15] It is worth noting that feminist work does not necessarily fall under the easily named categories of genre, source, author, date, and so forth. Any of these scholars may touch on one or several of these traditional topics, but only to the extent that it opens doors into deeper concerns.[16]

---

13. The point in Galatians 3.28 that I emphasize is Schüssler Fiorenza's point about what Paul is doing here. He is not simply saying that we should not regard one another according to "Jew" or "Gentile" associations, slave or free, and male and female. Rather, the issue, for Schüssler Fiorenza, is that the roles and identities associated with each of those labels within the socio-political realm do not apply within the body of Christ. Thus, "male and female" connotations, roles, prescriptions and expectations do not hold within the *ekklesia*.

14. Charles Talbert, ed., *Perspectives on First Peter* (NABPR, Special Study Series 9; Macon: Mercer University, 1986).

15. There is relatively little done with the mention of the "co-elect woman" at the end of the letter. See Judith K. Applegate, "The Co-Elect Woman of 1 Peter," in *A Feminist Companion to the Catholic Epistles and Hebrews* (Amy-Jill Levine, with Maria Mayo Robbins, eds; Cleveland: Pilgrim, 2004), 89–102.

16. Mark Dubis, "Research on 1 Peter: A Survey of Scholarly Literature Since 1985," *Currents in Biblical Scholarship* 4/2 (2006): 199–239. Mark Dubis highlights quite nicely, and presumably unintentionally, the (un)natural divide between traditional malestream scholarship and anything that stands outside

Precipitating Circumstances and Initial Recipients

With a renewed interest in the impact of the context on the letter, scholars tried to assess the circumstances that inspired the letter and the make-up of the community in general. Most notably, in addition to Balch and Elliott's work, were the contributions of Paul Achtemeier, Reinhard Feldmeier, and Elisabeth Schüssler Fiorenza.[17] Achtemeier, countering both Elliott and Balch, interprets the *paroikoi* and *oikos* terminology as a part of the larger controlling metaphor, and thus not something to be taken literally, and suggests that acculturation cannot be in view, since the community members are encouraged to make a break with their past way of life. Reinhard Feldmeier focuses upon the *parepidemoi* ("strangers") designation as it resonates with passages in the Hebrew bible where a stranger was someone who did not know the God of the Israelites. The application of it here is an ironic one because now the strangers are the chosen people of God. The issue, according to Feldmeier, is not one of either straight assimilation or sectarian division, but of who is in and who is outside the people of God.[18]

For Schüssler Fiorenza, however, the terms *parepidemos* and *paroikoi* are somewhat ambiguous, but primarily accentuate the political-individual aspect of the recipients.[19] Furthermore, she insists that it is necessary to delineate one's overall interpretive framework and method before making claims regarding the nuances of the meanings intended by the use of the terms *parepidemos* and *paroikoi*.[20] In other words, the relative sub-ordinate status of the recipients, noted by the terms used, which has caused their suffering to begin with, is reinscribed by the letter and ensures that the communities will be marked by kyriarchal relations of dominance. Schüssler Fiorenza sufficiently problematizes the labels, in contrast with other scholars who valorize, or at the very least accept as beneficial, these sub-ordinating labels.

---

of those rigid confines. In his 2006 "comprehensive bibliography" of scholarship on 1 Peter since 1985, there is not a single "feminist" contribution listed, though most feminist work on 1 Peter falls into those intervening 20 years. His bibliography is a perfect example of the way hegemonic malestream scholarship perpetuates the false idea that feminist critical scholarship, among many voices in biblical scholarship, is peripheral and thus secondary to or inconsequential for traditional biblical studies.

17. Paul Achtemeier, "Newborn Babes and Living Stones: Literal and Figurative in 1 Peter," in *To Touch the Text: Biblical and Related Studies in Honor of Joseph A. Fitzmyer* (Maurya P. Horgan and Paul J. Kobelski, eds; New York: Crossroad, 1989), 207–36. Reinhard Feldmeier, *Die Christen als Fremde: Die Metapher der Fremde in der antiken Welt, im Urchristentum und im 1. Petrusbrief* (WUNT, 64. Tübingen: Mohr-Siebeck, 1992). Elisabeth Schüssler Fiorenza, "1 Peter," in *A Postcolonial Commentary of the New Testament* (The Bible and Postcolonialism Series; Fernando F. Segovia and R. S. Sugirtharajah, eds; Sheffield: Sheffield Academic, 2007), 380–403.

18. Feldmeier, *Die Christen als Fremde*, esp. 92–6.

19. Schüssler Fiorenza, "1 Peter," 383, 386–89.

20. Ibid., 389.

1 Peter's Christological Content
Next, the Christology of the letter serves as an overarching topic that includes the issue of suffering and discipleship.[21] For Goppelt the letter was written to encourage faithfulness in following after Christ, no matter the circumstances. Christ in his sufferings stood as an example to follow, though Christians' suffering would have different ends, as it could not be salvific as Christ's was.[22] Stephen Bechtler, drawing upon Victor Turner's concept of liminality, sees the Christian communities as living in a temporal and socio-political liminal state. God bestows on these people a new form of honor through the suffering they were experiencing due to their religious beliefs; it is an honor that will sustain them in their state of liminality.[23] Sharon Pearson represents those who study the Hebrew bible hymnic sections of the letter, all of which she sees as Christological.[24] Hers is a study that addresses textual echoes, but does not address cultural or contextual issues.

Kathleen Corley is interested in pointing to positive places in the text with which women can identify. Her main concern is that suffering should never be affirmed for its own sake, but that it should always be in the service of making something better.[25] In a similar vein, Betsy Bauman-Martin strongly critiques feminist theologies of suffering that ignore the reality that some women cannot change their life situation, no matter how much they might want to, and argues for a feminist theological approach to suffering that focuses upon granting women agency and autonomy in the midst of these horrific situations.[26] Corley's and Bauman-Martin's efforts indicate that there can be helpful pastoral and ecclesial applications, most specifically offering empowerment for women who *cannot* change their life circumstances and must find a way to endure them. At the same time, it does not seem fair to suggest that all women in abusive relationships are powerless to change their situation. If this is the case,

---

21. Many scholars see an eschatological focus as one of the primary aspects of this letter. I have touched upon many of the scholars who take this line. For a more in-depth analysis of such content, see Mark Dubis, *Messianic Woes in First Peter: Suffering and Eschatology in 1 Peter 4:12-19* (SBL 33; New York: Peter Lang, 2002).

22. Goppelt, *A Commentary on I Peter*; Paul Achtemeier, "Suffering Servant and Suffering Christ in 1 Peter," in *The Future of Christology: Essays in Honor of Leander E. Keck* (A. J. Malherbe and Wayne A. Meeks, eds; Minneapolis: Fortress, 1993), 176–88.

23. Steven Richard Bechtler, *Following in His Steps: Suffering, Community and Christology in 1 Peter* (Atlanta: Scholars Press, 1998).

24. Sharon Clark Pearson, *The Christological and Rhetorical Properties of 1 Peter* (SBEC 45; Lewiston, NY: Edwin Mellon, 2001).

25. Kathleen Corley, "1 Peter," in *Searching the Scriptures: A Feminist Commentary* (Elisabeth Schüssler Fiorenza, ed.; New York: Crossroad, 1994), 349–60.

26. Betsy J. Bauman-Martin, "Feminist Theologies of Suffering and Current Interpretations of 1 Peter 2.18-3.9," in *A Feminist Companion to the Catholic Epistles and Hebrews* (Amy-Jill Levine with Maria Mayo Robbins, eds; Cleveland: Pilgrim, 2004), 63–81.

the teaching regarding suffering that comes from this letter ought to be taken up and offered in relatively few scenarios, instead of taught to all women in all situations. In either case, it is emotionally, psychologically, and for many women physically problematic to connect suffering within a relationship to being or becoming more Christ-like.

Literary and Rhetorical Studies of 1 Peter
The third post-1981 trend, a resurgence in literary and rhetorical approaches to 1 Peter, is primarily driven by the thought that understanding these aspects of the letter will grant insight into its meaning and purpose. Lauri Thurén stands out for his rhetorical work on the letter. He suggests that the use of ambiguous participial phrases, which are at transition points in the letter, allows the author to address two major segments of the communities simultaneously: those who are actively resisting and those who are passively submitting to whatever befalls them.[27] Careful attention to the rhetorical devices (and verb tense), Thurén claims, provides much insight into the community and the author's intention in writing to them. Alternatively, Charles Talbert's assessment of "the plan" of the letter is determined by thoroughly analyzing the epistolary form of 1 Peter.[28] In other words, regardless of the author's or the recipients' context, the meaning of the letter can be found by understanding the flow of the argument. Bonnie Howe has recently published a book on the role of metaphor in this letter, most significantly pointing out how the use of family terminology (contained in the household code) will ensure a patriarchal familial structuring of the communities.[29] Many other scholars have tried to grasp the literary argument or rhetorical thrust as a means of understanding the letter's overall meaning, including three scholars who contributed to the recent *Reading First Peter with New Eyes: Methodological Reassessments of the Letter of First Peter*. Eugene Boring engages the function of the narrative world; Troy Martin does a classical rhetorical analysis of the letter that leads him to conclude that the journey motif makes sense of all the persuasion within the letter, which is geared toward having the recipients maintain conduct that is appropriate for their journey; and Robert Webb writes about the prevalence of apocalyptic

27. Lauri Thurén, *The Rhetorical Strategy of 1 Peter with Special Regard to Ambiguous Expressions* (Åbo: Åbo Academy Press, 1990).
28. Charles Talbert, "Once Again: the Plan of 1 Peter," in *Perspectives on First Peter* (NABPR Special Study Series, 9; Charles Talbert, ed.; Macon: Mercer University, 1986), 141–51.
29. Bonnie Howe, *Because You Bear This Name: Conceptual Metaphor and the Moral Meaning of 1 Peter* (BIS, 81; Boston: Brill, 2006).

material in the letter that he claims is what gives the readers motivation to remain steadfast in their challenging journey.[30]

These rhetorical studies stand in stark contrast with the feminist rhetorical work of scholars such as Elisabeth Schüssler Fiorenza, who is conscious of her own socio-political location and how that informs and motivates her rhetorical work.[31] She calls biblical scholars to defy the "academic credo of value-detached objectivism" by naming and articulating their own socio-religious and socio-political locations.[32] Since malestream scholars indirectly imply that their interpretations are value-neutral by not naming their socio-political location, their contributions have a tone of universal authoritativeness.

For example, Schüssler Fiorenza begins her commentary on 1 Peter with an explanation of her critical emancipatory interpretation of scripture, which requires conscientization and a systemic analysis of the letter as more than communication, but rather in terms of it being embedded within the power relations that were a part of the socio-political context out of which it came. Following Chela Sandoval, she also employs a double analysis of power that recognizes both the horizontal network of relations of domination and the vertical, pyramidal, kyriarchal system of power relations, recognizing that the kyriarchal system in particular is structured upon various forms of intersecting relations of domination, including but not limited to those of gender, class, race, empire, age and religion.[33] She clearly notes that, while a scholar may hold a "confessional stance" toward the biblical texts, one must move beyond this realm of identity politics in order to be open to critical evaluations of the texts themselves and the "inscriptions of power" within them, with the ultimate goal of finding liberative interpretations for the oppressed.[34] Finally, the explanation of her method sets the stage for her main interest, which is that of attempting to reconstruct the submerged voices that the author seems intent upon silencing by this text.[35]

An explanation of her method allows us to see that every aspect of her commentary is driven and informed by her own socio-political and socio-religious

30. Eugene Boring, "Narrative Dynamics in First Peter: The Function of Narrative World," Troy W. Martin, "Rehabilitation of a Rhetorical Step-Child: First Peter and Classical Rhetorical Criticism," and Robert L. Webb, "Intertexture and Rhetorical Strategy in First Peter's Apocalyptic Discourse: A Study in Sociorhetorical Interpretation," Chapters 2–4 in *Reading First Peter with New Eyes: Methodological Reassessments of the Letter of First Peter*, edited by Robert L. Webb and Betsy Bauman-Martin (New York: T&T Clark, 2007). See also, James W. Thompson, "The Rhetoric of 1 Peter," *Restoration Quarterly* 36 (1994): 237–50.
31. Schüssler Fiorenza, "1 Peter," 380–403. See also, Schüssler Fiorenza, *Rhetoric and Ethic*.
32. Schüssler Fiorenza, "1 Peter," 382.
33. Ibid., 381.
34. Ibid., 381.
35. Ibid., 396.

location, and is anything but value-neutral, as malestream biblical scholarship feigns to be. Her contributions on the understanding of the *parepidemoi*, or on the elements of valorized suffering within the text, or her final decolonizing interpretation of the text as a whole must all be understood in terms of her interest in emancipatory interpretations of biblical texts for the sake of well-being and wholeness of all people. Her interpretation of the religio-political status of the recipients, for instance, does not stand on its own, but is thoroughly informed by her feminist critical rhetorical decolonizing interpretation of the letter as a whole. In contrast, we see in most of the scholarship on 1 Peter a seemingly objective focus on the rhetoric of the letter, its "theme," or the bits and pieces throughout the letter that touch upon suffering or Christological content. While these efforts are certainly well intended, an engagement such as Schüssler Fiorenza's highlights the importance of eschewing the notion of objectivity and taking quite seriously the implications of these texts.

Since the early 1980s, the scholarship on 1 Peter has begun to move beyond the discussion of genre into the realm of assessing the contexts of both the author and the letter's recipients. While this move has deepened the "source" discussion in a way that has begun to draw out the socio-political implications of the adaptation of certain sources, it is merely a beginning. All such source and genre discussions remain positivistic until they begin to include a critical assessment of the implications of such matters.

Social and Theological Implications

David Horrell has provided a delightful assessment of the Balch-Elliott debate regarding the socio-political status of the recipients, and thus the need for scholars to find a way beyond it, and has suggested a postcolonial studies approach as a helpful way to make such a productive step.[36] Horrell does, in fact, find a way to harmonize Balch's and Elliott's diametrically opposed conclusions by bringing into the conversation the insights from James Scott, Homi Bhabha, Anuradha Needham, and Stephen Moore regarding the nature of resistance and the concept of hybridity.[37] He sees the ambivalence regarding the identity of the people as a symptom of "sly civility," or polite resistance. They are ascribed a

36. David G. Horrell, "Between Conformity and Resistance: Beyond the Balch-Elliott Debate Towards a Postcolonial Reading of First Peter," in *Reading First Peter with New Eyes: Methodological Reassessments of the Letter of First Peter* (Robert L. Webb and Betsy Bauman-Martin, eds; New York: T&T Clark, 2007), 111–43.

37. James C. Scott, *Domination and the Arts of Resistance: Hidden Transcripts* (New Haven: Yale University, 1990); Homi Bhabha, *The Location of Culture* (New York: Routledge, 1994); Anuradha Dingwaney Needham, *Using the Master's Tools: Resistance and the Literature of the African and South-Asian Diasporas* (London: Macmillan, 2000); and Stephen D. Moore, *Empire and Apocalypse: Postcolonialism and the New Testament* (Sheffield: Sheffield Phoenix Press, 2006).

hybrid identity, given that they are in that in-between space that is marked by a tendency to resist and simultaneously to conform.

His use of postcolonial critical insights is productive. There is but one piece of his contribution that distinguishes him from what Warren Carter has suggested in "Going All the Way." While Carter reads the command as a license to do whatever it takes to remain in good standing socially, Horrell sees the terminology used in reference to the emperor, "honor" versus "worship," as a clear line in the sand.[38]

Betsy Bauman-Martin's postcolonial assessment of the supersessionist character of 1 Peter is well done and much needed. In essence, she reads what the text accomplishes in terms of displacing the Jews as a whole with a particular branch of this people, which the Church over the centuries has accepted as a valid move. She claims that 1 Peter is a colonial rhetorical act because it is written for a subaltern people in the midst of a struggle, and it

> participates in the appropriation/plundering of the cultural treasures/resources of another group, rewrites the past of another group for its own benefit, endorses a hierarchy that includes the emperor, suggests, but rejects true hybridization and a real diaspora consciousness, highlights the concepts of chosenness and home-land, all through the utilization of the language of transcendence and inclusion/exclusion.[39]

The Church has colonized the "alien" identity that appropriately belongs to Israel, taken its history and stories and claimed them as rightly their own, and done so in such a way as to imply that it was what God had intended all along.

General Haustafel *Studies*

It is the household code[40] — also referred to as the "domestic" or "station" code[41] — that sets the background for the project of this book. David Balch's

---

38. Horrell, "Between Conformity and Resistance," 142.

39. Betsy Bauman-Martin, "Speaking Jewish: Postcolonial Aliens and Strangers in First Peter," in *Reading First Peter with New Eyes: Methodological Reassessments of the Letter of First Peter* (Robert L. Webb and Betsy Bauman-Martin, eds; New York: T&T Clark, 2007), 156.

40. From here on, for consistency, I will refer to this construct as the household codes. I prefer the term "household" to "domestic" as the former reminds me that we are discussing a social institution that included people beyond the immediate family; the latter term has too many modern connotations for my own preference.

41. Troy W. Martin, *Metaphor and Composition in 1 Peter* (SBLDS 131. Atlanta: Scholars Press, 1982), 124. The label "station" has been in use since Luther, who affixed this label above the Colossians 3.18–4.1 and Ephesians 5.21-33 passages, and perhaps was made popular by Martin Dibelius and more

work initiated a renewed focus and direction within scholarship in this realm. Before assessing this final segment of the body of work on 1 Peter, I offer a summary of the scholarship on the origin of the household code as found in new testament documents, the delineation of such a construct within the new testament, and the sources drawn upon for this form.

Origin of the Form

David Balch offers an excellent summary of household code studies in his contribution to *Greco-Roman Literature*.[42] His summary suggests two main strands of thought regarding the provenance of the household codes as we have them in the new testament: that of an adaptation of Stoic/philosophical thought, and that of an adaptation of ideas contained in Aristotle's *Politics* (I.2.i; II.2.ii) and other writings that reflect Aristotle's tri-partite division of households.

The first strand of research was begun by Martin Dibelius, who in his work on Colossians saw similarities with Stoic thought in phrases such as "as is fitting," and the use of "acceptable." He concluded that the household code was Christianized Stoic thought because of the addition of "in the Lord."[43] Karl Weidinger after him noted that Hellenistic Judaism had already made this step, thus he thought the household codes were from this tradition instead.[44] David Schroeder agrees with Weidinger and turns specifically to Philo whose discussion in *Decalogue* (165–7), he thinks, is similar to the new testament household code form due to the address to social classes instead of individuals. Philo assigns duties to pairs that are hierarchized, which is considered foreign to the Stoic value of individual self-sufficiency but is something that the new

specifically his student Karl Weidinger. Here is a quotation from a letter written by E. J. Goodspeed to Francis W. Beare in 1949 that addresses this very issue: "As for the haustalfeln idea, we at Chicago were never able to find any such 'haustafeln' as it had been claimed anciently existed. Most scholars simply accept Weidinger's say-so, but the natural explanation seems to be a germ in Col., expanding in Eph., and then in 1 Peter." Beare, *The First Epistle of Peter*, 195.

42. David Balch, "Household Codes," in *Greco-Roman Literature and the New Testament: Selected Forms and Genres* (SBLSBS 21; David Aune, ed.; Atlanta: Scholars, 1988), 25–50. See also James E. Crouch, *The Origin and Intention of the Colossian* Haustafel (FRLANT 109; Göttingen: Vandenhoeck and Ruprecht, 1972).

43. Martin Dibelius, *An Die Kolosser, an die Epheser, an Philemon* (HNT 12; Tübingen: J. C. B. Mohr, 1927). Karl Heinrich Rengstorf noted similar aspects of the *Haustafeln*, but claimed that the differences between the "Christian" versions and those of the Hellenistic and Jewish parallels were significant enough such that they should be regarded as uniquely Christian creations. This thesis, based upon the use of the "in the Lord" phrases, is sufficiently countered in the work of the other scholars mentioned here. Karl Rengstorf, "Die neutestamentlichen Mahnungen an die Frau, sich dem Manne unterzuordnen," in *Verbum Dei manet in aeternum. Eine Festschrift für Otto Schmitz zu seinem siebzigsten Geburtstaf am 16. Juni 1953* (Witten: Luther-Verlag, 1953), 131–45.

44. Karl Weidinger, *Die Haustafeln, ein Stück urchristlicher Paranaese* (UNT 14; Leipzig: J. C. Heinrich, 1928).

testament *Haustafeln* include.[45] One voice rejects the Hellenistic influence, Ernst Lohmeyer. He agrees that there must be some paraenetic unit upon which Colossians, as the earliest new testament version, is based, but insists that it was purely a Jewish source.[46] Finally, James E. Crouch also agrees that the Hellenistic Judaism origin is most likely, but emphasizes that it is a nomistic Pauline move within "Oriental-Jewish" thought that is brought in to counter the freedom within purely Hellenistic religious practices, such as behavior found in the worship of Isis.[47] He also draws upon Philo's *Apology for the Jews* 7.14 and Josephus's *Against Apion* (II.193–203), content that will be discussed further below. Curiously enough, this strand of scholarship does more work with the underlying socio-political implications of such an inclusion in new testament texts than the next strand does, though I do find this second strand a more fruitful point of departure for my own work.

The second main strand of scholarship on the provenance of the household codes includes, most significantly, Dieter Lührmann, Klaus Thraede and David Balch. They agree that it is from the philosophical genre, *peri oikonomias*. Lührmann notes that the household codes are "latently political"[48] and then later also notes an interesting three-phase development of thought from (1) the Pauline material, to (2) Colossians/Ephesians, and 1 Peter, to (3) the Pastorals, concerning content related to this topic.[49] Many feminist scholars make a similar assessment of the development of thought contained in the canon in general, though certainly evident in the texts Lührmann notes.[50]

45. David Schroeder, *Die Haustafeln des Neuen Testaments* (Hamburg Dissertation, 1959).
46. Ernst Lohmeyer, *Die Briefe an die Kolosser und an Philemon* (Göttingen: Vandenhoeck & Ruprecht, 1961), 152.
47. Crouch, *Origin and Intention*, 142.
48. Dieter Lührmann, "Wo man nicht mehr Sklave oder Freier ist. Überlegungen zur Struktur frühchristlicher Gemeinden," *Wort und Dienst* 13 (1975): 53–83.
49. Dieter Lührmann, "Neutestamentliche Haustafeln und antike Ökonomie," *NTS* 28 (1980), though this development of adapting this construct starting with Colossians, leading into Ephesians and later 1 Peter was noted by Goodspeed more than 30 years earlier.
50. For examples of scholars who discuss the progression away from a Pauline egalitarianism, seen in the writings from the end of the first century, see Elisabeth Schüssler Fiorenza, "Discipleship and Patriarchy: Early Christian Ethos and Christian Ethics in a Feminist Theological Perspective," *Annual of the Society of Christian Ethics* 2/1 (1982): 131–72; William O. Walker, "The 'Theology of Women's Place' and the 'Paulinist' Tradition," *Semeia* 28 (1983): 101–12. William O. Walker claims that nothing in the "genuine" Pauline corpus says anything about women's subordination but only of egalitarian views and practices. See also, Mary Rose D'Angelo, "Colossians," in *Searching the Scriptures* vol. 2 (Elisabeth Schüssler Fiorenza, with Shelly Matthews, eds; New York: Crossroad, 1993), 313–24; E. Elizabeth Johnson, "Ephesians," in *Women's Bible Commentary, Expanded Edition with Apocrypha* (Louisville: Westminster John Knox, 1998), 428–32, "Colossians," in *Women's Bible Commentary, Expanded Edition with Apocrypha* (Louisville: Westminster John Knox, 1998), 437–9; Susan Brooks Thistlethwaite, "Every Two Minutes: Battered Women and Feminist Interpretation," in *Feminist Interpretation of the Bible* (Philadelphia: Westminster, 1985), 96–107; and Carolyn Osiek, "The Bride of Christ (5:22–23): A Problematic Wedding," *BTB* 32/1 (2002): 29–39; Dennis Ronald MacDonald, *The Legend and the Apostle:*

Klaus Thraede suggested that what we see in the household codes is a rational middle ground between complete egalitarian dynamics and unqualified patriarchal structures, drawing upon Neo-Pythagorean literature as important sources.[51] Balch finds this view of Thraede's a bit too simplistic, but more importantly, as noted above, he suggests that in 1 Peter the adaptation of the *peri oikonomias* material is a subtle *critique* of patriarchy, and as such it continues the thoughts and actions we have of Jesus in the gospels. Balch also suggests that the work of Dionysius of Halicarnassus, to be discussed below, should be considered as relevant to the household code forms that we have in the new testament materials.

Delineation of the New Testament Haustafeln

As one might expect, the delineation of what counts as *Haustafel* material is directly related to a scholar's understanding of the purpose of such material and to some degree to her or his view of its provenance. There are six general categories scholars have used to define what content is household code material and what is not.

The first category is the most strictly defined, held by Karlheinz Müller. He asserts that only Eph. 5.21–6.9 and Col. 3.18–4.1 can be considered true examples of the household code in the new testament, as they are the only ones that reflect both parties in the three types of relationships that Aristotle mentions in his writings.[52] Müller's standard and respect for keeping a particular form is understandable, but an all-or-nothing perspective suggests that we should see new testament letters as philosophical treatises, which does not seem appropriate. It also overlooks the city management aspect of the original form, which can be addressed without reproducing all three pairs of relations.

The next category includes texts where any household members are mentioned, with or without reciprocity. William Knox-Little, requiring reciprocity, would add 1 Pet. 3.1-7 to Müller's list, as this section refers to both wives and husbands.[53] J. Paul Sampley, who does not require that both members of

The Battle for Paul in Story and Canon (Philadelphia: Westminster, 1983); Margaret Y. MacDonald, *The Pauline Churches: A Socio-Historical Study of Institutionalization in the Pauline and Deutero-Pauline Letters* (New York: Cambridge University, 1988).

51. Klaus Thraede, "Zum historischen Hintergrund der 'Haustafeln' des NT," in *Pietas: Festschrift für Bernhard Kötting* (Ernst Dassmann und K. Suso Frank, hrsg.; JAC 8. Münster: Aschendorff, 1980): 361, 365, 367.

52. Karlheinz Müller, "Die Haustafel des Kolosserbriefes und das antike Frauenthema: Eine kritische Rückschau auf alte Ergebnisse," in *Die Frau im Urchristentum* (G. Dautzenberg, et al., eds; Freiburg: Herder, 1983), 263–319.

53. William J. Knox-Little, *The Christian Home: Its Foundations and Duties* (London: Longmans, Green & Co., 1895).

a duality be addressed, extends the 1 Peter passage to include 2.17–3.9 (an extension that covers the exhortation, "Honor all, love the brotherhood, fear God, honor the king," the words addressed to the slaves, and verses 3.8-9 that encourage good behavior in all people), as well as 1 Tim. 2.8-15, 6.1-10 and Tit. 2.1-10.[54] These pastoral passages include directives for women, words addressed to slaves, and exhortations to men in general as the implied leaders in the communities.

Martin Dibelius exemplifies the third category of scholars who look for exhortations to submit to others as the determining factor.[55] Thus Dibelius adds the (in)famous passage of Rom. 13.1-7 (which discusses relations with governors or rulers) and Tit. 3.1-9, which also addresses being obedient to rulers and endorses simply good behavior. Cannon, drawing upon the idea that the author of Colossians was using a traditional paraenetic unit,[56] also suggests that with Dibelius's reasoning 1 Pet. 2.12-17 should be added to the list.[57] This section is framed by admonitions regarding obeying governing rulers.

The fourth category is championed by Crouch, who suggests that any text that addresses old and young, men and women, bishops, presbyters, deacons, widows and the state also fall under the rubric of household codes.[58] Thus his category includes all content mentioned so far, which is socio-political in focus, and adds passages with admonitions to church leaders or regarding church order. It is noteworthy that this definition assumes that one knows when church leaders are being addressed, though this topic itself is a matter of great debate. Additionally, though Crouch does not address this dynamic, the inclusion of church leadership here highlights both the political implications and the kyriarchal nature of the *ekklesia*, since it is clearly adapting the household structure.

Fifth, David Balch asserts that any text that has admonitions to "do good" ought to be included, as these directives share with the household codes the motivation of contributing to social stability.[59] Thus Balch extends the 1 Peter material to begin at 2.11 and end at 3.12. Sixth and finally, Leonhard Goppelt makes a clear distinction between "household codes," which strictly address

54. J. Paul Sampley, *'And the two shall become one flesh': A Study of Traditions in Ephesians 5:21-33* (SNTSMS 16; Cambridge: Cambridge University, 1971), 19.

55. Dibelius, *An Die Kolosser*, 48. George E. Cannon, *The Use of Traditional Materials in Colossians* (Macon, Ga.: Mercer University, 1983), 99.

56. Cannon, *Traditional Materials in Colossians*, 96.

57. Ibid., 99.

58. Crouch, *Origin and Intention*, 12–13. Please see Chapter 4 for more discussion on this point of church leadership.

59. David Balch, "Early Christian Criticism of Patriarchal Authority: 1 Peter 2:11-3:12," *USQR* 39 (1984): 161–73.

household roles, and the more general and broad concept of "station codes."[60] Here Goppelt defines a person's "station" as the role in society to which a person is assigned by God's sovereignty.[61] His clear delineation is worth noting for two reasons.

The first is that he states that he is drawing upon the term "station" as it was used in the Reformation.[62] Asserting that "station codes" is much more appropriate than "household codes" based on Luther's terminology may be a move to appeal to tradition, but that claim alone does not make it definitive. It is also just as arbitrary as claiming that "household codes" *can* embrace more than just household duties. Balch makes such an assertion when he explains that household relationships were important for city management. Thus the charge in 1 Pet. 2.13 to be obedient to the emperor and his governors is appropriately placed within what Goppelt considers to be the household code, 1 Pet. 2.11–3.12.[63]

Along the same lines, Cannon notes that the *Haustafeln* are to be understood as addressing household issues as well as the concerns of the church. In fact he claims that these segments of the new testament are more ecclesiological than socio-political.[64] In all three categories offered by Goppelt, Balch and Cannon, the scholars make definitive, authoritative claims about the household code, though their conclusions are not compatible. Their different perspectives come from the way each reads the household codes and from how each understands the connection between the household and society in the first century CE. This is, of course, understandable, but does raise the question of the appropriateness of such definitive claims.[65]

The second reason I highlight Goppelt's claim is that while he sees a clear differentiation between the household roles and all other social roles a person might have, that does not mean that the line between these realms actually ever existed, and even if it did that line has certainly been blurred over time. Wishing, even willing, these realms to remain separate does not make it so.

60. Goppelt, *A Commentary on I Peter*, 162–3.
61. Ibid., 165.
62. Ibid., 165, n.10.
63. Balch, "Household Codes," 34.
64. Cannon, *Traditional Materials in Colossians*, 100.
65. I do not mean to imply that I am free of such influences or tendencies in my own work. The reason I include that piece is to highlight how well-meaning scholars can come up with mutually exclusive interpretations of these texts, and all claim to have "the" correct interpretation. Another fine example of such a move is found in Stephen James, "Divine Justice and Retributive Duty of Civil Government," *Trinity Journal* 6/2 (1985): 199–210. James completely denies any relation between the civil and legal structure of society and the work of Christ. "The saving work of Jesus is effective only with respect to the eternal and direct sphere of divine justice, and has no bearing on the indirect or civil sphere" (210). He makes this claim in an article that draws from Romans 13, 1 Pet. 2.13-14 and some of the gospels.

More importantly, it is clear that, at the point in time in which this letter was written, the faith communities were meeting within the household spaces. It is ludicrous to claim that the line separating roles as leader of a household and leader of a household of God was well maintained once this vocabulary was being used in the assemblies.[66] Goppelt serves as a prime example of how a person's wants or needs shape that person's interpretation of the texts.

Sources for this Construct

Discussing the sources that are assumed to be relevant for understanding the household code material is the best way to highlight my critique of what has been published on the topic. The present discussion will be limited in scope. For a more thorough handling of it, see Abraham Malherbe.[67]

The primary ancient author who comes into the picture of the scope and form of the household code is Aristotle, specifically in his *Politics*.[68] He begins his treatise on politics speaking of partnerships: every state is a partnership and every partnership aims at some good. The political association is the greatest of all partnerships and includes all partnerships that human beings create (I.1.i). He then moves on to speak of two necessary "couplings." The first is the husband and wife, for the sake of continuing humanity, and the second is the natural ruler and natural subject, for the sake of security (I.1.iv). This first coupling establishes a household; a partnership of households creates a village; and a partnership of villages creates a city-state. For Aristotle, we must note, the whole takes precedence over the parts, because each part is dependent upon the whole for safety and sustenance (I.1.iv–v). Then he speaks of the three dualistic components that make up any household, each in terms of the role the male head of the household plays. The master/slave relationship is one of mastership; the husband/wife piece is a republican relationship; and the father/

---

66. On the matter of household roles becoming synonymous with roles within the *ekklesia*, I refer the interested reader to Jorunn Økland, *Women in Their Place: Paul and the Corinthian Discourse of Gender and Sanctuary Space*, JSNTSup 269 (New York: T&T Clark, 2004). Økland suggests that Paul may have been interested in respecting the sacred space of worship in light of the meetings taking place within the homes. The introduction of household code terminology does seem to break down such well-intended barriers.

67. Abraham Malherbe, *Moral Exhortation: A Greco-Roman Sourcebook* (Philadelphia: Westminster, 1986).

68. Aristotle, *Politics*, Loeb Classical Library 264 (H. Rackham, trans.; Cambridge University, 1998. Original printing, 1932, reprinted 1944). Concerning the primary sources for this household code content, in addition to Aristotle's *Politics*, several scholars also turn to his *Nicomachean Ethics*. In v.6.viii–ix he discusses matters of justice, in particular between two people. In book VIII, on friendships, scholars tend to be drawn to his discussion of friendships between unequals, or to the passages that discuss what is just in a friendship. While I am aware of the political, unequal-power nature of friendships in antiquity, that this content is in the background of household code content in the new testament seems tangential at best. Aristotle, *Nicomachean Ethics* (LCL 73; H. Rackham, trans.; Cambridge, Mass.; 1934).

children dynamic is a progenitive and monarchic relationship. Each of these dualistic relations is also, according to Aristotle, a partnership (I.2.i).[69]

The nature of the various partnerships and the reasons for who rules over whom are discussed throughout the treatise. His concluding thoughts in Book I are quite to the point:

> Since every household is part of a state, and these relationships are part of the household, and the excellence of the part must have regard for that of the whole, it is necessary that the education both of the children and of the women should be educated with regard to the form of the constitution, if it makes any difference as regards the goodness of the state for the children and the women to be good (I.5.xii).

Though this quotation touches upon two matters that are well beyond the scope of this project, that of education and the constitution of the city-state, the underlying message is that for the state to succeed, the households must be run with an eye toward the state and all members of the households are to be trained/educated with the goals of the state in mind. Thus we can see in Aristotle's work both the basic tri-partite form of the "household code" and a socio-political motivation for the maintenance of the household.

The remaining ancient sources are typically drawn upon secondarily to Aristotle, in light of chronology and relevant content. Dionysius of Halicarnassus spent 22 years learning Greek and compiling sources for his writing. His most influential work for our purposes is *Roman Histories*, written about the founding of Rome, presumably in order to calm the Greeks from being angry at being ruled by Rome/Romans. Of relevance for household code form and content are two passages. The first, II.16.1, refers to the third policy that Romulus prescribed, which was

> not to slay all the men of military age or to enslave the rest of the population of the cities captured in war (or land to go to pasture) . . . but send settlers . . . to possess some part of the country by lot and to make conquered cities Roman colonies and even grant citizenship to some of them.

This is a practice that the Romans continue into the first few centuries of the Common Era. Keeping this *modus operandi* in mind has produced fruitful

---

69. Aristotle has a great deal to say about the nature of a slave and the natural relations between a slave and his [or her] master (esp. I.2.ii; I.5.vi–vii). This is content that could be helpful for projects focusing upon the slaves within household code content in the new testament.

insights in scholarship on 1 Thessalonians and Philippians, thus could be helpful for similar work on 1 Peter.[70]

The second Dionysius passage (II.24.i) notes that one particular law of
Romulus's illustrates "the character of the rest of his legislation." He took care
of all situations related to "marriage and commerce with women" in one law,
which said that a woman joined to a husband in holy marriage should share
in his possessions and sacred rites (II.25.ii). This law ensures that a woman
takes on the religious practices of her husband and considers his belongings her
own, so that her cares and concerns are bound up with his. At the same time,
it was essential for the husband to take care of his wife and to "rule her as a
necessary and inseparable possession" (II.25.vi–v). We can see how these ideas
are similarly reflected in various household code forms in the new testament,
and the issue of a wife taking on the religious practices of her husband is most
relevant for 1 Peter.

Several scholars have turned to segments of the writings by Seneca, Philo
and Josephus, along with various Apostolic Fathers and Neo-Pythagorean
writers as additional sources that resonate with and/or shed light upon the
household code material.[71] Seneca's Epistle #94, "On the Value of Advice,"
addresses the three main roles of the *paterfamilias*: that of the husband, father
and master. Couched in terms of differentiating between two types of philosophy — for individual cases and for humanity at large — Seneca's thoughts
highlight the fact that there was an understanding of individual action, though
always directed ultimately toward the corporate realm.

Philo and Josephus are most often employed in this discussion for their
thoughts on the tri-partite roles of the head of the household, reflected in
Apology for the Jews and *Against Apion*, respectively.[72] In 7.1-14, Philo offers
a summary of the constitution of the "nation of the Jews," in which he exhorts
wives to reasonable obedience in all things because the husband is endowed
with abilities to interpret the laws sufficiently for his wife, the father to children,

---

70. See Joe Marchal, *Hierarchy, Unity and Imitation: A Feminist Rhetorical Analysis of Power
Dynamics in Paul's Letter to the Philippians* (Academia Biblica 24; Atlanta: Society of Biblical Literature,
2006), 99–112.

71. For primary sources on the Neo-Pythagoreans, see Malherbe, *Moral Exhortation.* I list here the
relevant Apostolic Fathers passages because they are of interest in the development of this form and content
within the church tradition, but are not as helpful in establishing sources upon which other new testament
authors may have drawn. *1 Clement* 3.21.6-9 and 38.1f; *Barnabas* 19.5-7; *Ignatius to Polycarp* 4.1–6.1;
Didache 4.9-11; *Polycarp to the Philippians* 4.1–6.3.

72. Philo, "Apology for the Jews," from *The Works of Philo: Complete and Unabridged, in one volume*
(C. D. Yonge, trans.; Peabody, Mass.: Hendrickson, 2000), 742–46. Josephus, "Against Apion," from *The
Works of Josephus: Complete and Unabridged* (William Whiston, trans.; Peabody, Mass.: Hendrickson,
1987), 806.

and the master to slaves. Focusing upon the collective people instead of on the marriage institution, Philo's philosophical treatment of the topic also indicates the subtle, although essential, connection between the household realm and the socio-political matrix. As we see a concern for personal possessions in Seneca, so too does Philo assert that each person is lord over their own possessions (7.3). I will address this concern with possessions again below, as it shows up in Xenophon's treatise as a matter of particular interest for this project.

In *Against Apion* (II.199-203) Josephus claims that "scripture" says that "a woman is inferior to her husband in all things." Many scholars have noted that though this section may be relevant to the household code discussion, it is limited in scope as it reflects more the concerns of the Decalogue than those of the household in general. Nonetheless, both Philo and Josephus illustrate the general framework that Aristotle set forth in his *Politics*, regardless of the emendations each may have made for their specific contexts.

Now let us turn to Xenophon's *Oeconomicus* (*Oikonomikos*),[73] which is a fine example of an ancient document that sheds light upon possible socio-political and economic undercurrents associated with household matters, yet is not dealt with to any large degree by biblical scholars.[74] While *oeconomicus* is the term from which we derive "economics," it is also helpful to keep in mind that its Greek rendering is, woodenly, "law of the house." Thus, the very foundation of discussions of economics, whether of first or twenty-first century CE, is the household and its maintenance and operation. Even Cicero himself is a witness to this interconnection, when he praises Xenophon for the eloquence of his writings that address managing estates.[75]

As Sarah Pomeroy has noted, we would do well to reconsider the importance of the productivity and labor of the wife, children and slaves within the households, or should we say "estates," of the Greco-Roman era.[76] Many of the philosophers I have briefly touched upon above note that the male heads of households are responsible for and appropriate the goods of the households

73. Xenophon, *Memorabilia; Oeconomicus* (LCL 168; E. C. Merchant and O. J. Todd, trans.; Cambridge, Mass.: Harvard University, 1992). I can only assume that most scholars today refer to this piece with the Latin translation, instead of in Greek (*Oikonomikos*), because the ancient authors who referred to Xenophon's work also wrote in Latin. I have not found a discussion of this minutia but I do find it to be an interesting one, since this move has colonizing overtones and serves to erase part of Xenophon's identity and to align him with all that is Latin in language, thought, or culture.

74. Several of Xenophon's other writings deal strictly with economic concerns, specifically *Revenues*, *Cyropaedia*, and *Anabasis*.

75. Cicero, *De Senectute* (William Armistead Falconer, trans.; Cambridge, Mass.: Harvard University, 1996; reprint of 1923 edition), XVII.1.

76. Sarah B. Pomeroy, *Xenophon, Oeconomicus: A Social and Historical Commentary* (New York: Oxford University, 1994), Introduction.

within society, but they do not discuss how the men were simultaneously dependent upon and could not survive without the members of the household. It is this additional component that, to this day, goes significantly unappreciated.

There are subtle ways that Xenophon proves to be a bit more progressive than Aristotle, most strikingly in the fact that he can allow for a woman's intelligence to be developed, something that was by nature impossible, according to Aristotle. Xenophon also gives full recognition to a wife's role or contribution within the household, making him one of the first, if not *the* first, philosopher to do so in his writings. He does not describe her as a parasite or "necessary property" as Aristotle and Dionysius do, though to support his view of interdependence Xenophon sees different aptitudes in men and women, which leads to inevitable gender roles.

More to the point, though, are the following insights gathered from this treatise. Estate management is considered in the same branch of knowledge as medicine, smithing and carpentry. Clearly it is a highly valued endeavor. Every good thing a person possesses (even in another city) is a part of his estate; these possessions include anything that is beneficial to the owner (I.7), and should be well maintained (I.7-12) and organized (III.3). Xenophon speaks about Cyrus and what it was that made him great, which was his focus upon farming/ agriculture and war. For our purposes, I think it is important to keep in mind that the agriculture and war efforts, while separate endeavors, were mutually dependent upon one another. Finally, in order to indicate the importance of the "professional" role of being a housewife, Xenophon tells a young couple's story. It exemplifies his beliefs that the way the husband treats the wife is central to their success and that it is the husband's fault if he does not train his wife well and they fail (III.10).

The story is about Ischomachus and his wife, who was 15 when they married. She had been carefully watched over prior to marriage, which meant that she knew that she was to "see, hear and speak as little as possible," and that she had been taught some important essentials: how to take wool and make a cloak, control her appetite and give tasks to slaves (VII.1-7), all of which when added to self-control would lead to the greatest increase in their property (VII.17). Once Ischomachus's wife was "tamed and domesticated," i.e. she could carry a conversation, he sat her down for a talk or for specific training in running the household; namely, how to treat the servants, organize their belongings most efficiently, and utilize her powers of memory and concern in order to protect and manage their household. Her ability to heed well Ischomachus's words makes her a virtuous woman of high-mindedness, which is likened to a "masculine intelligence." This is intended to be high praise indeed.

Ischomachus offers one final example of her virtue and quick obedience, an example that I find intriguingly relevant to 1 Pet. 3.1-6. It is an anecdote about her appearance. Right there in the midst of a discussion on household management, Xenophon includes this insight on what it is that makes a woman most beautiful. Ischomachus says that his wife does not need to wear make-up or jewelry because in her unadorned state she is most becoming; in fact, he compares her with horses who are most beautiful just as they are to other horses. And what *does* make her beautiful: teaching what she knows best about running the household and learning in the areas where she lacks.

Clearly these ideas from Xenophon's treatise are not lacking in content to critique from a feminist, postcolonial, materialist perspective. My comments here, however, will be in keeping with the specific focus of household codes and their derivation, form and content.

First, it seems to me that bringing in a text such as this one helps to support all the arguments for how different the Christianized versions of the household code are, in that they speak directly to the women and slaves instead of to and through the male head of the household. It seems a shame that it has been left out of these discussions in the past.

Second, all of the scholarship that focuses purely upon form, thus only draws upon texts that reflect or are similar to Aristotle's tri-partite division, is not dealing with textual evidence for the reasoning behind such a structure. It seems to me that contextualizing the socio-political motivations behind a well-run household would be essential to a responsible interpretation. Beyond the basic assumption that a well-run household is an essential contribution to the well-run state, which is an idea we clearly receive from Aristotle, Xenophon's story makes clear the ways the husband is truly in control of all aspects of the home and is responsible for his wife's training for her professional role as housewife. Here we see clearly what Rosemary Hennessy speaks of when she critiques a kyriarchal structure of knowledge and empowerment: what we do impacts what we can know; what we know impacts what we can do — this is the "materiality of knowledge."[77]

Third, when we combine Xenophon's insights with Dionysius's on the law that women should take on their husband's possessions and religious practices, we have a much more visceral image of the socio-political motivations behind the well-run household. We are also in a position to see that the section in 1 Peter on women's adornment is not out of place in these exhortations to women, but may have actually been included because of the association that one has with the other. We are then invited to analyze the admonitions regarding

---

77. Hennessy, *Materialist Feminism and the Politics of Discourse.*

women's adornment and behavior as intimately related to the surrounding content.

Fourth and finally, as Elisabeth Schüssler Fiorenza has noted, leaving an analysis of the household codes at the level of derivation, form and content of the tri-partite roles and power relations "occludes how kyriarchal relations of domination still determine people's lives and consciousness."[78] In other words, leaving the discourse at the level of source or "meaning" ignores and thus leaves unchallenged the implications of those meanings when put into practice.

I find Xenophon's work on household management, which foremost includes economic concerns and the wife's role in sustaining them, helps make a connection between the household and the socio-political realm. It is with these things in mind that I build upon the scholarship that has come before me on 1 Peter's *Haustafel*.

Uniqueness of 1 Peter's Haustafel

Now at last we have come to the discussion of scholarship that pertains to the uniqueness of the household code in 1 Peter. There are three pieces of this text that scholars have focused upon: the fact that the majority of this section is addressed to the house-slaves and wives and the implications thereof, what exactly was intended by making reference to Sarah as an excellent foremother of faith to emulate, and how does this exhortation section relate to the command to honor the emperor?[79] Let us begin with the corpus discussing the slaves and wives as direct addressees.

Address Directed Toward Slaves and Wives[80]
The fact that house-slaves and wives are addressed directly is a significant move away from the Aristotelian form of simply referring to and acknowledging the

78. Schüssler Fiorenza, "1 Peter," 381.
79. Sharon Ringe's contribution to the *Global Bible Commentary* is not specifically addressed here, due to the brief nature of the commentary, yet also offers a pointed feminist critique of 1 Peter that touches upon the implications for women as well as some liberationist and postcolonial concerns. Sharon Ringe, "1&2 Peter, Jude," in *Global Bible Commentary* (Daniel Patte, Teresa Okure, et al., eds; Nashville: Abingdon, 2004), 545–52.
80. Very little has been done with the brief address to the husbands in this passage. Carl D. Gross has put forth the theory that the wives of these men were not members of the community and thus were not "Christian." It is a textually reasoned thesis, though one that draws upon some modern psychological assessments. Carl D. Gross, "Are the Wives of I Peter 3.7 Christians?" *JSNT* 35 (1989): 89–96. Ultimately my focus will be upon the implications of these directives to the wives/women. Though I am keenly aware of the possibility of including the slaves/house-servants in this analysis, more pointedly of the need for such an analysis, in this project I focus on the production and maintenance of subjectivities of the women in 1 Peter 2.18–3.7. Chapter 5 in *A Woman's Place: House Churches in Earliest Christianity* (Carolyn

male head of the household. Several scholars have noted this change in focus and see it as a liberating development, since it acknowledges these groups of people and gives them some agency.[81] Others see it within the context of the overall development of the Christian movement and conclude that it prescribes roles and realities for these groups of people that are more restrictive than what they could have expected previously within this faith community. Ironically, I can refer to Balch for both positions. He considers 1 Peter to be rejecting and thereby critiquing Aristotle's view of women and slaves that is embodied in the repressive, hierarchical and patriarchal Roman society. This somewhat liberative view sees the letter in line with the behavior of, and stories about, Jesus and his interactions with people. The problem is that, according to Balch, any liberative potential has been erased by the trajectory of interpretation and application of this passage.[82] Therein lies the crux of the interpretations on this part of 1 Peter's household code: is it liberative or restrictive for the slaves and wives?[83]

Though the degree to which scholars need to "redeem" the text varies, positivistic interpretations of scripture are rooted in the belief in the ultimate authority and usefulness of scripture.[84] Unfortunately, these interpretations are

Osiek and Margaret Y. MacDonald, with Janet H. Tulloch; Minneapolis: Fortress, 2006), "Female Slaves: Twice Vulnerable," points to some of the possible dynamics at work for slaves that are different from wives, which reinforces the need to treat servants/slaves separately from the wives in order to begin to do justice to their particular situation, toward which Jennifer Glancy has made great strides. Jennifer A. Glancy, *Slavery in Early Christianity* (Minneapolis: Fortress, 2002). It is also important to note that these two particular groups are significant within this context of a materialist critique, due to their role (being "needed") in maintaining the structure of society as it was. See also, Clarice J. Martin, "The *Haustafeln* (Household Codes) in African American Biblical Interpretation: 'Free Slaves' and 'Subordinate Women,'" in *Stony the Road We Trod: African American Biblical Interpretation* (Cain Hope Felder, ed.; Minneapolis: Fortress, 1991), 206–31.

81. For instance, Franz Laub, *Die Begegnung des frühen Christentums mit der antiken Sklaverei* (Stuttgart: Katholisches Bibelwerk, 1982), focuses on the message of agape and the fact that the slaves are actually addressed in the new testament versions of the household code. Catherine Clark Kroeger, "Toward a Pastoral Understanding of 1 Peter 3.1-6 and Related Texts," in *A feminist Companion to the Catholic Epistles and Hebrews* (A.-J. Levine, with Maria Mayo Robbins, eds; Cleveland: Pilgrim, 2004), 82–8. Robert L. Richardson, Jr., "From 'Subjection to Authority' to 'Mutual Submission': The Ethic of Subordination in 1 Peter," *Faith and Mission* 4 (1987): 70–80.

82. Balch, "Early Christian Criticism," 169.

83. Ibid., 170.

84. Regarding positivistic interpretations of this passage, see, for example, Kroeger, "Toward a Pastoral Understanding," 82–8 and Richardson, "From 'Subjection to Authority' to 'Mutual Submission,'" 70–80. Kroeger is critical of any interpretation of scripture that negates biblical equality of men and women, but does not find anything problematic in drawing upon Sarah as an example for women in this context or in the charge to women to submit silently. Kroeger thinks that both instances are about piety and doing what is right, so Sarah being used as an example overrides any potentially negative connotations, it seems. Robert L. Richardson, Jr.'s word study on *hupotassesthai* and *tapeinophrones* also seems to be driven by a need to be able to embrace this passage, and concludes that mutuality is the final note that modern Christians are to take from this letter.

examples of idolatry at its best, privileging words on a page over the real-life experiences of people who are energized and inspired by the life-breathing spirit of God, whom they claim also inspired the texts. I note these authors for the sake of acknowledging that positivistic perspectives on this text do indeed exist.[85] When *all* scriptural injunctions to men and women are understood to be God's will, all manifestations of them must be understood as just and holy and good.

Balch is not alone in his assessment of seeing a trend toward more restrictive or oppressive social and relational constructs.[86] In a move to help give reasoning for this particular command toward women, Margaret Y. MacDonald makes sense of this piece of the text in terms of the overall threat to social stability and the possible or probable roles women may have been playing within this burgeoning movement. This appraisal ties in with some of the underlying issues of the Pastoral Letters and her own work on the "hysterical woman" in particular. She suggests that we would do well to comprehend the kind of

85. Wayne Grudem, "Wives Like Sarah, and the Husbands Who Honor Them: 1 Peter 3:1-7," in *Recovering Biblical Manhood and Womanhood: A Response to Evangelical Feminists* (John Piper and Wayne Grudem, eds; Wheaton: Crossway Books, 1991), 194–208, goes into great detail defining submission and listing its benefits for women/wives, which Grudem suggests goes hand-in-hand with considerate leadership on the husband's part. James Slaughter, in addition to a three-part discussion of this topic within the journal *Bibliotheca Sacra*, also suggests "Peter's message must be understood and practiced by husbands in their efforts to represent Christ to their wives. Otherwise the marriage dynamic is weakened by the absence of a crucial biblical element. Only with the consistent application by Christian husbands of Peter's instructions in 1 Peter 3:7 can marriage truly be all God intends it to be" (James Slaughter, "Peter's Instructions to Husbands in 1 Peter 3:7," in *Integrity of Heart, Skillfulness of Hands* (Grand Rapids: Baker Book House, 1994), 185). See also his three-part series entitled, "Instructions to Christian Wives in 1 Peter 3:1-6": "The Submission of Wives (1 Pet 3:1a) in the Context of 1 Peter," *Bibliotheca Sacra* 153 (1996): 63–74; "Sarah as a Model for Christian Wives (1 Pet. 3:5-6)," *Bibliotheca Sacra* 153 (1996): 357–65; "Winning Unbelieving Husbands to Christ (1 Peter 3:1b-4)," *Bibliotheca Sacra* 153 (1996): 199–211. Mary Shivanandan, "Feminism and Marriage: A Reflection on Ephesians 5:21-33" *Diakonia* 29/1 (1996): 5–22. Though this is an article on Ephesians, it represents a similar perspective on the roles of men and women as taken from scripture, as she concludes that in the divinely created order, the man has the initiative and the woman is to submissively respond (9).

86. Schüssler Fiorenza, "Discipleship and Patriarchy," 131–72; Thistlethwaite, "Every Two Minutes," 105; Johnson, "Ephesians," 431; Johnson, "Colossians," 437; Osiek, "The Bride of Christ," 29–39; and D'Angelo, "Colossians," 314. Susan Brooks Thistlethwaite also reads the lack of "male and female" in the Colossian domestic code as a loss of the earlier egalitarian Jesus movement. E. Elizabeth Johnson notes that the adaptation of the domestic code signifies a step away from the freedom in the early church: "Ephesians is concerned that the church faithfully mirror the creation [thus enters the reference to Gen. 2.24] and that the household mirror the church." In Colossians, as well, Johnson notes the role of the Church/household in reflecting the redeemed creation. This domestic code is for her a "reassertion of patriarchal morality." Carolyn Osiek notes that the combining of images sets up a relational dominance within the church — she does not state it clearly, but I see her suggesting that there was a move toward a more hierarchical structure than what was present at the beginning of the movement. Mary Rose D'Angelo suggests that, "While some of Colossians' reformulations of Pauline motifs could have been used to challenge patterns of domination and subordination, the new theological picture formed by shifts in eschatology, ecclesiology, and parenesis facilitated the enforcement of patriarchy" (314).

"equilibrium" the author was attempting to find.[87] More specific to the 1 Peter situation, though, she suggests that when making "house calls," where only the women were believers, the wives could go in unnoticed and would not cause the stir, or possibly scandal, that a man visiting them might. She also suggests that any exhortation in relation to the being yoked with non-believers issue may simply reflect a frustration that the church leaders had in watching the unstable behavior of the wives of non-believers.[88] MacDonald's scholarship is quite helpful for a deeper understanding of possible dynamics at work in these communities, but like so many other scholars she does not deal with the socio-political realities that this letter creates when it becomes normative for the church.

Jeannine K. Brown compares and contrasts 3.1-6, addressed to wives specifically, and 3.14-16, which is directed to the community members in general (i.e. to the males).[89] These two sections are "strikingly similar" in terms of the vocabulary they share. Both passages refer to the realm of the heart (4, 15), address proper conduct (1-2, 16), mention reverence and gentleness (2-4, 16), and refer to holiness and sanctification and note hope as a value (5, 15). In addition, both groups are prohibited from fearing (6, 14) and are commended for doing good (6, 16). In light of these similarities, many (including Elliott) have suggested that women were exemplary models for the other members of the community, which means that characteristics attributed to wives become commended to all Christians. While there may not seem to be a problem with attributing women with exemplary status, Brown notes two significant issues this idea raises. The first is that in skipping over the dissimilarities, they are not held up for critique. The most poignant difference is seen in that the wives are told to endure silently and the community in general is to be prepared to speak, ready with a verbal defense of their Christian hope. The second issue Brown notes is that of the problematic of valorizing suffering at all, even more so for the most vulnerable people of a society.

If suffering makes one Christ-like, then there is no motivation to try to alleviate the source of the oppression or abuse. Betsy J. Bauman-Martin suggests that for many women today, however, who have no option of escaping abusive situations, this passage can be empowering and sustaining.[90] I think that this

---

87. Margaret Y. MacDonald, "Early Christian Women Married to Unbelievers," *SR* 19 (1990): 221–34; also *Early Christian Women and Pagan Opinion: The Power of the Hysterical Woman* (New York: Cambridge University, 1996).

88. MacDonald, "Early Christian Women," 221.

89. Jeannine K. Brown, "Silent Wives, Verbal Believers: Ethical and Hermeneutical Considerations in 1 Peter 3.1-6 and Its Context," *WW* 24/4 (2004): 395–403.

90. Bauman-Martin, "Feminist Theologies of Suffering," 63–82.

is an important and vital way of reading this passage. Bauman-Martin is not denying that this passage has significantly contributed *to* the ethos that causes or allows such terrible situations for women to develop; she is simply looking for a way for women who cherish these texts to read them for their benefit. I affirm her choice to find something life-sustaining in this text, and maintain my purpose of seeking out and naming the oppressive and abusive realities that this text has been used to engender.

Mary H. Schertz offers an important critique of this text when she sees in it continuity between the slavery and wifely submission pieces. If we choose to enforce the wifely submission, then we must also accept all that is associated with the kind of slavery at work in households at that time, as well as be willing to say that exploitative actions lead people to Christ.[91] Her conclusion, however, locates her with Bauman-Martin in the sense that, for those with no other options, nonretaliation is not a bad strategy.[92]

Each of these "feminist" contributions is helpful for understanding the text and some of what was "in the air" as the letter was written. Simply trying to understand the content of the text and the possible circumstances to which it was addressed does not go far enough, in my estimation of the matter. What I am trying to address is the distinction between this passage offering hope in a hopeless situation and it being a cornerstone in the constructed identity of women within these faith communities, a construction that has carried through the centuries and that indeed does contribute to maintaining and remaining within abusive relations.

Reference to Sarah

Several scholars have noted the intriguing reference to Sarah in the passage directed toward the women, which falls immediately after the exhortations regarding adornment and the beauty of the inner spirit:

> For in this way in former times the holy women also, who hoped in God, used to adorn themselves, being submissive to their own husbands; just as Sarah obeyed Abraham, calling him lord, and you have become her children if you do what is right and are not frightened by anything that causes fear (1 Pet. 3.5-6).

---

91. Mary H. Schertz, "Nonretaliation and the Haustafeln in 1 Peter," in *The Love of Enemy and Nonretaliation in the New Testament* (W. H. Swartley, ed.; Louisville: Westminster John Knox, 1992), 283.

92. Schertz, "Nonretaliation," 285. Warren Carter, "Going All the Way? Honoring the Emperor and Sacrificing Wives and Slaves in 1 Peter 2.13-3.6," in *A Feminist Companion to the Catholic Epistles and Hebrews* (A.-J. Levine, ed., with Maria Mayo Robbins; Cleveland: Pilgrim, 2004), 14–33. Bauman-Martin, "Feminist Theologies of Suffering," 63–81.

Granted, it is such a brief excursus on Sarah, it is easy to disregard it. This is precisely the point. What may seem like an off-handed reference to Sarah must have carried some weight or had some effect on the recipients. Otherwise, why bother? Was it a passing thought that the author felt like including at the last minute? Was it a story that is often told among or to wives when the issues of jewelry and wanting to be outspoken arose? Perhaps it is something much more subtle, as Mark Kiley and Dorothy Sly have suggested,[93] or simply the most obvious choice given the Hebrew bible references in the first two chapters of this letter.[94]

The conversation between Kiley and Sly is focused upon the claims in the letter that Sarah called Abraham "lord" and that in this reverence for her husband she is to be emulated. The first point is noteworthy since the only time Sarah *does* refer to Abraham as "lord" is in Gen. 18.12 when she is laughing about bearing a child: "After I have become old, shall I have pleasure, my lord being old also?" This is clearly not an instance of obedience to or reverence for her husband.

The way the second claim is worded has almost frightening implications: how exactly does Sarah function as the mother of those who "do right and are not frightened by anything that causes fear"? It is assumed that Genesis 12 and 20, which discuss Abraham handing Sarah over to the Egyptian Pharaoh and the King of Gerar, respectively, are in the background of this passage. Both situations for Sarah and Abraham appear to take place in a somewhat hostile environment in a foreign land, settings that resonate with the situation at hand for the communities in Asia Minor. According to the way the stories are told, Kiley claims that Sarah's outward beauty played a significant role in causing the predicaments, thus it makes sense to him that she would come to mind for the author at this point in the letter given the previous reference to outward adornment and inner beauty.[95] Kiley thus concludes that Sarah is a model for those women suffering unjustly because she submitted to the unjust treatment and "less-than-noble-will" of Abraham.[96]

On the other hand, Sly suggests that the author of 1 Peter was intentionally choosing to portray Sarah in submissive and typically Hellenistic terms in much

93. Mark Kiley, "Like Sara: The Tale of Terror Behind 1 Peter 3:6," *JBL* 106 (1987): 689–92; and Dorothy I. Sly, "1 Peter 3:6b in the Light of Philo and Josephus," JBL 110 (1991): 126–9.

94. See also Magda Misset-van de Weg, "Sarah Imagery in 1 Peter," in *A Feminist Companion to the Catholic Epistles and Hebrews* (A.-J. Levine, ed., with Maria Mayo Robbins; Cleveland: Pilgrim, 2004), 50–62.

95. Kiley mentions one final textual resonance between Gen. 20 and 1 Pet. 3.3-7. In 1 Peter there is a claim that the husbands' prayers will not continue to be hindered if this advice is followed, just as we see in Gen. 20 that Abraham was able to pray to God on behalf of Abimelech.

96. Kiley, "Like Sara," 691.

the same way that Philo and Josephus re-wrote parts of the Abraham/Sarah story.[97] The matter of Abraham submitting to Sarah's ideas in Gen. 16.2, 6, and 21.12 had become embarrassing, an issue Philo solved by allegorizing Sarah as wisdom and Josephus solved by simply re-writing the events entirely. Since these two men were comfortable making these emendations, Sly suggests that it is likely that the author of 1 Peter did the same thing. Sly's article is brief, as any textual note would be, so she does not tease out the implications of her fascinating proposition. In addition to erasing or taming the image of Sarah, this move reflects a freedom to manipulate women and the texts that give voice to them. Given the significance of narratives in forming the Judeo-Christian traditions, this kind of freedom has far-reaching effects.

There are, of course, plenty of positivistic interpretations of this reference to Sarah as a model for women in difficult situations. James Slaughter offers an interpretation of the "holy" wives of 1 Peter as women who willingly submitted to the unjust treatment of their husbands. He claims they did so not because they were avoiding hardship or were attempting to manipulate their husbands, but because their quiet confidence that God would save them allowed them to submit to their husbands without fear of harm.[98] This interpretation does nothing to address the emotional, physical or sexual harm that the women, nonetheless, experienced, as alluding to it in the letter implies. As well intended as this and similar interpretations are, when applied as pastoral advice, abused women are counseled to stay in abusive relationships. Reading "with the text," or what I have referred to as offering positivistic interpretations, can indeed be harmful for some followers of Christ.[99]

While the specific stories about Sarah in the Hebrew bible may reveal as much independent thought and action on her part as obedience, the choice to appeal to the wife of the father of Israel is perhaps more impressionable in this context. The first chapter and a half of this letter draws heavily upon the narratives, promises and traditions of the people of Israel. The fact that Sarah is depicted here as much more subservient than she appears in the ancient texts is, in my opinion, a mere ideologically driven literary device.[100]

---

97. Sly, "1 Peter 3:6b," 129.

98. Slaughter, "Sarah as a Model," 359.

99. I discuss more fully in Chapter 5 this matter of the harm that can come to a follower of Christ as a result of taking these admonitions to heart.

100. I do try to keep in mind the fact that we are able to go back and re-read the stories as they have been passed down to us in writing, which was not always the case for people in the first century CE. We have the ability to compare "original" stories with the various allusions to them in these later texts. It seems that so many arguments or absolutist claims are made based upon such comparisons without allowing room for the significant difference between the way the stories would have been heard and remembered in the first century CE. and how they are passed along, fastidiously studied, and taught today.

Cultural Significance — Imperial Pawns?

James W. Aageson has published an article that touches upon many of the typically feminist interests in this section of the letter. He highlights the problematic implications of emulating the suffering of Christ, of framing obedience in terms of a theological mandate, of power relations and the social status of the recipient communities then and now, and the issues associated with cross-cultural translation, canonization, and honor-shame dynamics.[101] With all of these factors noted, it is somewhat disappointing that he can appropriately note that emancipatory movements are struggling, still, against such violations of the humanity of women that were a part of the social realities in the first-century Greco-Roman world. Various forms of slavery and women's subordination continue to be realities in the twenty-first century, due in part to texts such as this one in 1 Peter and other similar biblical mandates that have had a significant role in forming the socio-political ethos of the dominating Western world. It is simply not enough to note that our values have changed when the texts of our religious communities have not, in particular when those texts have been so formative for the kyriarchal structures and power relations within family, church and governmental roles in the dominant powers of the West.[102]

As noted above, David Horrell suggests that we consider approaching this passage with the dynamics of resistance and hybridity in mind.[103] Resistance is characterized by ambivalence, "attraction and repulsion at the same time,"[104] and hybridity is what happens to people in that in-between space, where they embody the ambivalence of resistance and conformity. What is strikingly missing, however, is an assessment of the implications of this ambiguous, hybrid identity.

In her ever direct manner, Schüssler Fiorenza has had plenty to say regarding the implications that the household codes have for women, preferring to call them "patterns of patriarchal submission."[105] She then suggests that explaining away the accusations that the Christian mission was a subversive movement does a disservice to this letter. One of the social implications of this movement

---

101. James W. Aageson, "1 Peter 2.11-3.7: Slaves, Wives and the Complexities of Interpretation," in *A Feminist Companion to the Catholic Epistles and Hebrews* (Amy-Jill Levine and Maria Mayo Robbins, eds; Cleveland: Pilgrim Press, 2004), 34–49.

102. Edward Said, *Orientalism*, 5. I am keenly aware of Edward Said's claims about the formation and construction of the ideas such as "West" and "East" or "Orient" and their role in religio-political discourses today. I do agree that such labels are mere constructions and should be problematized or at least that we raise awareness of identity and labeling that such language impacts. At the same time, I think it is important to claim or own the inheritance that such constructions have given us.

103. David G. Horrell, "Between Conformity and Resistance," 111–43.

104. Moore, *Empire and Apocalypse*, 109.

105. Schüssler Fiorenza, "Discipleship and Patriarchy," 141.

was that it disrupted, at least early on, the patriarchal rule of the households. The fact that we see the inclusion of the household code in the relatively later (canonical) documents, Ephesians, Colossians and 1 Peter could very easily be explained by a need (perceived or actual) to re-establish the traditional patriarchal order within these *ekklesia*. There is no doubt that this was an order that would appease government officials.[106] Many scholars have admitted that this may have been a motivating factor in the adaptation of the household code, but are not willing to consider the ways this structure and behavioral prescription become real in the church and in people's lives.

Instead of rejecting the kyriarchal structure of the household and society, the ethos of the *Haustafel* is right in line with it, making these communities perfect targets for political cooptation by the Roman Empire. One of the most significant relationships within the community, the husband/wife relation, is defined by submission and obedience. The movement as a whole, then, will be defined and structured by such a dynamic.[107] Many of the scholars I have addressed above speak to these issues, though none as directly and forthrightly as Schüssler Fiorenza.

Her feminist postcolonial rhetorical analysis of 1 Peter is the most developed critical feminist postcolonial contribution to 1 Peter studies to date,[108] and subsequently becomes a part of the method I will employ in my critical reading of this text. She offers a critical feminist decolonizing analysis of the letter as a system of communication that goes beyond holding meaning for communities to constructing relations of power, affecting both horizontal and vertical relations.[109]

She names four steps that summarize her approach. She begins by exploring the socio-religious location of the author of the letter and its recipients. Second, she looks for power relations that are inscribed in the argument of the letter. Third, she analyzes the rhetorical strategies of the letter as well as the way subsequent scholars have interpreted the rhetoric. Finally, she wants to retrieve the voices that this letter has silenced. Her overall goal is to ask whether this letter engenders "emancipatory dissident consciousness" and egalitarian relations or whether it re-inscribes a dominating kyriarchal ethos and structuring of relations within the communities. It is the first three steps that are essential for my own project on the household codes.[110]

---

106. Ibid., 143.

107. Ibid., 148. See also, Nancy C. M. Hartsock, *Money, Sex, and Power: Toward a Feminist Historical Materialism* (Boston: Northeastern University, 1985), 155.

108. Schüssler Fiorenza, "1 Peter."

109. Ibid., 382.

110. Ibid., 381.

The fourth step of reconstructing the submerged voices and arguments is one that I think is worth attempting. Unfortunately, we will never be certain that we are accurately identifying the voices that were originally silenced, though I do think that such silencing took place. I think it is just as important to address the effects of the power dynamics embedded in these texts whether or not someone was objecting to them in the first place.

My point here is that a) some of those who objected may not have actually made their objections known, such that what we have in the letter may reflect more the fears of the author than actual issues that had already arisen; b) many of those who *should* have objected to such language may not have due to their enculturation and the extent to which they had internalized the *habitus* in which they lived; and c) ultimately this text was canonized and thus it is a part of the collective consciousness of the Christian tradition, whether or not people acknowledge it as such. Therefore, I am more interested in focusing upon the materiality of this text — i.e. the way it is embodied in various ways in our lives — which is a piece I see Schüssler Fiorenza concerned with, as well,[111] than in offering my version of Schüssler Fiorenza's fourth step.

In reference to 1 Pet. 3.1-6, the section addressed specifically to the wives, Misset-van de Weg has noted that this passage has been read prescriptively and from this vantage point has influenced the formation of Christian marital ethics and the role of women in Western churches and society. This fact alone, she claims, makes it worthy of more study.[112] She has touched upon two fundamental feminist and materialist concerns regarding this text and its effects or materiality, because she hints at the specific construction of women and the circumscription of roles for women that this text engenders. Of course there are nuances within both of these realms of discourse that I will address, but her basic claim is one that rings true for me, and this project is intended to be one piece of that further study of which she speaks.[113]

---

111. Schüssler Fiorenza, "Discipleship and Patriarchy," 159. "Such a hermeneutics [that solely focuses on the liberative aspects of the bible] is, as a result, in danger of formulating a feminist Biblical apologetics instead of sufficiently acknowledging and exploring the oppressive function of patriarchal Biblical texts in the past and in the present. It would be a serious and fatal mistake to relegate the *Haustafel* trajectory, for example, to culturally conditioned Biblical traditions no longer valid today and thereby overlook the authoritative-oppressive impact these texts still have in the lives of Christian women."

112. Misset-van de Weg, "Sarah Imagery in 1 Peter," 50.

113. Magda Misset-van de Weg, "Een vrouwenspiegel, 1 Petrus 3,1-6," *Proeven van Vrouwenstudies Theologi*, Keel IV (A.-M. Kort, et al., eds; IIMO Research Publication 44; Zoetermeer: Meinema, 1996), 145–82, offers a detailed account of 1 Pet. 3.1-6's application and effect in Church doctrine and belief.

Conclusion

As I hope this review of the scholarship on 1 Peter's *Haustafel* indicates, my own feminist, postcolonial, materialist engagement of this passage builds on the foundation of much of the scholarship on 1 Peter from the past 30 years. It is essential to take into consideration the precipitating event(s) for this letter, as well as the socio-political climate in which, and to which, it was written. I take seriously the Christological and theological content, given its implications for people of faith who are dealing with various forms of unjust suffering and most specifically in terms of the message this letter has for women in abusive relationships or marriages. I also think it is important to engage the rhetoric of the letter and the power relations embedded within it, primarily because most scholarship on this passage reads with the text or simply points to potential issues within it without teasing out the implications of such issues. As a component of the Christian bible, this letter has power and functions among faith communities to put into motion the ideas contained within it and to construct the subjects as they are addressed by the author. We can no longer afford to read "with the text" potentially oppressive ideas and theologically justified commands that are more helpful for maintaining kyriarchy than for endorsing liberation and fullness of life. The matter of how I suggest we could read biblical texts, then, is the focus of the next chapter.

2

A New Methodology

Introduction

In addition to the fact that a feminist, postcolonial, materialist critique has not yet been done on 1 Peter, there is not presently a method, to my knowledge, that will sufficiently direct such a critical analysis of a biblical text using the intersection of these three specific lenses. There are many avenues for feminist critical approaches to biblical texts, and postcolonial studies are gaining ground among biblical scholars, in particular within the area of the new testament. At this point, however, there are very few examples that combine these two particular approaches, much less that incorporate the type of materialist analysis that I am seeking to produce. It is the purpose of the remainder of this chapter to set forth the parameters of such a multidimensional critique.

Naming a method with various qualifying descriptors is simultaneously misleading and freeing. It is misleading in the sense that it projects to the reader that the totality of the dimensions named, in this case "feminist," "postcolonial," and "materialist," will be represented in the critique. The reality is that there is a spectrum of feminist concerns in any field, thus one can still question to what this qualifier, "feminist," refers and the same is true for the qualifiers "postcolonial" and "materialist."

The freeing aspect in naming a critical approach is that it allows people to locate themselves within a general range of discourse. Claiming particular labels is also a way of acknowledging that there are various socio-political dynamics that have an influence on one's understanding of the texts. Ultimately, I think that labels are more harmful or detrimental than helpful because they are based upon a system of knowledge and power that needs to contain and circumscribe discourses. Until the day comes that we can throw off the yoke of containment, however, I will participate in the discourses of power and choose my own labels, while trying to create new visions of possibility for engaging knowledge, power and social relations. The next step, then, is to set forth my understanding of what each of these three specific components — feminist, postcolonial and materialist critiques — address.

Feminist Studies

As alluded to in the introduction to this chapter, the reality is that one cannot neatly list, package, and hand on to a novice all the feminist concerns that are to be brought into conversation with biblical texts. Who we are, and the experiences we have had, directly affect the kinds of questions and insights we bring to any text in our efforts to interpret it. Thus, it is important to me as a feminist scholar that the centrality and relevance of our social locations be acknowledged in our interpretations. This means that Euro-centric white malestream scholarship does not get the final word, nor does it deserve to be normative or elevated to the place of most esteemed or "orthodox" interpretation. Since our social location is informed by many aspects of our lives (race, gender, sexuality, age, religious beliefs, etc.), as a scholar I try to bring as many of these dynamics as I can to bear in my engagement with biblical texts. The term "feminist" technically denotes an interest in gender equality, however, so for the sake of theoretical clarity, I will discuss this component here in such terms.

Representation: Speaking for and Standing in

There are two significant aspects of the concept of representation within feminist discourse[1] that I would like to highlight. The first addresses the false assumption that men[2] can speak for and represent the beliefs, viewpoints and life experiences of women. The second aspect addresses how "the feminine" or concepts related to "women," femininity, and the female body are invoked in order to minimize or denigrate certain behaviors, beliefs, relations and other people.

Traditional Western discourse is critiqued for projecting universal representation and objectivity in its claims to truth, in its interpretations of human relations, and, in this context, in biblical interpretations. Given the Christian bible's location within the Church, which is today predominantly led by males, and the Church's history of male-dominated leadership and biblical translations and interpretations, this step to question exactly who is represented by a (typically white) male biblical scholar's interpretation is an essential component of my approach to biblical interpretation. The matter is similar to having US

---

1.   Here and throughout the book I use the term *discourse* to refer to the verbal exchange(s) of ideas, whether this verbal exchange is in written or oral form. I deem the former possible given the influence the writings contained within the new testament have had over the centuries to define communities and their standards and behaviors.

2.   I am well aware that using terms such as "men," "women," "male," "female," "feminine" and so on perpetuate the dualistic worldview that I am trying to critique. This situation is much like my choice to use or claim labels for my methodology — they are both choices made in order to be understood within a certain discursive context.

Senators and Representatives who understand us, our concerns, our perspectives on how the Federal government functions, and so forth. People tend to vote for and support people whom they relate to or who they think holds similar views to them. Why in the world would we not also apply this logical approach to engagements with, and interpretations of, the sacred texts of the Church? For far too long white malestream interpretations have been allowed to predominate in this realm, which has created the false sense that a handful of men are "speaking for," or on behalf of, all women and men.

Due to the nature of inculturation and the power of the *habitus*[3] on the formation of ideological beliefs, it is not simply white Western males of privilege and power who create and perpetuate this false sense of universal interpretations of biblical texts. Many women[4] internalize the particular worldview that has subjugated and oppressed them. Thus they are often not even aware that their own beliefs, and applications of biblical interpretations, are keeping them from fullness of life.

The other aspect of representation, that of invoking gendered images or labels for the sake of denigrating or minimizing someone or something else, is similarly pervasive throughout Western cultures and societies. "Feminizing" language serves to justify the domination of one group of people over another. It is based upon another false belief that women are in essence ontologically weaker and less intelligent than men and in need of protection and care from some other entity.[5] Thus anything that is "appropriately" associated with the feminine can be controlled, subjugated and treated as property. Unfortunately, this use of language has a way of perpetuating itself: the belief that women are lesser beings than men justifies using female-gendered language as a way to indicate the inferiority of what is being described. The socially sanctioned "approval" of the use of gendered language for such purposes then perpetuates a belief that women indeed are lesser in value than men.

Both aspects of representation — representing others' perspectives and invoking "feminine" language in derogatory ways — continue even in our

---

3. Here I am drawing upon Pierre Bourdieu's concept of *habitus*, which is discussed more thoroughly in the "Language and Power" section in the concerns of postcolonial studies. Pierre Bourdieu, *Language and Symbolic Power* (Gino Raymond and Matthew Samson, trans.; John B. Thompson, ed.; Cambridge, Mass.: Harvard University, 1991).

4. I use this term, "women," to refer to all people who are oppressed or silenced by malestream society. See Schüssler Fiorenza, *Rhetoric and Ethic*, 1–14, for more explanation on the terms "women" and "malestream."

5. While the various forms of media are not the only place this is relevant, I am constantly baffled by the number of people who are numb to the way the media depicts women as in need of protection. We can see this depiction of women in song lyrics, music videos, movies that portray traditional relationship dynamics and expectations, TV sitcoms and series, news reports, advertisements, and so forth.

own society today. If we can see this still happening in various institutions of Western cultures in the twenty-first century, we most certainly are justified in looking for and highlighting the same concerns about ancient texts.

Essentialism and "Othering"

Essentialism in this context reflects a way of thinking that contends that one can describe or capture the "essential" core element of a given subject, whether it is in ontological, moral or behavioral terms. This essence is understood to be universal, thus it can be used accurately and appropriately to refer to all subjects to which this essence is ascribed. Essentialism is one of the primary factors contributing to the belief that one person can speak on behalf of the rest of humanity, and in particular within the context of men representing women.[6] Thanks to post-modern and deconstructionist thought that eschew objectivity, hail the relevance of context and admit that as human beings we are constantly changing, essentialist tendencies no longer rule the day. At the same time, that does not mean that they are completely eradicated.

Any claim such as, "women are more emotional than men," "being a mother makes a woman complete," or "that's just the way men behave," reflects essentialist thought. While such claims are only a problem if people start to believe them and behave accordingly, these kinds of stereotypical and essentializing phrases are commonplace in popular social discourse. There are plenty of people who do actually believe such claims. Within the context of engaging the bible, then, a reader is advised to pay attention to discourse in the bible itself as well as in the interpretations of it that label women with specific subjectivity or address women in such a way that one aspect of their being becomes definitive of their entire being.[7]

The concern of "othering" goes far beyond the male/female divide, given the racial, socio-political, cultural, tribal, and theological "others" that are denounced within the Christian canon. For many feminist biblical scholars including myself, then, all aspects of inequality and oppression that are justified or maintained by an "othering" within these texts fall under the scope of their feminist critical scholarship. At this point, however, I will continue to focus the discussion on the othering that takes place within the male/female dichotomy, and the specific concerns raised by its representation within biblical texts.

---

6.   Ellen Armour, "Essentialism," *Dictionary of Feminist Theologies* (Letty M. Russell and J. Shannon Clarkson, eds; Louisville: Westminster John Knox, 1996), 88; Peter Sedgwick, "Essentialism," in *Cultural Theory: The Key Concepts* (Andrew Edgar and Peter Sedgwick, eds.; New York: Routledge, 2002), 131–2.

7.   Similar concerns can be raised regarding the essentializing claims in terms of males within biblical texts and the interpretations of them.

It must be noted that there is both a positive and a negative way to approach "others." Positively, scholars speak in terms of mutual understanding that comes from acknowledging and learning from people who inhabit a social location different from one's own. This line of thought is similar to something we can see in Mikhail Bakhtin's work, as he discusses how a subject cannot fully know herself without the vision of the "other" filling in what she cannot see. She needs the other in order to be full and fully known, know herself fully, and the other in turn is more fully known in the process.[8]

Of course, this simple dichotomy, which I understand for Bakhtin is based upon a reverence for humanity and the depth, simplicity and power of relationships, can also be used in incredibly oppressive and demeaning ways. Within the realm of specifically gendered discourse, negative "othering" draws upon essentialist views of anyone who is not heterosexual male. Pointing to the difference in this "other," the heterosexual male — or anyone who affirms the values of heterosexual androcentrism — identifies with what has been socially determined to be normative and the power that is ascribed to it. As with any hierarchy or dichotomy, this identifying with normativity creates an unequal power relation. In an ironic twist, that which is considered normative and is most highly valued is only possible or necessary when an "inferior" party is present. The superior *needs* the inferior. One might think that this grants the inferior a certain amount of autonomous power, but this would be the case when that power can be acted upon independently, and it is only granted in light of being other than or less than the superior group.

Essentialist thought and commands based upon essentializing claims can be found throughout the Christian scriptures. Any time there is a reference to how "wives" must behave or to what "husbands" are to do in their marriage, we are witnessing the application of an essentialist belief system that all wives or all husbands can be neatly grouped together and told to behave the same way. "Othering" is also quite common in new testament texts. Whether it is in terms of the depictions of "the Jews" in the gospels or Paul's opponents and Gentile sinners in his letters, for instance, we can find such polarizing and one-up/one-down language throughout the sacred writings of the Church.

Language/Discourse

The concern regarding language from a feminist perspective highlights that our language and discourse are created by and from the perspective of a

---

8. Mikhail Bakhtin, *Art and Answerability: Early Philosophical Essays* (Michael Holquist and Vadim Liapunov, eds; Vadim Liapunov, trans.; Austin: University of Texas, 1990). Focus on the "self" and an individualistic view of the world are certainly foremost in this kind of discourse, for better and for worse.

predominantly "male" society, which creates the false sense that male perspectives are normative. If male is normative, then the use of language in a way that supports this "reality" is also normative. Any discourse that counters male-centeredness is typically viewed as subversive or threatening to the stability of society in some form. At the same time, any use of language or social discourse that affirms or acknowledges other allegedly "non-normative" realities can do so only by the fact that it is defined in terms of not being what is centrally normative. By being labeled as other or peripheral it maintains the normative or central status of "what has always been." So even the effort to give full legitimacy to realities on the periphery must first acknowledge their non-normative status, which can serve to maintain the peripheral status of those voices.

When new knowledge is created within western malestream social and political discourses, it creates a place for itself only to the extent that it expands the realm in general. It does not displace malestream language or realities from their central and normative location. It must remain on the periphery, all the more accentuating the power and prominence of "normative" language. In the same way that patriarchal or kyriarchal binaries define one element of a pair in contrast to the other, instead of on its own terms, so too the language of patriarchal and kyriarchal structures can allow a certain amount of newness only to the extent that it is defined in terms of "what has always been."

From the perspective of biblical studies and biblical interpretation, we would do well to assess the ways malestream language serves to repress all peripheral or non-normative voices, both within the bible itself and in the scholarship and interpretation of it. Luce Irigaray speaks of this silencing in the texts of a culture or society as the "procedures of repression."[9] The repression itself happens on several levels simultaneously. She urges us to analyze the way the structure of our discourse serves to define and separate the true and meaningful from the false and meaningless, and the way our discourse itself is sexualized, which means that the "true" and "meaningful" is also gendered. We must also attend to what does not get articulated, the pieces that are denied utterance.[10] The exclusion of women and/or our perspectives from the dominant, male-determined discourse is still internal to the overall order: women are confined within, yet

9.   Luce Irigaray, *This Sex Which is Not One* (Catherine Porter with Carolyn Burke, trans.; Ithaca: Cornell University, 1985), 75.
10.   Irigaray, *This Sex*, 73–5. Hélène Cixous and Catherine Clément also speak of the repressed words of women and the need for a new or transformed language and literature, in a space that does not allow for the male gendered hierarchical 'principles' of culture as it stands today (xviii). Hélène Cixous and Catherine Clément, *The Newly Born Woman* (Betsy Wing, trans.; Minneapolis: University of Minnesota, 1986).

excluded from; they are necessary for sustaining the system, yet this is so only as long as women are defined by this system as "other" or as lacking.

Women and women's words and stories are silenced by or subjugated to the malestream tradition because they are an internal threat to the kyriarchal system and the discourse that forms, establishes, and maintains this system.[11] The impulse to circumscribe in socially constructed roles over half of the population[12] requires a means by which to designate the weak and the strong, or the superior and inferior, or whatever hierarchical binary works best for the reader. These designations are justified by essentialist thought and maintained by othering rhetoric. The irony is that all people are affected by socially constructed roles. It is just that those who fit the norm or are more centrally located within the social relations of power do not have to acknowledge or contend with theirs.

Power

As words such as "maintain," "define," and "confine" indicate, language and discourse are ultimately related to power. "What is it that we are trying to verify or justify in asserting that [some set of knowledge] is 'scientific'? Proving the 'validity' of a method or set of knowledge is an attempt to invest that discourse with the 'effects of power.'"[13] As Foucault says of scientific knowledge, so we can say about attempts to create and assert correct dogma, theology, or structural relations: they are efforts to imbue certain beliefs and behaviors with power.

Thus we must address the genderedness of power as we find it within the Christian canon, since power structures the human community and defines how "legitimate" communities function.[14] Given that only male voices were canonized, as far as we are aware, and that the communities are ordered and structured in hierarchical/kyriarchal ways, it is clear that the early Christian communities were constructed by and for "male" constituencies. This means that these texts and the social relations within them are characterized by malestream kyriarchal images, assumptions, and experiences and ultimately serve malestream kyriarchal interests. These texts become the elements that create and maintain the social exchanges within the faith communities and in this way

---

11. Irigaray, *This Sex*, 91.

12. In a dualistic understanding that allows for only male or female, we are told that roughly 51% of the world's population is female — a statistic that itself is highly skewed given that its provenance is Western European studies. Not only is this particular binary often used to subjugate females to males, it also overlooks or denies the reality of those who see their "gender" as fluid or simply as something that is neither male nor female, strictly speaking.

13. Michel Foucault, *Power/Knowledge: Selected Interviews and Other Writings, 1972–1977* (Collin Gordon, et al., trans.; New York: Pantheon, 1980), 85.

14. Hartsock, *Money, Sex and Power*, 6.

are imbued with power. So we have come full circle back to the discussion of language and discourse. Knowledge, language, and power are intimately related, thus they must all be taken into consideration in a feminist critique.

Sex and Power

A feminist critical methodology would hardly be complete without bringing in the realm of sex or sexuality and the power associated with it. Within the realm of biblical studies this conversation becomes more than typically charged. There seems to be an unspoken assumption for many people that (I am exaggerating in order to make a point) unless someone is "begetting" a child or the passage specifically discusses a rape, then sex is not a part of the biblical stories. What this perspective overlooks is the ever-present dynamic of control through sexual relations, control of women's sex, and the power associated with both that are all a part of patriarchal or kyriarchal systems. In other words, to critique the patriarchal nature of the texts of the Christian canon or of the society in which those texts were written *is* to raise the question of the role of sexuality within those texts and that society. Carol Pateman has suggested that, "Domesticated feminism denies that sexual domination is at issue."[15] Since the field of biblical studies seems averse to the s-word in general, I do not expect to be warmly greeted when I apply this insight to new testament writings and say that sexual *domination* is present in the ethos of these texts. This does not mean, however, that Pateman is not correct or that we should not be looking for such dynamics.

Not only do we need to be aware of the power of sexuality within biblical texts, but we would do well also to attend to the power that the bible has in defining normative sexuality. The heteronormative presuppositions within the household codes must be noted as relevant to this discussion. In addition, the asexual treatment of passages such as the household codes stands out as a symptom of highly spiritualized interpretations of scripture in general. The "purely" religious treatment of the household codes does not remove the sexual power implications or the power to define normative sexuality that are embedded within them. On the contrary, in much the same way that ignoring political issues within biblical texts does not neutralize their political impact, denying the impact in defining "normal" sexual relations that a text such as this one has does not cancel out such effects, but only allows them to continue without being critiqued.

---

15. Carole Pateman, "Introduction," in *Feminist Challenges: Social and Political Theory* (Carole Pateman and Elizabeth Gross, eds; Boston: Northeastern University, 1981), 5.

Feminist Summary

When brought into the realm of biblical or religious studies, all of the factors mentioned above take on the added element of being ordained; that is set in place, by a Creator or Divine Being. There is no question that there is a great deal at stake in the handling and interpretation of the Christian scriptures. All the more so do feminist critical engagements need to be welcomed into the conversation.

Given the issues raised by feminist critiques, it will be important for me to look for ways that the text: 1) speaks on behalf of women or directly to them from a place of power over them; 2) uses an essentialist description or assumption when individuals or groups of women are addressed; 3) uses gendered terms to establish or perpetuate a relational hierarchy or to justify possessing or dominating over someone; 4) uses malestream language which serves to repress all peripheral or non-normative voices and to reinscribe those that resonate with androcentric kyriarchal views; and 5) represents sexuality and the power it ascribes or denies to a person.

Postcolonial Studies

Though there can be multiple ways of applying the critiques that come from postcolonial studies, they all, by definition of the geo-political nature of any kind of colonial discourse, address the dynamics and exchanges between a central dominant power and the colonized or de-colonizing peoples on the periphery. Colonial studies proper refers to work done analyzing the exploitation and other effects of colonization on political and social structures, or literary works that represent or reflect upon such structures.[16] Two of its primary concerns focus upon analyzing the dynamics of representation and mimicry and how they contribute to or justify the colonizing project. It raises questions such as, "How does the dominant body represent the dominated, and vice versa?" and, "In what ways can we see the colonized imitating the relations of power and the social structures of the colonizer?" In the discussion below, one can see that there is some overlap in the particular realms of concern that I raise for a feminist and a postcolonial critique. How they differ is in terms of the starting point or perspective from which the topic is analyzed. I will be discussing matters of representation, mimicry, language and power, bodies and sex, and economic issues for this postcolonial critical method.

---

16. Bill Ashcroft, Gareth Griffiths and Helen Tiffin, *Post-Colonial Studies: The Key Concepts* (New York: Routledge, 2002), 40–50.

Can we do "Postcolonial" Studies on Ancient Texts?

Kwok Pui Lan has asked how a twenty-first century scholar, living in an era of decolonization and some forms of "postcolonialism," is able to undertake postcolonial studies of an ancient, pre-modern text.[17] I am primarily using a "postcolonial" critique in the sense of analyzing the effects of the presence of the Roman Empire on these sacred texts of the church. It is because of the insights that have been gathered by scholars such as Edward Said, Gayatri Spivak, and Homi Bhabha — the "trinity" within postcolonial theoretical work — and Kwok Pui Lan, Fernando F. Segovia, and R.S. Sugirtharajah — three biblical scholars whose work has significantly informed my own — that I am able to apply reading strategies that look for colonial epistemological frameworks within these ancient texts.[18]

Having grown up and lived in the United States my entire life, I cannot escape having traces of colonialist rationale, which then influence my own motivations and goals. Depending upon your understanding of the global role of the U.S. and the responsibility its current citizens have for past atrocities, I can be understood to be a colonizer, a member of the elite within a global empire, a victim due to my sex and my political beliefs, or some other combined form of objective and subjective relation to the U.S. governmental powers. However one might define my socio-political location, postcolonial studies have helped me to make a connection between the religious and political realms of the society in which I live, and then to have a critical engagement of the bible with this connection in mind.

Representation

There are two sides to the issue of representation within postcolonial studies that I bring to bear in my engagements with the bible. The first deals with how people are represented, whether it is the image of the colonizer by the colonized in a way that intends to be subversive or at times collusionary, or that of the colonized by the colonizer in a way that justifies the domination of those particular people. For this situation of a postcolonial engagement with new testament biblical texts, then, we are to look for representations of the Roman

---

17. Kwok Pui-lan, *Postcolonial Imagination and Feminist Theology* (Louisville: Westminster John Knox, 2005), 2. For a discussion of the distinctions between colonialism, postcolonialism, decolonialism and neo-colonialism, see Ania Loomba, *Colonialism/Postcolonialism* (New York: Routledge, 2002), 1–103.

18. Kwok, *Postcolonial Imagination*, 2. For more information on reading strategies from a postcolonial perspective, see also, Fernando F. Segovia, *Decolonizing Biblical Studies: A View from the Margins* (Maryknoll, NY: Orbis, 2004) and Miguel De La Torre, *Reading the Bible from the Margins* (Maryknoll: Orbis, 2002).

Empire within these writings. Scholars ask whether the authors of these texts that depict imperial powers are doing so in such a way as to suggest a resistance to these powers or were they perhaps hoping to encourage the communities to align with the dominant powers? For many people within the church today, the second possibility raises the additional concern of whether the authors of these texts were conscious of their political alignments. While we will never be able fully to determine intentions of authors, we can assess some of the implications of the content of their efforts.

The second issue of representation, most notably addressed by Gayatri Spivak, is an issue of whose version of the representation is considered valid and true.[19] Do "subaltern" peoples have enough of a grasp of the global socio-political relations that affect them to be able to present their own perspective of it? Is it not true that requiring that the subaltern represent themselves according to the standards of the system that is causing their oppression is yet another form of oppression and restriction? Yet, if they cannot fully grasp or put words to the socio-political dynamics they are facing, who else is able to speak for them? How do people of any form of privilege presume to be able to represent the realities of others, realities they have never experienced firsthand? Clearly the issues of "voice," power relations, and language are intimately related to the matter of representation, both here and in feminist discourse. What I find most relevant for a postcolonial approach to biblical studies, then, are the direct and indirect representations of Rome/the Roman Empire and being able to question, that is to apply a hermeneutics of suspicion to, the texts that provide some sense of mediation between the Christian communities and the socio-political realm.

Mimicry

The issue of mimicry is closely tied to representation, and brings into the discussion ideas such as ambivalence, hegemony, and hybridity.[20] Mimicry is what we see colonized or occupied peoples doing in attempts to imitate the social and cultural standards and behaviors of the colonizer/occupier. According to Bhabha, there will always be a slippage in this attempt to imitate; that is, the imitation will be not quite perfect. Some may think of this slippage as a gap between the original and the imitation. Whatever one's understanding of it, the ambivalence is seen in the colonized teetering back and forth between desiring to emulate the colonizer — which is what the dominant power would like, as it

---

19. Gayatri Spivak, "Can the Subaltern Speak?" in *Colonial Discourse and Post-Colonial Theory: A Reader* (Patrick Williams and Laura Chrisman, eds; New York: Columbia University, 1994), 66–111.

20. Bhabha, *The Location of Culture*, 85–122; and for a lay-person's brief explanation of these ideas, see Ashcroft, Griffiths and Tiffin, *Post-Colonial Studies*, 139–42.

confirms its ruling position — and desiring to create a subversive parody of the colonizer. Ultimately, it does not matter what the intentions are. The imitation of a dominating or imperial presence assures that the new system in question will also be characterized by a dominating, hierarchical/kyriarchal structure and ethos. We should expect to see in this imitation the same methods of creating and maintaining control and order that are employed by the imperial power.[21] This particular dynamic is supremely relevant when studying epistolary writings, in terms of both the power assumed by and ascribed to the author as well as the nature of the commands given in the letters.

Language and Power

The issues of language and power are relevant to feminist and postcolonialist discourses in complementary ways. At times it is difficult to know when a critique is grounded in gender and when in political matters, which is entirely appropriate given how interconnected all of these pieces are in reality. Theoretically speaking, however, a postcolonial critique of language focuses upon the propagandistic aspect of language as it functions to promote and maintain social and political structures, creating and defining "others" in such a way that justifies their subjugated position. The combination of language and power, then, functions quite powerfully within the realm of the collective psyche of a people, in what Pierre Bourdieu has called the *habitus*.

Bourdieu defines the *habitus* of a society as the "dispositions [that] generate practices, perceptions and attitudes which are 'regular' without being consciously co-ordinated or governed by any 'rule.'"[22] This definition is strikingly similar to some definitions of ideology, and has a hint of hegemony to it. In choosing the term *habitus* he places an emphasis upon the way the dispositions are embodied and lived out on a daily basis. This idea goes beyond a controlling or hegemonic ideology that the ruling powers need to reinforce constantly; the *habitus* addresses the beliefs that people unconsciously realize — bring into being — in their lives. Much like ideological beliefs, it is the fact that aspects of the *habitus* go unspoken and unnamed that makes them so powerful and so difficult to counter. Thus, I find that speaking about the *habitus* of a people creates a space for assessing the effects of the combination of language and

---

21. For recent studies on such methods, see Joseph A. Marchal, *Hierarchy, Unity and Imitation: A Feminist Rhetorical Analysis of Power Dynamics in Paul's Letter to the Philippians* (Academia Biblica 24; Atlanta: Society of Biblical Literature, 2006) and *The Politics of Heaven: Women, Gender, and Empire in the Study of Paul* (Paul in Critical Contexts; Minneapolis: Fortress, 2008). See also Elizabeth Castelli, *Imitating Paul: A Discourse of Power* (Louisville: Westminster John Knox, 1991).

22. Bourdieu, *Language and Symbolic Power*, 12. See also, Pierre Bourdieu, *Outline of a Theory of Practice* (Richard Nice, trans.; Cambridge: Cambridge University, 1977).

power in the socio-political realm. One can see how this concept applies to the early Christian communities and can be helpful when discussing the role the texts of the new testament played in creating this *habitus*.[23]

Bodies and Sex

While I am aware that bringing up the issue of sexual relations and abuses taps into a significant body of research and scholarship that I cannot fully represent in this setting, it is an important aspect of colonial discourse that must be mentioned. Jean Kim's feminist postcolonial interpretation of several stories in the gospel of John highlights the significance in people's lives of their sexual relations — whether exploitative, abusive, pleasurable, or pragmatic. These are realities that biblical scholars have done their share of overlooking. Colonialism and nationalism, being gendered in their basic construct, not only reinforce patriarchal and kyriarchal structures and systems, but they do this primarily through the regulation and control of women's sexuality.[24]

Saying that colonization is a gendered construct means that there is a connection between an empire's geopolitical domination over other peoples and territories and that empire's social norms that allow for or perpetuate the domination of men over women. This "power over" mentality then also extends to one class over another, one race over another, humanity over the earth, and so forth.[25] In all instances the "right" of one party to treat another inhumanely or unjustly is justified by these dualistic hierarchical and kyriarchal constructions embedded within societies. The horrific effects of such unjust treatment serve to maintain multiple levels of the dominant/dominated relationship, because it renders the oppressed unable to stand up for themselves. Not only does the dominating power structure seem inevitable and beneficial, then, but so does the gendered construct of the supremacy of males.

Coming back to the conversation of sexuality within the specific realm of postcolonial discourse then, we must be wary of texts that prescribe socio-political expectations of women that indirectly maintain control over their sexuality. Even to this day, our social consciousness reflects the underlying notion that

---

23. I do not mean to suggest that the *habitus* of the early Christian communities was the same from place to place. The fact is that there were many variations of how to worship or be a follower of Jesus in the first few centuries (not to mention today). Or to put it alternatively, we can see the need for so many letters that address 'correct' practices as an indication that communities embodied various practices and beliefs.

24. Jean Kim, *Woman and Nation: An Intercontextual Reading of the Gospel of John from a Postcolonial Feminist Perspective* (Boston: Brill, 2004). See also, Jenny Sharpe, "The Unspeakable Limits of Rape: Colonial Violence and Counter-Insurgency," in *Colonial Discourse and Post-Colonial Theory: A Reader* (Patrick Williams and Laura Chrisman, eds; New York: Columbia University, 1994), 221–43.

25. Jean Kim, *Woman and Nation*, 31.

women are the reproducers and stabilizers of any country or nation,[26] an idea that is directly contiguous with the thought behind the domestic codes of the philosophical treatises in the ancient world, for instance. Women are valued for their ability to produce the next generation, and in maintaining stable families they sustain the stability of the country or nation. We can see similar concerns at work within biblical texts of the new testament, in particular when authors seem concerned about sustaining the movement, and most poignantly so within the passages that contain adapted versions of household code structures and expectations. This control over women's (but not men's) sexuality is an example of a kyriarchal system flexing its muscles, so to speak, in order to keep its power intact. Since the expectation is framed in terms of the potential a female body has to reproduce, it represents an example of essentialist thought. In prescribing expectations for women that require the use of their vaginas for particular ends, males get to control the bodies and purposes allotted to females.

M. Jacqui Alexander and Chandra Talpade Mohanty describe their feminist postcolonial paradigm as one that foregrounds "decolonization which stresses power, history, memory, relational analysis, justice (not just representation), and ethics."[27] In so doing they highlight the multidimensional nature of geo-politics and the interconnectedness of all people in today's global reality.

While Alexander and Mohanty are explicating feminist postcolonial discourse within the twentieth and twenty-first centuries, I think that their theoretical analyses are relevant for first-century Greco-Roman dynamics precisely because our socio-political realities today in the "West" are based upon structures and expectations found within the Greco-Roman world. We may be able to trace the evolution of the economic structures or systems in place during these intervening two thousand years, but the fact that there are pieces of continuity throughout, specifically the role and subjectivity of women, indicates that there are components of the "ancient" system that have never been significantly re-envisioned or reconfigured within the dominant or hegemonic social and political discourse of the Western world. Alexander and Mohanty note how state practices and fundamentalist religious discourses focus upon women's bodies, minds, and the roles they are allowed to occupy in the service of maintaining kyriarchal control and regulating morality.[28] The reader can just as easily apply these observations to today's political realm, to

---

26. Ibid., 30. In particular Kim speaks of the familial language that is applied to nationhood: "mothers of the nation," the role that we assume women play in nurturing the next generation, and so forth.

27. M. Jacqui Alexander and Chandra Talpade Mohanty, "Introduction: Genealogies, Legacies, Movements," in *Feminist Genealogies, Colonial Legacies, Democratic Futures* (M. Jacqui Alexander and Chandra Talpade Mohanty, eds; New York: Routledge, 1997), xix.

28. Alexander and Mohanty, "Introduction," xxv.

that of what we see represented within Christian biblical texts, or to various times and locations in between.

> Zillah Eisenstein notes that in her own work, she start[s] with bodies because political states always have an interest in them; because politics usually derive from such interests; and because, as we move increasingly toward new technologies that redefine female bodies, we must recognize these interests as utterly political.[29]

If any move to re-define women's bodies is utterly political, then any rhetorical, philosophical, or theological move to maintain the definition of women's bodies is just as political.

I shudder to think of how trite the phrase, "the personal is political," has become. Its overuse or lack of contextualization as it is used and referenced contributes to an ability to disregard the implications of its claim. The political realm is one that contains or relates to all other aspects of life. Many biblical scholars and well-intentioned Christians over the centuries have denied the influence on socio-political systems and relations of power that the claims of scripture have. It must be noted, however, that their desire to see them as unrelated does not make it so. Here, once again, we see a symptom of the over-spiritualized interpretations of the writings in the bible. From a postcolonial perspective, bodies are subjects that can be regulated and controlled, used and abused.

Economic Issues

In his contribution to *Postcolonial Biblical Criticism*, Roland Boer made a compelling argument that we ought to consider the economic aspect of a society as foundational to postcolonial criticism.[30] The geo-political struggle presently at work in the twenty-first-century global community attests to the fact that economic exploitation goes hand in hand with political domination and control. The creation of "Free Trade Agreements" and the sanctioning of financial aid provisions by world leaders to members of the two-thirds world are just the tip of the iceberg of the manifestation of economic and political collusion. There can be no getting around this connection today. Though we do not have parallel documentation for the relations between Rome and its

---

29. Zillah Eisenstein, *The Color of Gender: Reimaging Democracy* (Berkeley: University of California, 1994), 171.

30. Roland Boer, "Marx, Postcolonialism and the Bible," in *Postcolonial Biblical Criticism: Interdisciplinary Intersections* (Fernando Segovia and Stephen Moore, eds; New York: T&T Clark, 2005), 105–25.

colonies in the first century, we can rest assured that similar forms of political and economic agreements were present then as well.

With these things in mind, we would do well to take into consideration the economic and political dynamics that are perhaps not named but are still relevant in any parable spoken by Jesus, his interactions with the Jewish leaders of the Temple, or in Paul's admonitions to the various *ekklesia* around the Roman Empire, for example. Given the clear social, political, and economic role that households held in the ancient world, a discussion of the new testament household codes would not be complete without perspectives of a geo-political or Roman imperial framework.

Postcolonial Summary

The pieces of a postcolonial critique that I think helpfully inform a method of biblical interpretation are the following: 1) assessing the portrayal of the Roman Empire or imperial representatives and the relation or interaction with them that is encouraged for members of the faith communities; 2) analyzing the various layers of language, knowledge, and power within a biblical text that are forms of mimicry of the imperial methods of control, relational structures, and geo-political interests; and 3) noting what we learn about the view of women, in particular how their bodies and their sexuality or sexual relationships are used as a part of these methods of structural and relational control, and thus how they might be circumscribed by the text.

Materialist Concerns

The materialist approach I am using reaches beyond the economic structure of households in first-century CE Asia Minor, the realm a reader may anticipate by the label "materialist,"[31] in order to assess the construction of meaning and social arrangements that the texts of Christian scriptures support and engender. This approach is based upon Rosemary Hennessy's particular interest in the systems and power relations that texts adhere to, perpetuate and set in motion. She reads "irruptions" in texts as "symptoms" of the hegemonic voice silencing the voice of others who pose a threat to its normative ideology. In her words, her symptomatic reading "draws out the unnaturalness of the text and makes visible another logic haunting its surface."[32] It is with Hennessy's terminology in mind that I attempt to point beyond a critique of a text with a feminist

---

31. The typical Marxian critique of the divisions of labor is not enough but must include a gendered/sexual, and I would add at least "racial," division of labor.

32. Hennessy, *Materialist Feminism*, 93.

postcolonial lens to an assessment of the subjectivities that are constructed and circumscribed and subsequently take on material reality because of texts from the Christian canon. In order to make such an assessment, in addition to the feminist and postcolonial contributions, we need to look at the creation of knowledge and construction of subjects.

Creation of Knowledge

The creation of knowledge touches upon several of the realms of concern already discussed, power and language in particular. According to Hennessy, discourse joins power and knowledge, in part because it typically comes about as a result of a struggle between unequal power relations. Thus discourse can be both instrument and effect of power.[33] Social discourse itself is a form of ideology that reflects the (often unconscious) political ideology of the one speaking or writing. I would suggest that the political ideology is embodied and passed along in part through the *habitus*, as discussed previously. So we can read texts looking for the ideology that they perpetuate, and in so doing, the realm of knowledge of what is normative for a particular community or its members.

Hennessy also suggests that the social discourse of the *habitus* is intended to take on hegemonic force, which means that we can expect that some voice or idea is specifically being targeted in order to be silenced. She then reads these silences in a text as "irruptions" in the narrative. One has to be attentive to what happens in a narrative or text: is there perhaps something missing or beneath the surface of the discourse? Does a particular claim seem out of place within the larger discourse of which it is a part, or does it stand out in the "thou pro-testeth too much" sense of things? These irruptions are entry points to discover counter-hegemonic voices behind the discourse that were silenced by those in power.[34] It is through what Hennessy calls irruptions that much reclaiming of women's voices in and behind biblical texts has already taken place.[35]

A Gramscian definition of hegemony tells us that there is a need to con-tinually reassert the ruling or dominating ideology. This happens because, though the ruling ideology is somewhat embedded within the social structures, behavioral expectations, and relations of power, there is a voice, resistance, or a

33. Ibid., 41, 42.
34. Ibid., xii–xvii, 94.
35. This was the approach employed in Schüssler Fiorenza, *In Memory of Her: A Feminist Theological Reconstruction of Christian Origins* (New York: Crossroads, 1992). See also Antoinette Clark Wire, *Corinthian Women Prophets: A Reconstruction through Paul's Rhetoric* (Minneapolis: Fortress, 1990); Elizabeth Castelli, *Imitating Paul*; and Joseph Marchal, *Hierarchy, Unity and Imitation* and *The Politics of Heaven*.

heteronymous way of viewing the world that is also present, such that the ruling ideology must be continually reinforced. Normative knowledge is maintained by the silencing, and denigrating, of alternative perspectives and voices. When we see behavior or beliefs being corrected or redirected by pronouncements and commands, often in an over-determined fashion, we can assume that some form of resistance or movement of change was/is afoot. This perspective is quite helpful when studying Paul's letters and will also prove beneficial for discussing the passage at hand.

Hennessy wrote with twentieth-century socio-political realities in mind in her discussion of creating new knowledge. She challenges her reader to conceive of altogether new paradigms and structures for understanding our world. The goal to create counter-hegemonic discourses, specifically counter-ing the dominant patriarchal/kyriarchal social system, is sought in part by the production of new feminist knowledge. It is important to emphasize the "new" aspect, since she seeks not simply a feminist revision of history and knowl-edge as currently promulgated by our institutions, but a creation of an entirely new sphere in and by which to create knowledge. It is not a coincidence that numerous feminist theorists speak of creating *new* knowledge as compared with simply revising what exists. It is not enough to "spin" malestream content from a feminist perspective. The new sphere or space allows for alternative social constructions and norms of relating, which support knowledge produced in and from various aspects of life. This task of creating new knowledge today is often addressed in terms of the content disseminated by universities through college courses but more importantly through journals and other publications.[36]

While journals do not have a direct parallel within the first-century Greco-Roman setting, I suggest that the production of documents and texts and the canonization process do reflect the same underlying agenda: the creation or construction of knowledge and behavioral standards for the sake of consistency and survival. Scholarship reflects the socio-cultural concerns of the context in which it is written, different fields have their own significant — and often unconscious — presuppositions, and all forms of scholarship bear the race, class, and gender perspectives of the person who wrote it.[37] The texts of the new testament were written and collected with many of the same socio-cultural factors present as we see in scholarship today. The processes and content of

---

36. For instance, see Patrice McDermott, *Politics and Scholarship: Feminist Academic Journals and the Production of Knowledge* (Chicago: University of Illinois, 1994).

37. Patrice McDermott, *Politics and Scholarship*, 5. I refer to these three general categories — race, class, and gender — well aware that they are not comprehensive in terms of identifying the aspects of a person's life that have an impact on the content of an author's scholarship.

textual and canonical creation are inherently political. These political texts, whether first-century CE ecclesial correspondence or twenty-first-century academic publications, determine normativity of thought, beliefs and actions. Thus I read new testament texts with an eye toward the knowledge they create or highlight as normative.

Construction of Subjects

The construction of subjects and creation of knowledge are intimately related. As Hennessy notes, "What we do impacts what we can know; and what we know impacts what we can do."[38] Subjectivities are discursively constructed, often very clearly delineated or "circumscribed" according to what is normative knowledge and behavior for a given situation or community. While we can see various aspects of language and power coming into play in the social construction of women, it is important to try to isolate, for the sake of creating a method, the particular dynamic of construction. It is a peculiar dynamic, in that the subject so constructed does not necessarily actually exist in that society. Rather, there is an ideal that is described, which then stands as a model for all recipients and, in the case of such subjects within the Christian canon, subsequent generations. The very nature of subject construction implies that there are counter-images simultaneously at work. There are images that the dominant discourse or ideology needs to denounce, silence, or eradicate. Thus it is through discourse that subjects are constructed, and it is when the discourse permeates the *habitus* that these constructions become embodied, realized or materialized by the people of a given community.

While defining a subject may seem to be an innocent, rather normal endeavor, the need to construct or define is ultimately a matter of power and control. It establishes correct behavior and circumscribes the realms of influence that are considered appropriate for the subject in question. When this subject is described within a sacred text, which is believed to be divinely inspired, the description of the subject takes on almost divine status. For example, since David in the Hebrew Scriptures is hailed as a man after God's heart, then males in the Church today are commended for seeking to be men after God's heart. Since it is a male in the scriptures who is given this title, then it is males today who are most commended for this trait; females have their own essentialist descriptions to emulate. Given the power that the Church has ascribed its texts for defining what faithful followers look like, this is not an arbitrary issue to address. This is not a blame game of pointing fingers; it is simply an exercise

---

38. Hennessy, *Materialist Feminism*, 7.

in addressing the implications of a social construction, the material realities of prescriptions of subjects.

When looking at biblical texts, we need to look beyond the particular relations it addresses to the underlying realms of life that are also affected by the prescriptions within the texts. These underlying relations are often more central to women's lives than the ones being addressed. Addressing a superficial relation as a means of controlling something deeper is in effect a type of irruption itself. Whether or not the author was conscious of the deeper impact is not the point.

Normativity of knowledge and of socio-cultural expectations, as defined within a kyriarchal system, however, do not give full value to the realities of subordinate members. The political ideology of a society or community, inasmuch as it is defined by kyriarchal rulers, is foreign to subordinate members to a large degree, as it is imposed from without and does not take into consideration or reflect their own experiences. It is in this way that certain discourses or kinds of language are silenced altogether. Since they are not reflected or recorded in the shared social discourse, they are not passed along for future generations. Their voices are not a part of the collective practices and perceptions. Yet the imposed ideology with its kyriarchal power relations becomes familiar, has a way of justifying itself and perpetuating itself as part of the status quo, and over time is even embraced by many who are oppressed by it, either because of a need to survive or a lack of will/resources to resist it. We can turn to the *habitus* again, the space in which language (discourse) and power (ideologies) come together, to understand or explain this phenomenon.

Let me reiterate Bourdieu's concept of the *habitus* of a society: it is the set of "dispositions [that] generate practices, perceptions and attitudes which are 'regular' without being consciously co-ordinated or governed by any 'rule.'"[39] In his definition, I understand the "dispositions" to be related to, if not the same thing as, Terry Eagleton's characterization of dominant ideology, which: *promotes* the beliefs and values that maintain it, *naturalizes* and *universalizes* them so that they are unconsciously embraced as self-evident, *denigrates* those belief systems that challenge or subvert it, *excludes* rival forms of thought from the common discourse, and *obscures* social reality in such a way as to promote itself.[40]

For the purposes of engagement with biblical texts, I do not think that one must choose to speak only in terms of either ideology or the *habitus*, given the social, often unconscious, nature of the power of both. We are invited, instead,

---

39. Bourdieu, *Language and Symbolic Power*, 12.
40. Terry Eagleton, *Ideology: An Introduction* (New York: Verso, 1991), 5–6.

to take seriously the role that the biblical texts had in the formation of both within the early Christian movement. We might ask what practices, perceptions, and beliefs needed to be specifically made regular within the early Christian communities. The answers are found within the writings that were collected and passed along by these communities.

The purpose of correspondence was to affirm some communities and to correct behavior that was incongruent with what someone (who?) had determined was appropriate for this burgeoning movement. Ensuring the perpetuity of the movement, at times by offering encouraging words for those in the midst of persecution, took precedence over perpetuating the initial purpose of the movement.[41] At times the letters were comforting and poetic, at times they were full of rebuke, and often they were a mixture of various types of content and purposes. In all cases there was something like the narrative of the faith communities contained within them. Though it may seem to be a bit of a stretch to call Paul's letters, and the other non-gospel writings that are collected in the new testament, narrative, at a basic level that is exactly what they constitute: the narrative of a young, burgeoning social movement.

Narrative is "essential for constructing the worlds we inhabit, sustaining the communities that hold us, and enlivening the rituals that shape us."[42] Stories, phrases, pithy sayings, myths, proverbs, poetry, lines from film and various other forms of writing make up our collective social consciousness today. How much more affective are such traditions and collected stories of legends and heroes in an age of papyri, scrolls and codices, and oral transmission? We construct meaning and identity, both individual and communal, through stories.

Joseph E. Davis claims that narrative is an essential element of any movement's discourse, and therefore becomes a productive source for analyzing the nature of the movement.[43] Similarly, Robert D. Benford focuses on how these narratives function as control mechanisms within social movements. Benford notes how the members of a movement actively, even strategically, engage in activities that uphold the narrative that defines the movement and even work to prevent alternative narratives from taking root or being disseminated. This adherence to the movement's narrative or story, he claims, creates uniformity

---

41. I am aware that there is no consensus on the matter of what the "original" purpose was of the Jesus movement. However, it is clear that if Jesus was indeed crucified by the Romans, it was his actions and reputation that led to it. Those of his later followers who were persecuted or killed were so treated because of touting his *name*, not necessarily for imitating his actions that had a socio-political thrust.

42. Herbert Anderson and Edward Foley, *Mighty Stories, Dangerous Rituals: Weaving Together the Human and the Divine* (San Francisco: Jossey-Bass, 1998), 5.

43. Joseph E. Davis, "Narrative and Social Movements: The Power of Stories," in *Stories of Change: Narrative and Social Movements* (Joseph E. Davis, ed.; Albany: State University of New York, 2002), 4.

by "channeling and constraining individual as well as collective sentiments, emotions, and action."[44] It is striking how well these insights drawn from observing nonviolent peace movements in the twentieth century reflect some of what we can see at work in the first and second century formative Christian communities.

The act of preventing alternative or competing messages runs throughout the Pauline corpus. Several of the Pastorals are aimed at constraining the actions and realm of influence of women, which is also tied to controlling the "story that is told about the movement." It is clear from the content of 1 Peter that the author was seeking to direct and control the actions and emotions of the recipients. It does seem that there is no other way to sustain or maintain a movement with any continuity with the past unless the beliefs, behaviors, and roles are clearly delineated. There remain two concerns regarding these well-intentioned efforts to sustain this movement. The first is that laying down such narrowly defined behaviors does not allow for that change that is inherent to human nature. The second is more germane to this paper and brings us back to the issue of constructing subjectivities: whose version of events, narratives, beliefs, and proper behavior is made the controlling paradigm?

The issue of constructing subjects taps into numerous socio-political dynamics of social acceptability and sustainability, vertical and horizontal power relations, essentialism and representation, and even mimicry and collusion. What we can do affects what we can know. What we can know is affected by the nature of the communities of which we are a part. When any of a community's power relations are marked by a domination/submission dynamic, then the nature of the community as a whole will be structured by domination.[45] Thus subjects within this community will be constructed accordingly.

Materialist Summary

The materialist critique that I will undertake in the following chapters reflects an assessment of the knowledge this letter creates by addressing the power struggles within and behind the text, seen in the irruption or the gap in the fabric of a narrative: what the text allows women to know. The construction of subjects that occurs as a result of biblical texts is addressed by granting the importance and influence of the content of ecclesial correspondence, naming the ideologies at work behind commands or prescriptions, acknowledging the

44. Robert D. Benford, "Controlling Narratives and Narratives as Control within Social Movements," 53–75 in *Stories of Change: Narrative and Social Movements* (Joseph E. Davis, ed.; Albany: State University of New York, 2002), 53.

45. Hartsock, *Money, Sex, and Power*, 155.

various aspects of women's reality that are affected by such prescriptions, and sorting through how actions and behaviors are circumscribed by a text. These two pieces — creation of knowledge and construction of subjects — are predicated upon an agreement with Hartsock's insight, that the relations that define and circumscribe women's activity are embodied in and perpetuated by their communities. Within Christian communities, the collected correspondence is the starting point for such assessments.

Weaving the Threads

The time has come to pull together the various strands of thought and inquiry that inform and direct this feminist, postcolonial, materialist engagement with biblical texts. I read for seven specific dynamics or components of the text:

1. How it speaks on behalf of women or directly to them from a place of power over them. What does this piece tell us that women can do and know?
2. The malestream language that, by definitive claims and commands, represses peripheral and non-normative language and experiences, noting for whose sake this occurs.
3. How it uses essentialist assumptions and descriptions in order to perpetuate kyriarchal relations and to justify dominating over or possessing someone.
4. Explicit or implicit reference to sexuality and other aspects of women's lives that are affected by these ascriptions and commands that are often overlooked in interpretations.
5. Portrayals of the Roman Empire and its representatives, and relations with them that are encouraged.
6. The layers of knowledge, power, and language of these communities that are impacted by imperial ideology.
7. What do we learn about the view of women, in particular how their bodies and their sexuality or sexual relationships are used as a part of these methods of structural and relational control, and thus how they are circumscribed by the text?

There are also two assumptions that I hold regarding Christian scripture in general that are important to note here. Put in terms of 1 Peter, specifically, they are: 1) the letter of 1 Peter is a system of communication that is embedded in and reinscribes power relations, and 2) the content of 1 Peter and other ecclesial correspondence was and still is taken very seriously in faith communities, noted by their use in worship services and in the belief that it is the primary source for guidance into God's will and for knowing God's Son.

Ultimately, these analyses brought together will inform my assessment that 1 Peter does less to engender "emancipatory dissident consciousness" and egalitarian relations than to reinscribe a dominating kyriarchal ethos and structuring of relations within the communities.[46] These insights in turn highlight the actions, behaviors, and knowledge that are circumscribed for women by this text.

---

46. Schüssler Fiorenza, "1 Peter," 381.

3

Reading the Rhetoric

For understanding, function is more significant than the origin.[1]

Introduction

This chapter is intended to look at the narratological and rhetorical effect of the content of the letter that precedes the *Haustafel* in 1 Peter. A full or thorough assessment along these lines would indeed require its own monograph. For our purposes, however, it is enough to highlight the overall importance of this particular content. The three main areas of focus are the two sets of labels "aliens and refugees" and "royal priesthood and holy nation" and the command to "honor the emperor."

As Alasdair MacIntyre has noted, "There is no way to give us an understanding of any society, including our own, except through the stock of stories which constitute its initial dramatic resources. Mythology, in its original sense, is at the heart of things."[2] Looking back from the vantage point of two thousand years of Christian traditions, it is easy to overlook the social and even psychological impact that the new testament texts might have had the first few times they were heard or read. Thus it is essential that we take the time to (re)consider what these texts, not as "given truths" but as performative and affective writings, tell us about the "heart of things" for early Christian communities: their identities, roles, and socio-political alignments.

If we think of the labels "aliens and strangers" and "royal priesthood and holy nation" as part of a new symbolic universe for the self-identity of the communities in Asia Minor,[3] then the letter of 1 Peter gives new life to old narratives and sacred stories. As Philip Wheelwright has noted, "What really matters in a metaphor is the psychic depth at which the things of the world,

1. Thurén, *The Rhetorical Strategy of 1 Peter*, 186.
2. Alasdair C. MacIntyre, *After Virtue: A Study in Moral Theory* (Notre Dame: Notre Dame University, 1981), 201.
3. Bechtler, *Following in His Steps*, 40.

whether actual or fancied, are transmuted" for the benefit of those who engage the metaphor.[4] Additionally, as Lakoff and Johnson note, the impact of metaphors can be seen in our daily lives, since the concepts that govern our thought also structure and govern how we understand what we perceive, how we function in the world, and how we relate with one another.[5]

Various groups of Christians throughout the history of the church have taken up images or labels such as "royal priesthood" or "aliens and strangers" in order to understand their own identity as a part of God's people.[6] There must be something in a narrative or a metaphor that rings true for the audience in order for it to have staying power. Since "it is the primary function of tradition to explain the new in terms of the old and in that way to authorize the new,"[7] we can safely assume that the author of 1 Peter drew upon familiar myths that would continue to touch "psychic depths." Consciously or not, he joined thought, feeling, imagination and language in the development of a new authoritative myth or symbolic universe.

The first part of the letter (1.1–2.12) is devoted to recalling several parts of an ancient myth/story, which is (re)adapted by these communities. The part immediately following this beautiful midrashic composition is an incorporation of a socio-political expectation, what we refer to as a "household code."[8] Its inclusion is often read today not as a symptomatic irruption but as a perfectly reasonable section of the letter. I suggest that its reasonableness is due to the blending of religious and socio-political language that occurs leading up to it. It remains an irruption in the text, however, because it departs from the traditional household code form, directly counters the non-gender-role-determined ethos that Paul spoke of, and it prescribes an over-determined circumscription of women — all are issues that I will address in the next chapter. For now, I will

4.　Philip Wheelwright, *Metaphor & Reality* (Bloomington, Ill.: Indiana University, 1962; repr. Eugene, Ore.: Wipf and Stock, 1997), 71.

5.　George Lakoff and Mark Johnson, *The Metaphors We Live By* (Chicago: University of Chicago, 1980), 3.

6.　A divinity school student recently informed me that her Easter sermon would contrast Jesus' testing in Gethsemane — the emphasis being on the testing, with which the members of her African-American church identify — with the church's identity as the "royal priesthood." Far from being a problematic theological justification for hierarchical relations, for this student and those who receive or claim this label it is an affirmation of God's love for them.

7.　Ferdinand Dienst, "Idealistic *Theologiegeschichte*: Ideology Critique and the Dating of Oracles of Salvation. Posing a Questions Concerning the Monopoly of an Accepted Method," *Studies in Isaiah* (Wouter C. van Wyk, ed.; Hercules, South Africa: NHW, 1981), 65.

8.　As noted in Chapter 1, the household code was never labeled as such in the ancient world. To refer to it as such is truly the reflection of a modern construct, though I will continue to do so because of its familiarity and convenience.

begin by addressing the first label or metaphor that comes from both 1.1 and 2.11.

"Aliens and Strangers" or "Immigrants and Refugees"?

The initial address of the letter contains one part of this label: "Peter, an apostle of Jesus, to the chosen *parepidēmois* of the diaspora in Pontus, Galatia, Cappadocia, Asia and Bithynia" (1P 1.1). Most English translations highlight the foreignness, transient, or alien sense of the term *parepidēmois*: "elect who are sojourners," "chosen exiles," "pilgrims," or "elect strangers in the world," for instance. For reasons that I will explain below, I prefer "refugees."

The familiar phrase "aliens and strangers" comes from the most common translation of 2.11,[9] "Beloved, I urge you as *paroikous kai parepidēmous* to abstain from worldly desires that wage war against the soul." Here we find the much more common term *paroikous* paired with *parepidēmous*; the typical rendering of this phrase indicates that translators see these terms as synonymous.[10]

Whatever is intended by these labels, however, there can be no doubt that some aspect of their social-political status is forefront on the author's mind in relation to these communities and the situation that he is addressing for them. It is understandable that subsequent interpreters of this letter have assumed that this terminology is intended to overshadow the content of the letter. The ongoing debate is, "in what way?"

What the term "stranger," a common rendering of either Greek word, might bring to mind today is not necessarily parallel to all that is implied by this term in its first-century context (or sixth century BCE, for that matter). The same is true of "alien," which perhaps invokes for Westerners thoughts of spaceships and multiple-headed beings or a person caught within the borders of a country that is not her homeland — though even with the latter connotation, the focus tends to be on whether she is "legal" or "illegal" as such, which completely avoids dealing with the underlying issues that force a person to relocate at all.

---

9.   The same language is also used in Ephesians 2.19: "So then you are no longer strangers and aliens, but you are fellow citizens with the saints, and are of God's household," a passage that picks up on the "stranger" (*xenoi*), "exile/refugee" (*paroikoi*), "citizen" (*sumpolitai*), and "house of God" imagery as well.

10.   This suggestion is confirmed by two observations. The first is that there is a lack of consistency in a term-for-term rendering in English translations. For example, while in 1.1 (*parepidēmos*) the translation might be "elect who are sojourners," in 2.11 (*paroikous kai parepidēmous*) it is "sojourners and pilgrims," flipping the order in relation to what is in the Greek text. The New Living Translation does something similar: "chosen people living as foreigners," and "foreigners and aliens." This is a minor detail, I realize, but it does indicate a certain amount of interchangeability between these two terms. The second observation is that any form of *parepidēmos* is exceedingly rare in both the new testament and the LXX, and when the LXX uses it, it is paired with *paroikos*.

It seems appropriate at this point to take a brief look at some Hebrew bible parallels of these terms in order to demonstrate my rationale for a somewhat distinct rendering of these labels, "immigrants and refugees."[11]

The Hebrew word *gēr* is translated with both *paroikos* and *parepidēmos*. A common word in labeling those in the Hebrew bible who were not a part of the 12 tribes, *gēr* is often used to refer to a hired employee of a household. It implies someone clearly not a member of the family and yet distinct from the slaves of the house. It appears that the term is also used within the Hebrew bible to refer to a non-native resident who does not have full citizenship.[12] Many of the common modern translations have more of a transient sense than what I see in the various bible dictionaries and encyclopedia[13]: in particular, the Levites are told to be *gērim* among the rest of the Israelites and *gēr* is used to refer to God's presence at times. I do not see why either one of these contexts implies transience, and prefer to interpret the connotation of the term with a more socio-political focus.

Additionally, since the Israelites were *gērim* in their time in Egypt, it seems that the economic and political factors that precipitated the move to Egypt or later into the "promised land" should be considered in the assessment of these terms in context. I am taking up this word study at some length because, for instance, Elliott has based his theology of the whole letter, and by extension the purpose of the church, on his understanding of this one phrase in 2.11, which he translates as "resident aliens and visiting strangers." While I find his interpretation to be on the whole a helpful and productive one, I also think that it is lacking in political implications in the way he applies it, which is actually somewhat contradictory to his overall project.[14]

In fact, the more I look at the Hebrew bible references to *gēr* the more convinced I am that a helpful modern parallel to these *paroikoi* and *parepidēmoi*

11. See also R. S. Sugirtharajah, "Postcolonial and Biblical Interpretation: The Next Phase," in *A Postcolonial Commentary on the New Testament Writings* (Fernando F. Segovia and R. S. Sugirtharajah, eds; Sheffield: Sheffield Press, forthcoming), 463–65.

12. Within the Roman Republic and Empire, however, the parallel term or concept to the Hebrew word *gēr* is taken up to refer to native residents who do not have full citizenship. Especially given the importance of land and belonging to a particular geographical location as a part of one's identity, this subtle shift is somewhat noteworthy.

13. Daniel I. Brock, "Sojourner; Alien; Stranger," in *International Standard Bible Encyclopedia*, vol. 4 (Geoffrey Bromily, ed.; Grand Rapids: Eerdmans, 1988), 561–4; T. M. Mauch, "Sojourner," in *IDB* vol. 4 (George Arthur Buttrick, et al., eds; New York: Abingdon, 1962) 337–9; John R. Spencer, "Sojourner," *ABD* vol. 6 (David Noel Freedman, editor-in-chief; New York: Doubleday, 1992), 103–4.

14. Elliott touches upon the literal, instead of merely metaphorical or spiritual, homeless in the United States in his work, *A Home for the Homeless*, leading me to believe that economic and political factors of our society are important to him.

would be immigrants from Central and South America[15]; or in the case of the Israelites who had returned to Jerusalem from Babylon, I see today's prisoners of war of various forms, even sex slaves such as the "comfort women" in Japan, as appropriate parallels. We do the text and the early Christian communities a disservice if we de-politicize these labels and downplay the desperation that accompanied being in such a position.[16] Thus, I have chosen "immigrants and refugees" in order to highlight the three concerns of: the lack of citizenship and "belonging," bearing the brunt of the labor that sustains the region or simply fulfilling work that no one else would choose, and the continual state of being at the mercy of others.

Contrary to what Elliott has said about *paroikoi*, which is that this term focuses upon their social estrangement,[17] Michael Ivanovitch Rostovtzeff suggests that this term was applied to *native* people who "cultivated and inhabited" extensive tracts outside the major cities. "From the Roman point of view these villages were 'attached' or 'attributed' to the city; from the Greek point of view the villages were inhabited by 'by-dwellers' (*paroikoi* or *katoikoi*) who never had had and were never destined to have the full rights of municipal citizenship."[18] In other words, according to Rostovtzeff this was a label used by the elite within the cities to refer to the peasants in the outer-lying areas, those who worked the land and were ultimately the foundation of the economic system.[19]

Some regions of Asia Minor had a predominance of cities, but much of the inner part of Asia Minor did not.[20] Given the five regions of Asia Minor that

15. The story of Jacob taking his entire clan to Egypt is usually told from an entitled position — since they were God's chosen people they were entitled to seek a place where they would survive. We might benefit from seeing the same right or entitlement to seek ways to survive motivating those "illegally" crossing the border between Mexico and Texas, for instance.

16. In spite of many white Western males' assertions to the contrary, the typically white-Western privileged church in the United States today hardly reflects the socio-political realities that I imagine are going on for the communities in Asia Minor. Thus, wealthy members of mega-churches today, for instance, would do well to reconsider to whom and how easily they assign these "sojourner," "stranger," and "alien" labels.

17. John H. Elliott, *1 Peter: A New Translation with Introduction and Commentary* AB 37B (New York: Doubleday, 2000), 458–9, 476–83. While Elliott notes the political implications for the native tenant farmers (478), he then returns to using "social" terms, as if the vast array of political dynamics is sufficiently represented by the "social realm."

18. Michael Ivanovitch Rostovtzeff, *The Social and Economic History of the Roman Empire* (New York: Oxford, 1926), 236–7. One might also ponder the racial/ethnic undercurrents that may have been at work here, though they would not have been labeled as such at the time. If someone who was native to a particular area was still seen as a "by-dweller," it raises the question as to what part of him or her evoked such othering language.

19. Dio of Prusa spoke to the tension created by this socio-political issue, suggesting that a *sunoikismos* be created, a social and economic unity between the city and countryside villages.

20. Rostovtzeff, *Roman Empire*, 239.

are named in 1.1, perhaps we should assume that the letter was addressed to and read in communities in both urban and rural areas, with the potential to have constituents of varying political and economic standings. Whatever the case, we cannot lose sight of the opening line that describes all the recipients as "chosen refugees," a label I maintain is best understood in politico-economic terms.[21] J. W. Pryor adds that "it is just not imaginable that a group of churches in Asia Minor at this time would be made up of one social class, that of 'resident aliens,'"[22] which I take as a helpful warning against taking any of these terms too literally.

The method proposed in Chapter 1 raises two important points about this label, "immigrants and refugees." The first is that it draws upon the reality lived by those most exploited by the kyriarchal socio-economic structure. The label only makes sense as long as the exploitative system remains in place. Second, the socio-political relations that the kyriarchal system requires are not necessarily scrutinized or critiqued.[23] In identifying with these members of society the author acknowledges their relative powerlessness and voicelessness that is created by the system. When taken in conjunction with the other labels of the letter, however, we will see that their real social location is to be traded in for a metaphorical identity that resonates with the very institutions that exploit them. Additionally, what this label cannot do is acknowledge the additional layer of oppression or powerlessness that women have in this situation.

Royal Priesthood and Holy Nation

The realms of priesthoods and leaders of nations are typically inhabited by men, often chosen by God (or the gods) for such prestigious roles. Because of the theocratic nature of Israel there was for them no boundary preventing one institution from influencing the other, the way we might think of them as separate entities today. Because the language used here in 1 Peter bears the imprint of religious and political terminology, the new identity becomes a fascinating example of mimicry of both realms, and ultimately resonates with imperialist ideology.

21. See also Edgar Krentz, "Order in the 'House' of God: The *Haustafel* in 1 Peter 2:11-3:12," in *Common Life in the Early Church: Essays Honoring Graydon Snyder* (Julian Victor Hills and Richard B. Gardner, eds; Harrisburg, Pa.: Trinity, 1998), 279.

22. John W. Pryor, "First Peter and the New Covenant (II)," *RTR* 45, no. 2 (1986), 45.

23. It can be posited that in the author's calling attention to their plight there is an underlying critique of the system that holds them in it. For me, however, that critique does not go far enough.

Of Priesthoods and Nations

The text that most closely reflects the labels of "royal priesthood and holy nation," is that of Exod. 19.6, which begins, "And you shall be to me a kingdom of priests and a holy nation. These are the words that you shall speak to the sons of Israel."[24] The issue of what these phrases meant in the Hebrew bible's initial context is certainly one of debate, as one might expect. It is beyond the scope of this project to do a full analysis of any kind on the Exodus passage in question, though I direct the interested reader to John H. Davies' recent work as a starting point for such a focus.[25]

The label "royal priesthood" draws upon the communal aspect of their calling and indicates an access to the divine presence reserved for the priesthood;[26] it also resonates and identifies with kingdoms and their ruling powers. Similar to Davies' understanding of the Exodus passage, I see these descriptors primarily marking the relationship between the chosen people and their God;[27] any residual effect on the faith communities' relationship with outsiders is secondary, though certainly significant. For our purposes, it is important to stay attuned to the fact that, at least for Israel, the members of priesthoods and the rulers of nations are men, and both realms are kyriarchally structured.

Davies reminds us that "any depiction of relationship between deity and humanity must necessarily strain the limits of language, and any neat packaging of that relationship into formulas may do as much or more to obscure than to enlighten."[28] At the same time, however, I am reminded that these texts are the words of humans. They reflect the needs, visions and desires of those with influence in these communities. The language used reflects an androcentric bias, represents male experiences, and in this situation defines the communities with institutions reserved for men[29] — institutions associated with great power

---

24. Various translations use the wording, "royal priesthood," or "priestly kingdom" instead of "kingdom of priests." A minor detail, but it is worth noting that in the LXX it is *basileion hierateuma kai ethnos hagion*, the same short phrase we have here in 1 Pet. 2.9 which is consistently translated as "royal priesthood and holy nation." There is one exception, of course, which is John H. Elliott's translation in his Anchor Bible commentary of 1 Peter. His choice is to translate *basileion hierateuma kai ethnos hagion* as: "a 'royal residence,' a 'priestly community,' a 'holy people,'" treating the first two words as two substantives, but the last two as one concept. My point here is that scholars are making distinctions between a Hebrew bible and a "New Testament" usage of the same phrase, presumably to fit their own theological presuppositions, as if the "intention" for such a transformation was already there in the document.

25. John H. Davies, *A Royal Priesthood: Literary and Intertextual Perspectives on an Image of Israel in Exodus 19.6* (JSOTSS 395; London: Continuum, 2004).

26. Ibid., 98.

27. Ibid., 102.

28. Ibid., 137.

29. An objection may be raised that women were judges over Israel, for instance. Not only was judge not the same role as a king/emperor but Deborah stands out as an exception to the "norm." Though there were some priesthoods that included or were exclusively women, the fact that they are either not spoken of

and leadership, and structured according to the roles and realms of royalty and priesthoods.[30]

Ambivalent Mimicry

As Homi Bhabha has explained, the dynamic of mimicry is a multi-layered phenomenon.[31] The ambivalence of this socio-political development is noted by the colonized people wanting to both reflect the ways of the colonizer for the sake of survival or acceptance and subversively redefine the ways and structures of the colonizer for the sake of resistance. In terms of the letter of 1 Peter, its author, and its recipients, then, we might expect to see this mimicry in the structuring of the community, based upon a kyriarchal system, which includes the identity of these people and the ways in which they relate with one another. It may also be present in the roles and expectations placed upon members of the communities, or in the values that direct what is esteemed and encouraged.

When we read the text of 1 Peter today, we must consider the fact that the communities in first-century Asia Minor would have received such a correspondence from the center of the Roman Empire fully aware of the religio-political implications of these metaphors. These faith communities were given appellations that resonate with and counter two different dominating influences in their lives. Even though the effort to counter an oppressive regime is intended to be liberatory for its constituents, when it draws upon the basic structure of the oppressor it ensures that the new community will also be structured upon kyriarchal power relations.

Israel's Tradition Superseded

The use of the term or image of "priesthood" in this particular letter may not strike modern readers as out of the ordinary. After all, Christianity is based upon the traditions and texts of the Hebrew bible and the religious communities that identified with them. The role of the priest within these texts is central to the worship context, and it is by worshipping their particular God that the people are set apart and given their identity.

Drawing upon this priestly tradition, the new testament book of Hebrews is concerned about Jesus' relation to the order of Melchizedek and various other priestly issues. Hebrews is also the only place in the new testament where we have a theologian working out the sticky issue of Jesus being both the sacrifice

---

in Christian literature or are denigrated when they are brought up indicates the gendered role expectations that "won."

30. Lakoff and Johnson, *Metaphors*, 5.
31. Bhabha, *Location of Culture*, in particular Chapter 4, "Of Mimicry and Man."

and the priest who offered it — clearly an indication that priestly matters and the sacrificial system in general were important to the communities for whom that particular writing was intended (curiously enough, in light of it being written post-70 CE). The continuation today of the use of priest and related concepts in various branches of the Christian church indicates that the terminology is still affective.

Even though, aside from 1 Peter, the label of royal priesthood itself is not taken up in the new testament as a way to describe the developing Christian communities, it has taken on something of an endearing quality for theologians throughout the centuries.[32] For instance, referring to a theologian of the twentieth century, Michael G. Cartwright explains John H. Yoder's vision of the church as "Royal Priesthood":

> The apocalyptic writings of the apostolic communities of faith . . . exhibit the awareness that there is "no crown without a cross" and, thereby, no sharing in the kingly reign of God without sharing in Christ's sacrificial servanthood. In *these* practices of discipleship the "royal priesthood" of the church is made visible in the world wherever Christians may gather.[33]

Royal priesthood language applied to the church is quite appropriate, it seems, since its constituents will be sharing in the "kingly reign of God." I find it to be a doubly tragic metaphor since in this case it is affirmed by a passionate pacifist.

Yoder simply takes for granted that the church's identity is that of a priesthood. "The church's royal priesthood is ultimately validated not by economic standards or efficacy but by its capacity to manifest the continuing relevance of the servant-like work of Christ as *the sign* of the lordship of Christ."[34] Yoder continues on about the royal priesthood's role to "serve God and rule the world," a perspective shared by many. One wonders if the genderedness of

---

32. I would note that Rev. 1.6, 5.10, and 20.6 all make reference to the followers of the Lamb as having been made into priests for their God, perhaps more out of countering the priests of the emperor worship than out of an adaptation of this Exodus passage. There is obviously a connection to "priesthood," but the specific label "royal priesthood" has direct supercessionist implications that "priest" alone does not.

33. Michael G. Cartwright, "Radical Reform, Radical Catholicity: John Howard Yoder's Vision of the Faithful Church," in *The Royal Priesthood: Essays Ecclesiological and Ecumenical. John Howard Yoder* (Michael G. Cartwright, ed.; Grand Rapids: Eerdmans, 1994), 2. I would also refer the reader to other works, such as Craig Bartholomew, et al., eds, *A Royal Priesthood? The Use of the Bible Ethically and Politically: A Dialogue with Oliver O'Donovan* (Grand Rapids: Zondervan, 2002), and Thomas Forsyth Torrance, *Royal Priesthood* (Edinburgh: Oliver and Boyd, 1955). The label "royal priesthood" is assumed to be appropriately ascribed to the Christian church in both of these works and is the foundational image of the political assessments, so claimed, within each, though 1 Peter is not referred to in the discussion of the theological-political ethics discussed.

34. Cartwright, "Radical Reform, Radical Catholicity," 2.

the concept or the sacrificial system that it originally implied, not to mention the supersessionist issue, have been considered by Yoder.

In his book, *The Elect and the Holy*, Elliott notes the premise of the super-session claim. His extensive chapter on the history of the transmission and interpretation of Exod. 19.6 includes the following succinct comment: "It is the continuation of Israel as the elect and holy people of God, her abiding relationship with God, and her continued preservation through Him which are important here."[35] This understanding of what was at stake makes perfect sense, given that those themes play out in the biblical traditions and history of the people of Israel. Yet noting the development and seeking to justify the supersession are two very different endeavors.

What I see happening in the choice by the Christian community and the author of 1 Peter to adopt these promises is a colonization of the texts and traditions of another people.[36] Several scholars have noted that 1 Peter does not actually refer to these communities as the "new" Israel[37] — this is a label that is the product of new testament scholarship, not the content therein. Perhaps this is an indication that the author clearly saw himself as still a "true Jew," and not yet a member of a splinter group, but the ultimate development of the concept of the Church being the "new Israel" is quite justified based upon this letter.[38]

There is no getting around the fact that 1 Peter makes a move to take over what belonged to another group of people, justified by the claim that those traditions were intended for the new group all along (1.10-12, 17b-20).[39] The

35. John H. Elliott, *The Elect and the Holy: An Exegetical Examination of 1 Peter 2:4-10 and the Phrase* basileion hierateuma (Leiden: Brill, 1966), 126. There are several non-canonical texts that are also important for this thesis, in particular, Jubilees 16.18, 33.20; Philo's *De Sobrietate* 66; and 2 Macc. 2.17.

36. While the initial disciples were Jews and many of the members of the faith communities being addressed in this letter may have been as well, there is no question that the Jesus followers represent at best a new sect of Judaism, and Christianity as a movement would quickly become antithetical to its mother religion.

37. Schüssler Fiorenza, "1 Peter," in *A Postcolonial Commentary on the New Testament Writings*, (Fernando F. Segovia and R. S. Sugirtharajah, eds; Sheffield: Sheffield Academic, 2007), 387; Elliott, *1 Peter*, 472; and W. Edward Glenny, "The Israelite imagery of 1 Peter 2," in *Dispensationalism, Israel and the Church* (Draig A. Blaising and Darrell L. Bock, eds; Grand Rapids: Zondervan, 1992), 156-87.

38. For a more thorough handling of the colonizing and supersessionist implications of this letter, see Betsy Bauman-Martin, "Speaking Jewish," 144–77.

39. 39 Pet. 1.10-12: "Concerning this salvation, prophets who prophesied about the grace that was to be yours searched and investigated it, investigating the time and circumstances that the Spirit of Christ within them indicated when it testified in advance to the sufferings destined for Christ and the glories to follow them. It was revealed to them that *they were serving not themselves but you* with regard to the things that have now been announced to you by those who preached the good news to you through the holy Spirit sent from heaven, things into which angels longed to look." 1.17b-20: "Conduct yourselves with fear during your time as refugees, realizing that you were *ransomed from your futile conduct, handed on by your ancestors*, not with perishable things like silver or gold, but with the precious blood of Christ as of a spotless unblemished lamb. He was known before the foundation of the world but revealed in the final time for you." (italics added)

author suggests that the ancestors in this faith tradition were not entirely on the right track, but were merely pawns for the sake of preparing the way for Jesus' followers. We could look at this assertion through the lens of colonization that justifies claiming someone else's land or that explains the desire to "civilize" another people is a part of God's will for all involved. In both cases — the efforts to colonize or to supersede another — something that the original people have is desired by a group that comes after them, and the original people group is spoken of in demeaning terms in order to create the illusion that the new people are justifiably in charge. Most notably, both efforts are supported and driven by claims to theological certainty and divine right. Thus we see Israel's traditions and covenant snatched away from them with the same certainty they had when originally claiming the promises for themselves.

"Holy Nation" in relation to Empire

For reasons that I imagine have to do with a linguistic connection, "royal priesthood" receives much more attention in biblical scholarship than does "holy nation." Yet with postcolonial lenses on, it seems that the claim to be a (separate) holy nation would be more disturbing for imperial rulers than the claim to be a priesthood of some sort. Just as Israel, the original holy nation in this tradition, is represented as an independent nation at times, the application of this covenantal promise also holds resonances of autonomy for these communities.

W. Edward Glenny applies a "typological-prophetic hermeneutical" approach to the metaphors in 1 Peter. While his interpretation is but one of many, and is different from my own, I refer here to his work as representative of apolitical interpretations of the new testament writings. "Israel is a nation, and the national, political, and geographic applications to Israel in the Old Testament contexts are not applied to the church, the spiritual house, of 1 Peter."[40] His explanation offers a nice way to avoid supersessionism. According to Glenny, the Church does not fulfill the national, political, and geographical prophecies of Israel — since it is not the *new* Israel — but is built upon the prophecies of the Hebrew bible and in this way is the fulfillment of these texts, simply within the spiritual realm.[41] Even if the author had a "spiritual nation" in mind, however, he was still using nation language which carries with it socio-political implications. More importantly, the fact that Glenny must do such acrobatics to deny the religio-political connection that this text makes indicates how strong that connection actually is.

---

40. Glenny, "The Israelite imagery of 1 Peter 2," 186–7.
41. Ibid., 187.

Yahweh as God and King of Israel ensured that they were a theocratic people. Within the covenant established at Sinai, Yahweh claimed them as His own people and the people in return pledged to be obedient to Yahweh. This covenant reflects the needs of the people to feel secure and taken care of, an understandable motivation on their part. Their utter devotion assured their survival. They fought and conquered other peoples in the name of their God and with the command from their God to do so. Their communal identity was wrapped up in their relation to their God, thus legal and ritual, social and familial relations were all crafted in the light of their covenant with their God. In some sense, the divinity — in this case Yahweh — was never separated from the realm of political warfare and "national" well-being.

For the neophyte "Christian" movement then, claiming to be a holy nation is not necessarily mimicry of the imperial reign any more than it is an appropriation of a theo-political worldview. This worldview was not unique to the Israelites and their lineage. From coins to statues, temples to domestic altars, we have artifacts indicating the ways the gods were called upon or given credit for victory and peace.[42] The role of emperor veneration/worship in supporting the Roman Empire (see the "Honor the Emperor" section below) was in keeping with a general practice that was endemic to cultures in the Ancient Near East.[43] Emperors represented themselves as presciently chosen and approved of by the gods. Any citizen who was not forthrightly participating in the various rituals of emperor veneration, as Klaus Wengst suggests, would have "inevitably aroused the suspicion of fundamental political disloyalty."[44]

While the language "royal priesthood and holy nation" may have been borrowed from the sacred texts of a specific people, the general idea of ascribing royalty/kingly-ness to a priesthood and holiness to a nation were in concert with the way many people understood that the world naturally functioned. In fact, Fergus Millar suggests that the priesthoods within the Roman Empire were always a "significant medium of imperial patronage,"[45] which blurs the

---

42. J. Rufus Fears, Princeps a Diis Electus: *The Divine Election of the Emperor as a Political Concept at Rome* (Rome: American Academy in Rome, 1977).

43. While we may not refer to the practice with the same terminology today, "emperor veneration" is alive and well today. For example, "Long live the King!" is an expression of self-preservation as much as respect for the King, given that peace and prosperity were considered to be in the hands of the King. There are plenty of church traditions today that regularly pray for government officials and many of the members of such traditions hold the president of the United States to be most important in this matter, even though "in Christ" all people are equal.

44. Klaus Wengst, *Pax Romana and the Peace of Christ* (John Bowden, trans; London: SCM Press, 1987), 50.

45. Fergus Millar, *The Emperor in the Roman World (31 BC — AD 337)* (London: Duckworth, 1992), 355.

line between sacred and royal realms of interest, ultimately attributing all power therein to the emperor. The realm of the emperor cult certainly is a part of this dynamic as well. Thus, when a holy nation arises within the people under imperial rule, the challenge to imperial sovereignty cannot be missed. In adapting a familiar or traditional myth, the author is also making a statement against or in reaction to the *other* royal priesthood present in Asia Minor at that time.

Musa Dube's method of postcolonial feminist interpretation to the bible,[46] applied to this passage, produces the following questions: What does the inclusion/reinterpretation of the promises to Israel do within the letter of 1 Peter? What kind of a stance does this reclaimed covenantal promise establish for the Christian communities in relation to the Empire? And finally, do these texts encourage one to collaborate with, resist, or imitate the contemporary powers of domination?

I hope at some level I have addressed the first two questions. In claiming these central covenantal promises these new faith communities supersede that of Israel and its people. Given the theocratic nature of the people of Israel, the ideology imbued in their texts sets up these new communities to collaborate with imperial ideals, if not simply a mindset of political autonomy over and against that of the Roman Empire. The next section is intended to address the final question, which is related to the materialistic implications as I have defined them for this project.

Materiality of Metaphors

The author of 1 Peter employs several metaphors straight from the traditions of the Jews in the description of the communities in Asia Minor: immigrants and refugees, royal priesthood, and holy nation. The exclusion that we see in the Hebrew bible of this one people being chosen by God becomes a part of the Christian communities, since they now claim to be God's chosen people. Several aspects of what defined Israel as God's people — covenant, being chosen, being an example for the nations — are easily discussed as taking on new meaning in and through Christ. What is often overlooked is what lies beneath the promises and metaphors; the things that go unspoken because they are assumed to be objective realities that are most influential in the foundational structure and power relations within these communities.

---

46. Dube, *Postcolonial Feminist Interpretation of the Bible*, 135–41.

"He doth protesteth too much"

One of the ways these unspoken yet fundamental pieces make their way to
the surface is when theologians and biblical scholars go out of their way to
smooth over a seeming contradiction within Christian doctrine or a biblical text.
Within the scholarship on our text, we see this taking place most significantly
when scholars assert that the leadership roles implied with the "priesthood"
identity,[47] the section addressing young men and elders (*presbuteroi*) near the
end of this epistle, and the general household order are all intended to be kept
separate from one another.

It is almost humorous the way so many scholars attempt to separate the
"official leadership" from the role of the laity in ministry. Typically they treat
the "royal priesthood" designation with great importance for defining the
church but claim it has no direct correlation to actual ministerial roles.[48] From
this perspective, 1 Pet. 5.1-5 (which encourages young men to be respectful of
and submissive to male elders) is assumed to be foreshadowing the *episkopos*
and *diakonos* roles delineated in Titus and 1 & 2 Timothy,[49] and 1 Pet. 2.4-10 is
granted importance for its connection to Hebrew bible references (in particular
for its "cornerstone," "royal priesthood and holy nation," and "once you were
no people but now you are the people of God" language). According to these
same scholars, however, the labels used in Chapters 1 and 2 and the *episkopos*
and *diakonos* language do not meet or mingle in their meanings.[50] There is no

---

47. There are other textual resonances with priestly issues that could be mentioned here. In the saluta-
tion the author refers to these non-citizens as having been chosen in God's foreknowledge for obedience
and the sprinkling with the blood of Jesus Christ (1 Pet. 1.1-2), imagery that resonates with the sprinkling
of the altar in their own tradition and of initiation rites for priests in other contemporaneous religious
ceremonies; and the "ransom" language and Christ as the lamb imagery in 1.18-19.

48. For instance, Elliott makes the following claim: "The inner-directed ministry is comprehended
under the aspect of brotherly love and humility; *hierateuma*, under that of election and holiness. The former
is a consequence of the latter and not identifiable with it" (*The Elect and the Holy*, 195). Yet, several pages
later he notes, "Here in 2:4-10 the injunction to a holy life, brotherly love, growth in the word, and witness
to the world receives its most detailed support. Here the fundamental indicative for the entire epistle has
been spoken" (217). I agree with this statement, and do not find that a reader/hearer must separate these
various fields of responsibility the way he seems to think that the church has and ought to continue.

49. Again, in playing the "word study" game, even this claim is a bit shaky. The leadership roles
discussed in Titus and 1 and 2 Timothy are those of *episkopos* and *diakonos*. *Episkopos* is a name for Christ
used in the midst of the household code, "the shepherd and guardian of your souls" (2.25), and only shows
up in Acts once. *Diakonos* is not used in Acts at all, but does show up in various places throughout Paul's
letters. But 2 Timothy, on a quick reading, it seems to me has more household-type language (fathers and
sons, mothers and daughters, slaves and masters, women encouraged to be "self-controlled, chaste, good
homemakers, under the control of their husbands, so that the word of God may not be discredited," all such
commands are directly in line with household code instructions) than strictly deacon and leader language.

50. See, for example, John H. Elliott, "Ministry and Church Order in the New Testament: A Tradio-
Historical Analysis (1 Pt 5, 1-5 & plls.)," *CBQ* 32: 367–91.

acknowledgement that the brain makes connections in themes, even when those connections are not explicitly delineated in the text.

A question raised by Elliott, "How accurately and faithfully do even the Early Church Fathers represent the position of the New Testament [on leadership/ministerial roles], specifically 1 Peter?"[51] seems to me to miss the point. Aside from the fact that the early Church Fathers represented various trajectories of the Christian faith and its expressions, their interpretations *were* deemed to be faithful and accurate and were given authoritative weight. The question of "right" or "wrong" is not only impossible to resolve, it veils the deeper issue of the effect that their voices and texts did have and continue to have because of their role in shaping the early church, its traditions, and texts.

One of the main purposes of Elliott's book *The Elect and The Holy* is to address this very issue of leadership and ministerial roles. In his chapter, "Verses 4-5 and the Election and Holiness of the Body of the Faithful," he claims that there is a specific distinction between "ministry" and the role of the *hierateuma* (priesthood).[52] He asserts that since 1 Peter makes no clear connection between these two realms, ministry and the priesthood, we should not make that connection either. Again I say in response to this textual or vocabulary-based assessment that the connection does not need to be named in order for it to be in effect. The use of the priesthood and other familiar imagery in the first two chapters sets the stage, and thus has some staying power throughout the letter.[53] I do not wish to argue over details, but to point to the power of words to evoke various semantic and image-producing domains.

Some scholars, pastors, and general readers of the bible reject that the

---

51. Elliott, *The Elect and the Holy*, 14.

52. Ibid., 192. On this note, for instance, he claims that the term "ministry" implies only "'inner-directed' ministry within the body of the faithful" and is not to be used for the "'outer-directed' witness toward the world" (192). Aside from this being an arbitrary definition of "ministry," these two particular roles within the Church (inward nurturing and outward witnessing) are by nature related to one another, and the need to define them separately is driven by a need to control and compartmentalize, rather than by a free-flowing empowerment by the Spirit. I can anticipate an objection to this point, given the dating of the book. But if one consults Elliott's 2000 Anchor Bible Commentary, one would see his dependence upon his early thought. Even his foray into social-scientific theory did not alter his interpretation of this letter, but only solidified it.

53. Many scholars make claims about the "staying power" of terms and concepts referred to in the greeting and/or introductory sections of letters when they offer commentaries on various epistles. It is common to assume that a theme or concept mentioned within the greeting and/or introductory section will be actively playing out throughout the letter. Jerome Murphy-O'Connor suggests the nature of the description of the sender and the recipients tells us a great deal about the context in which and to which it was written and the nature of the relationship between the parties. Jerome Murphy-O'Connor, *Paul the Letter-Writer: His World, His Options, His Skills* (Collegeville, Minn.: Liturgical, 1995), 45–53. See also, for instance, Peter T. O'Brien, "Letters, Letter Forms" in *Dictionary of Paul and His Letters* (Gerald F. Hawthorne, Ralph P. Martin, and Daniel G. Reid, eds; Downers Grove, Ill.: InterVarsity, 1993), 551.

priesthood terminology anticipates purely male addressees by noting that it was typical to address a mixed group with male plural terms. This logic begins to break down, however, when we see the commands directed specifically to the wives and house slaves 2.18–3.7. Not only does the specific mentioning of these non-male and non-full-citizen people become a symptom or an irruption in the text — they *do* have specific role expectations — the roles and behavior encouraged for them utterly clash with the imagery used for the (male) priesthood. This dissonance belies the fact that the women and slaves were not, after all, some of who the author had in mind would embody the "priesthood" identities ascribed to the communities.

Populating a Priesthood

The constituents of a priesthood and their role as mediator between the divine and human realms is one of privilege and thus one of great power. As Davies has noted, priests are chosen and appointed by God. Their attire, a point of interest for parallels with the commands to wives in 3.1-6, is elaborate and regal, serving as a visual reminder of their status and role as mediator and their association with life and well-being.[54] There is much that is grand about the honor and respect ascribed to those in the role of priest. The additional socio-cultural expectation that only males are leadership material is part and parcel of the ideology of this letter and is perpetuated by the use of this kyriarchal metaphor, "royal priesthood."[55] The implications of these expectations, in particular as they have been adopted by the church, are that the ethos and structuring of the faith communities is kyriarchal and imperialistic, and the leaders are males who are not only set apart but set above, given great power and prestige.

Sacredness, being set apart, was an integral aspect of any priesthood. The sacred aspect of a priest or priestess's role was marked by some form of ceremony, rite, or ritual. Bourdieu speaks of the rite of circumcision, but his point can be extrapolated for the purpose of this discussion, which is that "the most important effect of the rite is the one which attracts the least attention: by treating men and women differently, the rite *consecrates* the difference, institutes it."[56] The language of priesthood invokes a consecrated role, which was reserved, at least within the Jewish communities at that time, for men. The "psychic depth" to which such defining characteristics of an institution inform what its members know and can do should not be underestimated.

---

54. Davies, *A Royal Priesthood*, 240. This point also has significant implications for the discussion on women's attire in Chapter 4.

55. Ibid., 102.

56. Bourdieu, *Language and Symbolic Power*, 188.

Rites actually serve to separate those who have undergone or will undergo the ritual from those who *will never do* such a thing, creating an inside and outside, which implies a superior and inferior, a primary and secondary participant. With this overarching theme of priesthood the community perpetuates a patriarchal structure: men as leaders, women as laity. The connection to royalty or kingly-ness reinscribes a theocratic and kyriarchal worldview. Thus imperialist and male language of the Hebrew bible is now employed for the communal identity formation of the early Christian communities, which ensures their conformity with an imperialist agenda as well.[57]

Living into the Labels

The social effect of a designation, then, is that a person is compelled to behave accordingly — to live into the name, to live within the boundaries of appropriateness for the role. It serves as much to keep the person in line (accountability) as it does to let others know where they cannot go.[58] The identities of the communities and of the members within them function as social control mechanisms, "channeling and constraining individual as well as collective sentiments, emotions, and action."[59] This is, in part, what I am calling the materiality of the text: the labels in the letter become realized in people's lives; they are not simply words on the page but they dictate real-life roles and expectations.

From the perspective of Rosemary Hennessy's claim that what a person does controls what s/he can know; what a person knows controls what s/he can do, both labels, "royal priesthood" and "holy nation," declare that women do not have access to power and leadership roles in these communities. They are then socialized to think that they cannot have such power. It is in this way that these two metaphors do have legitimate "symbolic efficacy in the construction of reality" for the early Christian communities.[60] Much like legal discourse, which "brings into existence that which it utters,"[61] the language of this epistle is creative speech that has brought into being the very imagery and power relations that it has "uttered."

---

57. Dube, *Postcolonial Feminist Interpretation*, 135–41.
58. Bourdieu, *Language and Symbolic Power*, 121.
59. Robert D. Benford, "Controlling Narratives," 53.
60. Bourdieu, *Language and Symbolic Power*, 105.
61. Ibid., 42.

"Honor the Emperor"

The final command in 1 Pet. 2.17, "honor all people, love the brotherhood, fear God, honor the emperor," inevitably evokes discussion about the imperial cult and the Christians' involvement in it. Just what does it mean, in that context, to honor the emperor? There is plenty that can be said, and indeed the region of Asia Minor seems to have a unique story to tell on this matter.[62] Nonetheless, I will keep the discussion of the role of the imperial cult in this region to a minimum, while touching upon the aspects of "honoring the emperor" that I think are the most relevant here: its kyriarchal presuppositions, the way it encourages collusion with Empire and the effects of this string of commands functioning as the preface to the household code.[63]

Kyriarchal Presuppositions

The command to honor the emperor as the ultimate element in the set of commands implies, among other things, that the emperor and the system he represents are necessary for peaceful existence. He is named last in a short list of relations central to daily life. This may seem like an obvious point to make, but consider how the verse would change without "honor the emperor" at the end. Its inclusion creates a subtle but powerful presence that connects these faith communities and the socio-political realm.

Emperor and Empire are Essential

There is no question that emperor worship/veneration was prevalent in the region of Asia Minor during the time that the letter of 1 Peter was written.[64] The pressing question seems to be, "to what extent did this dynamic affect the members of Christian communities, and in what form?" The persecution that the letter refers to has been assumed to be founded upon religious tensions, which are heightened when the followers of Jesus are perceived to be choosing to worship a heavenly emperor instead of the one in Rome and, in so doing,

---

62. See, Samuel Dickey, "Some Economic and Social Conditions of Asia Minor Affecting the Expansion of Christianity," in *Studies in Early Christianity* (Shirley Jackson Case, ed.; New York: Century Co., 1928), 406; Tenney Frank, *An Economic History of Rome* (Baltimore: John's Hopkins, 1927), 337–8; and Steven J. Friesen, *Twice Neokoros: Ephesus, Asia and the Cult of the Flavian Imperial Family* (New York: Brill, 1993).

63. I would also refer the reader to both S. R. F. Price, *Rituals and Power: The Roman imperial cult in Asia Minor* (Cambridge: Cambridge University, 1984; repr. Cambridge: Cambridge University, 1998) and to Friesen's short dialogue with Price's interpretation of the data, *Twice Neokoros*, 142–68. Additionally, it is worth noting that Allen Brent in his monograph, *Imperial Cult and the Development of Church Order* (Boston: Brill, 1999), only refers to 1 Peter twice, in reference to 5.1-5, and ever so briefly. Clearly the interpretation of the matter of how the developing Christian communities were to relate to the political powers is no less ideologically driven than any other realm of scholarship related (or not) to 1 Peter.

64. This claim remains true no matter when a person chooses to date the letter.

are not behaving in a manner supportive of Rome's Empire. Based upon this assumption, this letter is an attempt to help the members of these communities be faithful to both the Roman Empire and the "heavenly" kingdom.

We cannot determine with certainty who or what power initiated this persecution, nor what form it took. Duane Warden suggests that what Domitian did or required of Roman residents had little, if anything, to do with the persecution of Christians in Asia, but it was the actions of Roman governors in Asia that mattered in this instance, an insight I find particularly persuasive.[65] Some scholars, such as F. Gerald Downing, suggest that the lack of textual evidence implies that the suffering, whatever it was, was not intense.[66] Considering the fact that persecution will affect all aspects of one's life, and how difficult it is to communicate such effects in writing, it seems to me that a strict dependence upon textual evidence will not allow us to see the whole picture in any historical situation, in particular at this point in time.

On the flip side of Downing's assessment is John Knox's brief critical note,[67] which highlights the similarity between what Christians were being accused of in court and the language used in several places of 1 Peter. For instance, the author makes several references to the recipients being "slandered as evildoers," and in 4.15, we see what appears to be a direct reference to crimes Christians were accused of when brought before authorities and governors: "By no means let any of you suffer as a murderer, or thief, or evildoer, or a troublesome meddler (*allotriepiskopos*)." W. M. Ramsay suggests that the term *allotriepiskopos* should be read within a similar semantic domain or socio-political context that Knox suggests, since this term was one applied to Christians during Nero's reign for crimes they had committed.[68]

---

65. Duane Warden, "Imperial Persecution and the Dating of 1 Peter and Revelation," *JETS* 34 (1991): 203–12.

66. F. Gerald Downing, "Pliny's Prosecutions of Christians: Revelation and 1 Peter," *JSNT* 34 (1988): 105–23.

67. John Knox, "Pliny and 1 Peter: A Note on 1 Pet 4:14-16 and 3:15," *JBL* 72, no. 3 (1953): 187–9; and I would add 2.12-15 to this list. Comparing the correspondence of Pliny to Trajan with these verses of 1 Peter, Knox raises the question as to whether Pliny's letter informs more than the issue of "the name" for which Christians were persecuted, as historians have typically seen. He notes that in the section where Peter speaks of suffering as murderers, etc. that perhaps he is saying that they should not allow themselves to be persecuted as such, in the ways that Pliny indicates some of being falsely accused. It is a delightful take on these pieces of the letter — 4.14-16: "If you are reviled for the name of Christ, you are blessed, because the Spirit of glory and of God rests upon you. By no means let any of you suffer as a murderer, or thief, or evildoer, or a troublesome meddler; but if anyone suffers as a Christian, let him not feel ashamed, but in that name let him glorify God." Along a similar line of thinking, W. M. Ramsay, "The Church and the Empire in the First Century, III: The First Epistle Attributed to St. Peter," *Expositor* 4, no. 8 (1893): 282–96, suggests the same thing is at work behind the use in 4.15 of the term, *allotriepiskopos*, most often translated as "trouble maker" or "meddler."

68. Ramsay, "The Church and the Empire," 282–96.

Additionally, in a letter to Emperor Trajan, the governor of Pontus and Bithinia, Pliny notes that he had some Christians put to death due to their "obstinacy and unbending behavior." He explains, "For I held no question that whatever it was that they admitted, in any case obstinacy and unbending perversity deserve to be punished."[69] This confession on Pliny's part could explain why the recipients are encouraged in 3.15 to be ready to give a *defense* for their faith, and to do so with gentleness and respect.

While there was most likely no official persecution going on at the time that 1 Peter was written, this does not preclude unofficial persecution from taking place that would have had significant social and religio-political effects. A comparison with an event in our own day may help in understanding just how intense unofficial persecution can be.

After the events of 9/11 in the United States, there was no official persecution of adherents to Islam. To this day, however, people who even *appear* to be of Middle Eastern descent[70] are constantly ostracized — dare I say persecuted — in various forms, the most obvious taking place in airports, but certainly not restricted to such locations.[71] Unofficial persecution, which can be just as devastating as official persecution, tends to happen "under the radar," and will be undocumented precisely because it is unofficial. It is in this way that I imagine the members of the Christian communities might have been persecuted in Asia Minor near the end of the first century CE — unofficially, with governors and other leaders at least turning a blind eye, if not being complicit with it. Additionally, just as airports today are spaces where suspicions run highest in terms of potential threats to public safety, we might think in similar terms regarding the threat Christians posed, specifically in their worship practices or the lack thereof in terms of emperor veneration.

Whether or not the author of 1 Peter saw the emperor as other than or distinct from God/the Gods is another important issue in scholarship on this passage, and has an impact on what is meant by "honoring" the emperor. The distinction that some modern minds tend to draw between humanity and deity was not as

69. John Wayland Coakley and Andrea Sterk, eds, *Readings in World Christian History* (Maryknoll, NY: Orbis, 2004), 23.

70. I am having difficulty knowing how to refer to the phenotypical attributes that many people associate with a person from Iran, Iraq, Afghanistan, etc. I am aware of the dangers of making collective generalizations based upon resemblances, language, and culture; yet it is based upon such misguided generalizations that so many people in the United States have behaved in the past nine years. The racial aspect of this problem is highlighted when we consider the number of people of European descent who are Muslim but are not profiled as such precisely because of their physical appearance.

71. Wiretapping and surveillance of email and postal correspondence, which is sanctioned and monitored by the Federal government, can be considered official persecution.

clearly present, if at all, in the first century CE.[72] It is clear that the Christian movement adopted terminology that was used in various religious traditions. The emperors were called *Sotēr* because they saved their people from famine and foreign armies, and were referred to with *theos* (god) terminology for the way they provided for the people and created peace over the land. The more governance was placed in the hands of one man and the people could turn to their emperor in addition to their gods for their well-being, the more god-like this man became, both in perception and in relation to his power and control over people and their resources.[73]

So on a fairly basic level, the command to honor the emperor is a concession to the preeminence of the emperor in Rome and a charge to behave in such a way that reflects obedience to him.

"Honoring" is a Public Endeavor

What exactly did it mean to "honor the emperor" then? We may never be able to say with confidence what the author intended by this short exhortation, but many scholars have posed possibilities. Some suggest that it meant that they were to participate politically within society, others that they were to behave with "sly civility," and still others that it meant to be "unconditionally submissive."[74] Miroslav Volf has suggested that it was a "soft difference" that the author had in mind: "the open life-stance of the strong, who feel no need to support their own uncertainty by aggression toward others."[75] From the perspective of these scholars it is the involvement itself that is honoring to the emperor.

72. Lauri Thurén, "Jeremiah 27 and Civil Obedience in 1 Peter," in *Zwischen den Reichen: Neues Testament und Römische Herrschaft* (Tübingen: A. Francke Verlag, 2002), 219. I will never forget the day I realized, while reading the *Iliad*, that if a man did something heroic or savior-esque, and no one knew who his father was, then he was transformed from being called a bastard to being spoken of as a son of a God.

73. Andrew Wallace-Hadrill, "Patronage in Roman Society: From Republic to Empire," in *Patronage in Ancient Society* (Andrew Wallace-Hadrill, ed.; New York: Routledge, 1989), 63–85.

74. Lauri Thurén, "Jeremiah 27 and Civil Obedience in 1 Peter," 226; cf. Jan Botha, "Christians and Society in 1 Peter: Critical Solidarity," *Scriptura* 24 (1988): 27–37, who claims that Christians, as strangers to the world, were to live in critical solidarity with the world, seeking to do good and to be a positive example for those around them. See also Goppelt's understanding of the use of *hypotagete*: "order yourselves," in 2.13. He read this command as a counter not to rebellion but to "the flight of emigration" (Leonhard Goppelt, *A Commentary of 1 Peter*, 168). They were to enlist themselves in the organizations of their society, as Epictetus notes in his *Dissertationes* that the "role of a Man" was to be a citizen of the world which meant that one should bear in mind the proper character of a citizen (2.10.1) (171).

75. Miroslav Volf, "Soft Difference: Theological Reflections on the Relation Between Church and Culture in 1 Peter." *Ex auditu* 10 (1994): 24. Unfortunately, Volf also claims that "soft difference" is the "missionary side of following in the footsteps of the crucified Messiah" (25). I do not see the turbulence that the Messiah represents being embodied simultaneously with this kind of meekness or gentleness. But it does, also, seem to me to be the kind of interpretation that a privileged white Western male might come up with in peering into this letter.

Warren Carter and David Horrell take the approach that the honoring was some form of literal action or reverence directed specifically toward the emperor.[76] Carter sees this command as the author's permission for the recipients to "go all the way," in terms of emperor worship. Horrell, on the other hand, draws the line in the sand just short of this full commitment. While one can understand Horrell's desire to interpret the situation in this way, there is very little evidence to suggest that people in the first century would have seen "honoring the emperor" as any different in meaning from "worshipping a god."

C. Freedman Sleeper suggests that what the author meant by "honor the emperor" was to do good things, since 1 Peter makes use of terms employing the *agath-* and *kala-* prefixes several times throughout the letter, primarily within the household code.[77] Bruce Winter's work pushes this suggestion to the point of it being about the benefaction system.[78] Just as the emperors were praised and glorified for all the good deeds they did for various regions and specific cities, the author is, according to Winter, encouraging similar benevolent acts on the part of these communities.[79]

Winter's conclusion deserves some consideration, for what kinds of "good deeds" would a governor know of unless it was somewhat publicly demonstrated? If a Christian were honored for civic benefaction, then s/he would be publicly honored and/or crowned. Certainly any actions that were acknowledged by governors would silence any talk about Christians being ill-willed or haters of humanity and especially that of being a threat to the stability of the society.[80]

Whatever form of "honoring of the emperor" the author had in mind — that of veneration, political involvement, or public "good deeds" — there is clearly an element of public engagement involved. Choosing to honor the emperor by means of religious rituals and social benefaction is a choice to participate in and maintain the kyriarchal structuring of society.

---

76. Warren Carter, "Going All the Way?" 14–33 and David Horrell, "Between Conformity and Resistance," 111–43.

77. C. Freedman Sleeper, "Political Responsibility According to I Peter," *NovT* 10 (1968): 270–89.

78. Bruce Winter, *Seek the Welfare of the City: Christians as Benefactors and Citizens* (Grand Rapids: Eerdmans, 1994).

79. If we take Winter seriously the author was, at least in part, encouraging them to support other clubs and associations, perhaps as a way of starting new communities or simply to be seen being supportive of other associations in general. As William Countryman notes, clubs were usually dependent upon a patron for funds. The club gave the patron "honorary titles, decrees, crowns, inscriptions and even statues." The patron was typically not a member of the club, or even an officer, but was influential: "in fact, the club functioned almost as a client — particularly if it was a club composed of poor people." L. William Countryman, "Patrons and Officers in Club and Church," in 1977 SBLSP (Paul Achtemeier, ed.; Missoula: Scholars, 1977), 136.

80. Bruce Winter, *Seek the Welfare*, 39.

Encouraging Collusion

The grouping of commands, "honor all, love the brotherhood, fear God, honor the Emperor," is laden with political and social concerns more than those that define individual piety. It is directed toward collective behaviors and ways of relating both within the faith community and in the socio-political realm. This list of commands closes a short section (2.13-17) that encourages being subject to all authorities, in particular the emperor or his governors (*hegemosin*) sent to approve those who do what is good or right and reprove those who do what is evil or wrong. One can see how the domestic code is smoothly incorporated into this letter, coming after this exhortation on civic behavior.

In addition to encouraging "good deeds," the charge to honor the emperor engenders an attitude of submission and compliance toward the emperor and his representatives. A comparison between 1 Peter and the Apocalypse of John on this matter makes the issue a bit clearer. The latter condemns the emperor and his exploitative administration and any members of the local communities who were complicit with, and thus benefited from, this oppressive regime. The Apocalypse is written from the perspective of "the people" and with their best interests in mind. The author of 1 Peter is also, seemingly, sending exhortations with the best interest of the people in mind, since he is clearly trying to help them avoid unnecessary persecution. Yet the structures and systems that his advice draws upon and perpetuates are those that benefit the elite.[81]

The author does not criticize or condemn the emperor or his exploitative tactics; he does encourage participation within the kyriarchal social structure *as it was*. There is no indication within this letter that he wanted them to actively challenge or reform social structures and relations of power. In anticipating an objection to this comment, I fully understand that the author may have been specifically *not* taking this route for the sake of keeping the movement alive, which is my point entirely. He was helping them find a way to survive within the system as it was, which meant capitulating to all the exploitative or oppressive aspects of it. Countering unjust systems may not have been the author's intent, but when this kind of rhetoric and ideology becomes canonized, collusion with unjust systems is endemic to the movement.

2.13-17 as a preface to the Haustafel

Whether the author of 1 Peter made the connection consciously or not, the placement of his adaptation of the household codes immediately following

---

81. It is akin to what often happens in Christian churches today, where language that is patriarchal and kyriarchal by nature is employed, thus reinscribing and perpetuating the structures and systems that cause the sufferings that the people in those congregations often attend church to escape.

2.13-17 strengthens their socio-political implications. The content of this section is the focus of the next chapter, but for now I will note that whatever "Christianizing" of the socio-political construct is reflected in 2.18–3.7, it is not enough to neutralize the political aspects of it. Additionally, it creates a requirement of anyone who wishes to be obedient to Christ to be obedient to the emperor as a good citizen as well.

What Musa Dube has claimed in response to the gospel of Matthew can also be said of 1 Peter, which is that "paralleling faithfulness to an imperial institution, one that is fundamentally oppressive and exploitative, with faithfulness to God not only disguises its evil character but also sanctifies it."[82] The author of 1 Peter is encouraging faithfulness to the emperor and the imperial system, and such behavior is given the weightiness of being equivalent to fearing their God.

Conclusion: The Religio-Political Preface to the Household Code

In the same way that the symbol of God functions,[83] symbolic metaphors used to define the people of God function. If we heed the warning to examine the role "played by words in the construction of social reality" and the struggle that occurs in trying to define certain groups "in terms of age, sex or social position, [and] also clans, tribes, ethnic groups or nation,"[84] then we will take seriously metaphors that are at work in 1 Peter. The images drawn upon were familiar, thus their re-presentation struck deep psychic chords for the recipients of this letter. The metaphors employed in the defining of the Christian communities in Asia Minor effectively influence the structure of the movement as well as the nature of the ways people can participate within it.

The appellation "immigrants and refugees" highlights the socio-economic and political reality of being displaced and exploited. It has a strong connection with the plight of the people of Israel, or various specific individuals within it, linking the members of the Asia Minor communities with the sufferings of Israel as well as to the chosen-ness Israel claimed. Whether a person interprets these words, "refugees and immigrants," literally or metaphorically, we must contend with the implications of these social realities being juxtaposed with terminology of royalty, priests and emperors. The system that establishes both the emperor and the "by-dweller"/refugee/immigrant as recognizable social

---

82. Dube, *Postcolonial Feminist Interpretation*, 133.

83. Elizabeth A. Johnson, *She Who Is: The Mystery of God in Feminist Theological Discourse* (New York: Crossroad, 1998), 5.

84. Bourdieu, *Language and Symbolic Power*, 105.

locations significantly depends upon the socio-economic contributions of the latter category.

In a fanciful transformation from refugee to royal priest, the members of these communities are simultaneously liberated or empowered and made into a pawn of Empire. The true paupers now have no grounds by which they can challenge the injustices of their daily lives, because the theological ideology of these communities is now in line with and supports imperial ideology. One can also appreciate that women were, as always, subsumed under the general categories of roles allotted to men. "Immigrants and refugees" certainly included wives or women, but the new religious identity of priesthood and nation includes them only as "supporting actors."

The metaphors "royal priesthood" and "holy nation" not only stand in stark contrast with the socio-political nature of "immigrants and refugees," but also, due to their connection with leadership, become a part of the nature and determine the structure of the communities that adapt them. Because the language employed in 1 Peter is embraced by the followers of Christ, the systems and structures that are associated with priesthoods and nations are intertwined with the identity and behaviors of the movement. These metaphors are simultaneously religious and political, thus they play upon roles and terminology used in both realms with wildly successful results, for as Bourdieu suggests, "Religion and politics achieve their most successful ideological effects by exploiting the possibilities contained in the polysemy inherent in the social ubiquity of the language" of the culture.[85] The use of such polysemic metaphors ensures the perpetual mimicry of Empire and its power relations within these faith communities.

When a command such as "honor the emperor" is seemingly appropriately included in a letter to faith communities, we can conclude that what those communities stand for and how they interact with society must be conducive with honoring the emperor. Taken together with the various labels ascribed to these communities, this command becomes the unifying element and effectively locates the faith communities in a subservient position regarding Empire. Since we cannot serve two masters at once and please them both, submission to Empire and its rulers must be an aspect of submission to Christ.

85. Ibid., 39.

4

Components of Collusion

Western misogynism has its root in the rules for the household as the model of
the state.

A feminist theology therefore must not only analyze the anthropological dualism
generated by Western culture and theology, but also uncover its political roots in
the patriarchal household of antiquity.[1]

Introduction

Now that I have done a brief analysis of some of the religious and socio-
political aspects of the text leading up to the household code, I will turn to the
code itself. The ultimate goal of this project is to address how women/wives
are constructed according to 1 Peter: their circumscribed subjectivity prescribed
by kyriarchal structures and power relations, created and sustained by abusive
power dynamics. Given the nature of the household code, however, it will also
be helpful to address, ever so briefly, the components related to the slaves and
the husbands as well. In doing so, using the method proposed in Chapter 1, I
will discuss the "components of collusion" within this text.

Thus I will begin with a review of *Haustafel* concerns related to this project,
address the irruptions within the household code itself — in terms of the slaves,
the wives, and the husbands — link these irruptions with the role of households
within the Roman Empire, and conclude with an analysis of the ambivalent
mimicry contained within this section of 1 Peter and some of the implications
of its presence in the Christian canon.

Review of Haustafeln Background

As noted in Chapter 1, there is a general consensus among scholars that
Aristotle was the first to provide in writing the general tri-partite division of

1.   Elisabeth Schüssler Fiorenza, "The Praxis of Co-equal Discipleship," in *Paul and Empire:
Religion and Power in Roman Imperial Society* (Richard Horsley, ed.; Harrisburg, Pa.: Trinity, 1997), 240.

roles for the husband, or *paterfamilias*, within the household: husband over wife, father over child, master over slave. Thus discussions of how the household code was altered, or Christianized, in its application within Christian texts tend to use his work as expressing the normative form of these socio-political roles and expectations.

While Aristotle may seem more concerned about order, evidenced by the hierarchical structure he espouses, than the survival and prosperity of households, political and socio-economic dynamics were still a part of every household. It is precisely the fact that household management was tied to the economic prosperity of the family *in addition to* the maintenance of the political state that gives us a warrant for a postcolonial analysis of this passage, as well as reason to turn to Xenophon's *Oeconomicus* for deeper understanding.

There is an interesting twist in the adaptation of this structure in 1 Peter. Aristotle directed the content toward the head of the household in terms of what leadership or active administration he is to perform. The 1 Peter example is not simply directed to those who are to submit, but is done in such a way that *accentuates* their submission; it encourages and affirms a passive leadership for women.[2]

Luce Irigaray quotes Freud as having said that, "A marriage is not made secure until the wife has succeeded in making her husband her child as well."[3] While this idea might be disturbingly unsettling for many of us, it does, nonetheless, resonate with the line in the *Oeconomicus* where the husband says that the most pleasant experience for his wife is to make even him her servant. Including an extended excerpt at this point seems apt.

> But I assure you, dear, there are other duties peculiar to you that are pleasant to perform. It is delightful to teach spinning to a maid who had no knowledge of it when you received her, and to double her worth to you: to take in hand a girl who is ignorant of housekeeping and service, and after teaching her and making her trustworthy and serviceable to find her worth any amount. . . . But the pleasantest experience of all is to prove yourself better than I am, to make me your servant; and, so far from having cause to fear that as you grow older you may be less honored in the household, to feel confident that with advancing years, the better partner you prove to me and the better housewife to our children, the greater will be the honor paid to you in our home. For it is not through outward comeliness that the sum of

2. David Horrell, "Leadership Patterns and the Development of Ideology in Early Christianity," *Sociology of Religion* 58 (1997): 333, "though in these codes the focus is not upon the forms of leadership as such, but is often upon the appropriate submission expected of subordinate social groups."

3. Irigaray, *This Sex*, 133.

things good and beautiful is increased in the world, but by the daily practice of the
virtues (VII.41-3).

The way Xenophon narrates this marker of achievement it is difficult to tell
for whom it is such a "sweet experience," whether it is for the wife or for him.
It also conveys a false sense of the wife's authority since she is always under
the final authority of the *paterfamilias*. We still see such dynamics at work in
almost all facets of life today, when a woman is affirmed for her capabilities
and given leadership positions as long as it does not completely dismantle the
kyriarchal structures and relations of power that are already in place.

Though more than two thousand years separate Xenophon and Freud, there
is a common thread that connects their lines of thinking. What Irigaray sees
in Freud's comment is a deeper unconscious desire *for* these relations, for
the woman to nurture and mother the husband. Any hints of incest aside, the
suggestion that such roles, and lack of mutuality, would be desirable within
a marriage is still a disturbing possibility. Though it is beyond the scope of
this project to fully develop and analyze the affects of desire on our (sub)
consciousness, it is within the scope of this method to note that texts written
within kyriarchal social structures will be markedly influenced by the need
or the desire to maintain such systems. This influence suggests to me that we
would do well to look for what it is that is desired in a text, or what it is that
a passage, if fulfilled, would accomplish. Given the socio-political context in
which and to which 1 Peter was written, we are sure to find components of the
letter that collude with, instead of resist, dominating powers and structures.

It is also important to note that the injunctions within biblical texts only
represent an ideal, not necessarily the lived reality.[4] As many scholars have
noted, this very prescription of certain behaviors for wives in 1 Peter indicates
that the author of the letter heard about some behavior that was out of place
and, in his opinion, was in need of correction for the sake of the survival of
the movement or those particular communities. It is just as important to note
that we will never know to what extent the initial recipients heeded the advice.

What has endured, however, is the text itself and along with it the kyriarchal
structure and power relations that it espouses. Consequently, it also ensures
that these power relations are a part of the communities that embrace the text.
In other words the dynamics within the writing have "materiality," in that
they take on form in real-life faith communities. As a means of getting to the
materiality of this text, I will address its symptomatic irruptions — the places

---

4.   See also, Sharon Ringe, "1 and 2 Peter, Jude," 548.

where desires and matters of control and construction of "reality" urgently break into the narrative or surface of a text.

Symptomatic Irruptions

As Rosemary Hennessy suggests, we find symptoms or irruptions in a text when we pay attention to those moments where some urgent, often unconscious, desire of the author irrupts the flow of a narrative or discourse like a socially awkward person interrupting a formal party with a loud announcement. Since discourse does then, in turn, influence the structure of a culture or society — the discourse has "materiality" because people take it to heart — analyzing symptomatic irruptions is also working with the materiality of knowledge: what a person does informs what she can know and what a person knows informs what she can do. While the original experiences that the author of 1 Peter was responding to may never be recuperated, the startling symptomatic irruptions within this letter help us note when we can interrogate the text and its role in shaping what women "can" do and know. From this perspective, I would like to address the irruptions related to the slaves and wives, as well as the husbands, with an eye toward their indication of collusion with, versus resistance to, Empire.

Slaves and Wives
The scholarship on this section of the letter tends to skip past analyses of how women and slaves become a part of the households in the first place and focuses on questions drawn only from the content of the letter. Thus they leave uncriticized the various exploitative and objectifying practices that are already at work in a household and that would be in the backdrop of a passage such as this one in 1 Peter. This approach, within the context of two thousand years of church tradition, directs scholars to assume that the only concern related to husbands and wives that precipitated the writing of the letter was an issue of different religious practices. In terms of the slaves, scholars are often quick to note how different the institution of slavery was "back then," as if this justifies avoiding dealing with the fact that slavery is endorsed by the bible. It seems that these scholars are looking back to those situations with the sanitized views of Sunday morning "church" in the Western (developed) world in mind. This perspective does not do justice to the texts or to the people whose stories are co-opted and/or silenced in the service of the author's agenda. Thus, with an eye toward what the irruptions in the text betray about the author's collusion with kyriarchal structures, I will discuss the call to silent suffering, the issue of outward adornment and the reference to Sarah in this text.

The Call to Silent Suffering

Many scholars have noted that addressing specifically the slaves and the wives is an unusual move on the author's part, an irruption of sorts that has empowering possibilities, since the household codes within philosophical treatises are addressed to the male head of the household and all relations within the household are centered on him in typically dualistic terms. While the androcentrism, hierarchy and dualistic nature of the household codes is to be expected, these are not dynamics that we ought to expect within the household of God. (Or are they?) Some scholars suggest that these dynamics are turned on their head simply because the author is here speaking to the lowliest members of the community instead of to the *paterfamilias*. But we might ask ourselves if the subjects of the slaves and wives as constructed, still dualistically, by this letter are actually going to be able to do anything to overturn the androcentric nature of their society. Just acknowledging those members of the households does not, in itself, give them autonomy.

Jeannine K. Brown's insights into the silence predicated upon/of wives in 3.1-6 compared with the command to the community in general to be prepared to speak in 3.14-16 help to highlight the second particular irruption I see in the *Haustafel*. The community is to be ready with a verbal defense of their Christian hope; the women/wives are to let their actions speak for them.[5]

In other words, they were not allowed to speak, but were to let their actions, determined by a kyriarchal social expectation, speak on their behalf. Not only were their words taken from them, but the messages they were allowed to speak-in-action were those of the kyriarchal social system. The contrast between the wives and the male non-slave members of the communities is heightened by the terminology that the two sections share. They both speak of realms of the heart (3.4, 15) and the recipients' conduct (3.1-2, 16), the "reverence" or fear with which they are to behave (3.2, 16), a prohibition from fearing ill treatment from superiors (3.6, 14), a value placed upon holiness (3.5, 15),[6] and good conduct or doing good things (3.6, 16). Though many scholars have tried to see the positive side of these parallels, which is that it makes the wives strong examples in the communities, I cannot help but question whether such

5. Jeannine K. Brown, "Silent Wives, Verbal Believers: 1 Peter 3:1-6," *Word and World* 24, no. 4 (2004): 395–403.

6. The second instance, of commanding the community members to "sanctify Christ as lord in their hearts" (whatever that meant/s), resonates with the idea of setting something apart, as well as the sanctification associated with the jobs of priests. These choices on the author's part may be coincidental, or they may be another example of the way a theme or image once attributed to a group continues to function throughout the text.

a strong parallel would have been made (allowed) if it were encouraging the women to use their words and not just their bodies.[7]

Quite to the contrary, the application of this social construct removes any agency or autonomy that the slaves and wives might have experienced in the house-churches. The "fear" that is to be rendered to God in 2.17 is also the manner in which the slaves and wives are to interact with their superior, the head of the household. Whether written consciously or not by the author, it seems it is no coincidence that the male god-figure and the male head of the household are to be given the same treatment and "reverence."[8]

There is an additional theological implication in using the example of Christ suffering silently to affirm the abject position of the slaves and thus indirectly that of the women.[9] With a text like 1 Peter, we are missing one side of the dialogue; we do not know what the other side of the conversation was advocating or resisting. In this regard, the women are doubly silenced. The initial concerns about what was going on in the Asia Minor communities are lost but for this hint that is recorded in the response contained in 1 Peter. But the very fact that part of the problem was mistreatment at the hands of spouses or masters makes the command to quietly submit themselves to the *paterfamilias* an abusive command. What we see here is a primary level of silencing of the most vulnerable in those communities. The author's response to the problem is to silence the complaints and to send the women silently back into the mistreatment.[10]

While the slaves were being encouraged to silently endure mistreatment simply because it was in their best interests, for the wives it had missiological ends. Contrary to the advice to brides and grooms that the wives should take

7. J. Ramsey Michaels, "St. Peter's Passion: The Passion Narrative in 1 Peter," *Word & World* 24/4 (2004): 387–94. He claims that, "in 1 Peter the accent is *not* on Jesus' silence, possible because (except among Christian wives, 3:1) silence is not what he wants to encourage among those who follow Jesus" (391). I note this comment because it strikes me as almost clueless as to the effects of this one exception, as if this were a minor oversight on the author's part.

8. Mary Daly's oft-quoted line, "If God is male, then the male is god," lingers in the backdrop of such a correlation. Mary Daly, *Beyond God the Father: Toward a Philosophy of Women's Liberation* (Boston: Beacon, 1973), 19.

9. Leonhard Goppelt makes an interesting assertion that the theology of suffering that we see in 1 Peter is drawn from the martyrology that we see in the old testament/Hebrew bible, Daniel in particular, instead of Job, and on the beatitude regarding suffering for righteousness' sake (174). It seems that most of the commentators I have read stay only with Jesus' own suffering and death, and do not draw in the beatitude or the Daniel parallel. Leonhard Goppelt, *A Commentary on I Peter.*

10. Here I am reminded of Jean Kim's discourse on the ways the sex trade, or existence of comfort women, was covered up by the Korean government by destroying all records that indicate that they knew what was going on. Destroying the evidence is a form of silencing the complaints, and in both cases it is being done with an eye toward social and economic "survival." See Chapter 1 or the introduction of Kim's *Woman and Nation.*

on the gods of their husbands, Peter seems to be implying that they not only do not need to do so but should see their example as one that may win over their husbands to their own God.[11] I must note, however, that nowhere in the text does it say to what the husbands might be won over; in other words, Peter may simply be hoping for peace among households that are mixed in their religious practices.[12]

Additionally, if the gospel announces, to some degree, the liberation from all that separates us from our god, our neighbors and ourselves, then the call to silent suffering has no place within the kerygma of Christ. Much like Ann McGuire has said of Colossians, any biblical passage that adapts a social construct that counters full life for some people is an example of an internal contradiction. Such adaptation and accommodation should not be able to be embraced within the Church that is defined by seeking newness of life and freedom from metaphorical and literal death.[13]

On the one hand, if Jesus' example of suffering is truly as the Son of God, who is subsequently raised from the dead in order to overcome such death and suffering, then anyone who suggests that people ought to see suffering as making them Christ-like is only talking about the pre-resurrected Christ. If it is truly the resurrection that makes Jesus' death different from any other state execution, then there ought to be no room within the Church to suggest that suffering in itself can be redemptive or a part of making one more like Christ. This is even more so the case when it is the lowliest in the community, who have no "power from on high" that would give their suffering the potential to be redemptive, who are being held up as examples of Christ-like suffering and obedience.

On the other hand, if Jesus suffered in solidarity with the outcast and oppressed, he was still doing so as a male with a following. The power discrepancies between Jesus and the slaves and wives do not allow for a fair comparison. Turning to women and slaves as the embodiment of Jesus' example is again reinscribing the very structures Jesus was speaking against. In other

11. Krentz, "Order in the 'House' of God," 284, "Peter urges Christian wives to use their way of life as a means to convert their husbands to Christianity (3.1), and here he breaks the social mold of the time." See also, Brown, "Silent Wives, Verbal Believers," 400.

12. I am also somewhat suspicious of any attempts to claim that these women were giving up entirely the honoring and/or worshipping of their husband's gods. The popular religious practices that take place in the homes do not always conform to the official practices and expectations of the organized religions. See Phyllis Bird, "The Place of Women in the Israelite Cultus," *Women in the Hebrew Bible* (Alice Bach, ed. NY: Routledge, 1999), 3–21.

13. Ann McGuire, "Equality and Subordination in Christ: Displacing the Powers of the Household Code in Colossians," in *Religion and Economic Ethics* (Joseph Gower, ed.; Lanham, Md.: University Press of America, 1990), 65–85.

words, if Jesus died as one of the lowly, then his death was for nothing if the lowliest of the lowly continue to be persecuted. An act to reinscribe within the faith communities the hierarchical kyriarchal system that eventually put Jesus to death is to have his followers completely miss the point. They are embracing the systems that Jesus died to overcome.

For another perspective on the mistreatment element, I would like to raise the (strong) possibility that the women in these communities were from various living situations. The traditional view of women being sold from father to husband is certainly relevant, but does not represent the lives of all women. I suggest that we consider that some of the women had been part of the spoils of war, or that some of them were not living within traditional household situations. How would the exclusively coupled-centered discourse of the socio-political structural norm of the household codes sound to these latter groups?[14] For any women who were sexually "impure" due to the actions of men staking territory through the women's bodies, this kind of rhetoric judges them again for what has been done *to* them, and it repeals the freedom they might have initially found in an embracing, accepting and empowering community/situation.

The author also reinforces the silence with a charge that their holy lives win over their husbands (*tēn en phobō hagnēn anastrophēn*): the men will observe their wives, and see that their behavior is innocent, pure and holy. We can see that, though motherhood is not mentioned and children are not addressed at all in 1 Peter, the pure or innocent way of living for the wives *is* the focus of discussion. No matter how the women are addressed or what roles they are assumed to fill, their re-productive and sexual potential is in the background. In fact, the overtones of sexuality are present simply by the use of the terms "husband" and "wife." The combination of these overtones with pure and upright behavior is a powerful collusion indeed, in particular if one grants that the typical honor/shame social dynamic is actively influential in these communities.[15]

Constraining the sexuality of women, and implying that this aspect of their

---

14. Luise Schottroff, *Feminist Interpretation: The Bible in Women's Perspective* (Minneapolis: Fortress, 1998), 188; see also, Jean Kim, "Uncovering her Nakedness: An Inter(con)textual Reading of Revelation 17 from a Postcolonial Feminist Perspective," *JSNT* 73 (1999): 61–81.

15. Stephen Bechtler discusses the honor/shame system motivation as he sees it playing out in this letter. He sees three particularly relevant passages, 2.12-15, 3.13-16 and 4.14, contributing to a symbolic construction of communal self-identity for the addressees (honor/shame discourse primary here; it serves as a basis for constructing a new symbolic universe in which what used to accrue shame now attributes honor from God). Suffering and disgrace (loss of honor) are the problems that Peter addresses, and depends upon only *verbal* disgrace. Bechtler refers to the *dox-* root (14 times), *tim-* (6) and *epainos* (2) and dishonor: *kataisksunō* (2) and *aisksunomai* (1). He also notes the connection to gender in the honor-shame system, specifically in terms of the wife's sexual purity, which is what she contributes to the honor of her husband/family, which he suggests explains the commands to the wives regarding their behavior. Bechtler, *Following in His Steps*, 102–3.

personhood holds the key to whether or not they live uprightly, essentializes them as sexual beings. Within the overall context of this letter, then, the women/ wives in the faith community will all be sexually pure and innocent. The issue is not that I am trying to approve of licentiousness, but only to point to the material reality, the socio-political implications, of such rhetoric that mimics that of imperial ideology. These essentialized (a)sexual beings uphold Empire and the *ekklesial* gatherings alike.

Finally, we can also see a strong correlation between the submission of everyone in the communities to the emperor and the wives to their husbands. Submitting to every human institution (2.13) is clarified as being in terms of the emperor or his representatives. The subsequent directives to the slaves and wives (2.18–3.6) to then be submissive to their masters and husbands is equally under the same injunction.[16] The roles of emperor, his regional representatives, and the *paterfamilias* are all human institutions, and the men in these positions are all to be given reverence and authority.

Outward Adornment

Much has been made of this passage regarding the braiding of hair and wearing of fine jewelry, in particular in comparison with wealthy women's practices and adornment, as well as in light of positions of leadership in other religious contexts at that time.[17] This approach to the topic makes a basic assumption that these are the only (or most) relevant contexts for comparison. Yet even this tidbit is a curious symptomatic irruption within the fabric of new testament scholarship, as most male scholars go out of their way to explain why the household codes have nothing to do with leadership roles. So why would we make any reference to women in leadership in other worship contexts as a way to make sense of why this directive is needed? Perhaps there is a cue for us in this lack of alignment within the scholarship on this aspect of the

---

16. Schertz, "Nonretaliation," 258–86. Schertz sees a parallel between the slaves and wives which reinforces the unity of the sections, thus the injunctions can be assumed to be posed to all, though this possibility does somewhat break down, given that the section addressed to the husbands also begins with "likewise."

17. See 1 Cor. 11.2-16 and my chapter "To What End? Revisiting the Gendered Space of 1 Cor. 11:2-16 from a Feminist Postcolonial Perspective," in *The Colonized Apostle: Paul and Postcolonial Studies* (Christopher Stanley, ed.; Minneapolis: Fortress, forthcoming) for part of the picture surrounding hair and women in prophetic/leadership roles. There is also a general sense that, since the wealthy women in ancient Greece and Rome wore ribbons and jewelry in their hair and gold and jewelry on their body, we can assume that the author was trying to promote a counter-image of modesty among these women. Contemporary philosophers also spoke of this kind of modesty or of beauty being something that comes from within a woman.

passage, which indicates how relevant the roles within the household were for the worship contexts as well.[18]

In a world where women were commodities, and everything about their lives was ultimately under the rule of her husband, requiring one's wife to be unadorned can be viewed as serving the needs of the husband in some way. Here it is a direct command from an authoritative person who was in a position of power over the communities. It is a choice being made and prescribed for the women, one that is also reinforced with theological justification (3.4, "Let your adornment be the inner self with the lasting beauty of a gentle and quiet spirit, which is very precious in God's sight"). There is no representation of the women's perspective or even an acknowledgement that the matter is open for discussion. It is a foregone conclusion that the command will be heeded by the recipients. Again, whether or not the directives were actually followed is not something we can know with any certainty. It is the fact that such directives were appropriately included at this point in the letter that gives us something to address.

While the mention of outward adornment in this context of household relationships may seem like an irruption in the text for the modern mind, as I mentioned above it is actually a rather appropriate place for such a topic. While Xenophon reports that what makes a woman truly beautiful is her competency within the home and her ability to continue to learn and to teach others, it seems the issue for Peter is that a woman's beauty be derived from her gentle and quiet spirit and the "hidden person of the heart." This is a significant shift toward a focus on controlling the women. Every action of theirs will reflect, positively or negatively, the beauty of which the author speaks. All that the woman looks like and does reflects upon her husband. All that she can do and be is subsumed under his authority. What a difference this makes between Xenophon and Peter's ideals if we compare the direction of their trajectories.

There is nothing wrong with encouraging people to strive to embody a gentle spirit; the problem comes when this is coupled with injunctions to be silently submissive, which is then the ultimate marker of faith and godliness for one specific group of people.[19] This is a clear example of controlling women by

---

18. I do not intend to disregard all theory on how space is/was often demarcated by gender and that gender plays/ed a role in differentiating between "sacred" and "secular" space. I simply wish to point to the difficulty we have in making clear distinctions or of completely compartmentalizing and separating the social implications of structure and ritual in one space from that in another. See Jorunn Økland, *Women in Their Place*.

19. On one level this idea offers a wonderful critique of or counter to what is held out as "beauty" today in the United States in particular, and thus in other countries that are influenced by its cultural fads and norms. At the same time, however, it also allows for the body/spirit split to come into the discussion.

focusing on their bodiliness. In this case it is a refusal to appreciate the body or to resist adorning it for whatever reasons, both of which denied the "traditional hallmarks of feminine beauty [at the time]: skin, hair, clothes."[20]

Even if we choose to see Peter as in line with philosophical thought at the time, instead of actively denying the body and its beauty, we must also take his injunctions regarding outward adornment together with the rest of the admonitions toward the wives, and perhaps contemplate the striking difference there is between these comments and what Paul said on these matters. The lack of similar attention to women's appearance in Paul's writings can be attributed to the general apocalyptic urgency that many people see in his worldview. All the more, then, do we have recourse to note that the inclusion of this muted and simplistic requirement is in keeping with controlling the spirit and actions of the wives.[21] Then the symptomatic irruptions take on the force of circumscribing wives to, among other things, silent positions of submission in both the marriage and ecclesial contexts, roles that support kyriarchal power structures.

Parallel to Sarah — Symptomatic Irruption or Logical Conclusion?
A handful of scholars have noted the "strange" choice to refer to Sarah calling Abraham lord and her attitude toward him as an example of being submissive. According to the biblical stories, the only time she actually called him "lord" was in laughter, when God had said that she would have a child within the year. But the two times she notably submitted to Abraham was when they were in the Pharaoh's court and with the King of Gerar, and she was taken in as a member of the concubinage of each.

On one hand, referring to Sarah may have simply been because of the significant imagery drawn from Israel and their texts that is used in the first couple of chapters, in addition to the fact that Abraham and Sarah were in foreign lands

---

20. Richard Hawley, "The Dynamics of Beauty," 49. I am keenly aware that the sources and scholarship that I am working with do not include much in the way of Jewish voices, mostly due to the fact that I am more concerned with the effects than the sources of these commands. In terms of giving some insight into halachic views of dress, adornment and behavior, I would send the reader to Rabbi Pesach Eliyahu Falk, *'oz vǝhadar levushah: Modesty, as Adornment for Life: Halachos and Attitudes Concerning Tznius of Dress and Conduct* (Nanuet, NY: Feldheim, 1998). While this *sefer* goes farther in portraying one particular modern interpretation of halachah than some of the first-century views, it is helpful for the bridge that it creates between the two. For instance, "*tznius* does not deny the woman her natural requirements [for fine clothes and jewelry] and far be it from *Yiddishkeit* to prevent a woman having one of her innate and instinctive needs fulfilled. . . . To our good fortune, modesty and refinement are an intrinsic part of being a Jewish woman or girl. Women have inherited these treasures from the original 'mothers of *Klal Yisroel*', each of whom personified special modesty, bashfulness and *eidelkeit*. It is our duty to reawaken these partly dormant qualities once again within ourselves" (5). This is one of many views on this topic, but noteworthy for how it essentializes and naturalizes a "need" for outer adornment.
21. See Chapter 5 for a discussion of the connection between the external physical appearance and a person's internal mindset or spirit.

and were uncertain of their relationship to the ruling powers, much like the opening and some of the content of 1 Peter implies about its recipients. On the other hand, this particular confluence of elements can be said to stand out too much due to its unusualness. In this regard it is a symptomatic irruption in the fabric of the text, one that requires attention.

From the perspective of lifting out components of collusion, the kind of deference or reverence that is called for is aimed at keeping people in line and willing to comply with structures and systems instead of to resist them. I suggest that it is not a coincidence that 2.17–3.16 is replete with echoes of "fear." It modifies the way the wives were to relate to their husbands, the house-slaves to their masters, and all people to their king or the king's representatives.[22]

When I read through this part of the text, it seems that the line between mortal fear[23] and reverence for an authority is blurred. Being afraid of their husbands is quite different from being deferential to one's god or master. When read holding both types of fear in mind, this passage becomes an example of how easily a person in a position of power can disregard the various dynamics of the daily reality of those to whom he speaks. This approach of offering universal directives instead of truly empathizing with and understanding the people affected by the "solutions" is similar to the way white Western malestream biblical scholarship has proclaimed its own authoritativeness. In both cases, the voice with authority is heeded and what he says goes.

The author would have us believe that Sarah did not give in to the fear she must have experienced when in the possession of these men, regardless of whether or not she was raped or even touched at all. In addition to erasing or taming the image of what happened to Sarah, this move reflects a freedom men presume that they have to manipulate both the women in their lives and the texts that (could) give voice to them. For the interested reader, I do more fully address Sarah's role in this letter in Chapter 5.

In this adaptation of the household code, all of the directives or commands given, including the submissive and compliant behavior attributed to Sarah, are reflective of a model citizen of Empire. Since this text is beneficial to Empire, the author is, intentionally or not, colluding with imperial ideologies.

Husbands
While I am not working with this section of the household code as much as the pieces addressed to wives and slaves, I do find it useful to address briefly,

---

22. Fear (n): 1.17, 2.18, 3.2, 3.14, 3.16; fear (vb.) 2.17, 3.6, 3.14.
23. This topic, "mortal fear," is addressed in the following chapter.

particularly at this point in the project. Primarily, it serves to highlight a distinction between roles for women and men that are realized within faith communities.

Muted Directives: "showing consideration" versus "suffer in silence"
Jeannine Brown has noted the unexpected element here of charging husbands to show honor to their wives, in 3.7: "Husbands, in the same way, show consideration for your wives in your life together, paying honor to the woman as the weaker sex, since they too are also heirs of the gracious gift of life — so that nothing may hinder your prayers." This seemingly pleasant irruption — pleasant to the extent that showing consideration and paying honor to a person are welcome behaviors — should give us reason to pause, however. Within a kyriarchal society that depends upon all members to behave in ways that sustain that order, all relational dynamics must be analyzed for their contribution to maintaining the status quo.

As the name of this section notes, there is a significant distinction between the commands given to the wives and those of the husbands in these communities. Whether or not the husbands being addressed are married to women within these communities is not my primary concern.[24] The issue is that within the first-century context such distinctions between behavioral expectations of husbands and wives were typical, thus many scholars note that we cannot fault the authors of these texts for, in a sense, being products of their culture. They could not help but to think of women and men differently and thus to have very different directives for them. But this basic disclaimer preempts any attempt to critique that very socio-political reality in which the authors lived and which they in turn textualized in their writing endeavors.

The "love patriarchalism" analysis is one of the most common ways to justify or to get around holding these texts accountable for what they engender in faith communities.[25] All such endeavors remain on the surface of the texts: "what Jesus 'said' was more loving and accepting than . . .," or, "it was unheard of for someone to suggest that a man give honor to his wife, thus the Christian movement was quite progressive in its early formative years." This kind of

24. I refer the reader interested in this topic to Gross, "Are the Wives of I Peter 3:7 Christians?," 89–96.

25. Schüssler Fiorenza, *In Memory of Her*, 78–84. Gerd Theissen adopted Troeltsch's understanding of patriarchalism in order to explain why one particular early Christian trajectory "survived" or was "successful" beyond the second and third centuries. According to Theissen, the Christian communities blended an agapeic love with the patriarchal structures, hierarchies and roles. The result was a "willing acceptance of given inequalities" within the social sphere, while maintaining an equality "in Christ" within the religious sphere. Gerd Theissen, *The Social Setting of Pauline Christianity: Essays on Corinth* (Philadelphia: Fortress, 1982).

approach to the passage is understandable, in that it points to what the scholar perceives to be a positive aspect of the text.

But my concern is not to decide whether these claims are wrong or right, but to note how finding the affirmative aspects of texts without holding them accountable for the oppressive realities that they perpetuate is also an act of collusion with the texts. A "step in the 'right' direction," by this way of interpreting, is still a step within the kyriarchal framework. There is still a stark contrast in roles between wives submitting silently and husbands ruling, however considerately, and this text assures that both parties will behave accordingly.

Ultimately, there is a stark contrast between the silence of the wives and the "considerate treatment" that is expected of the husbands, in order that their prayers not be hindered. One group is silenced and the other's ability to voice needs and issues is protected within the span of seven verses! The deference required of wives toward their husbands was not a new idea in terms of the socio-cultural expectations of that time, nor was the suggestion that husbands treat their wives well. They do clearly endorse behavior constituent of kyriarchal power relations, however, and in this sense are examples of components of collusion.

Role of Overseer in the Home and Ekklesia

In addition to the general dynamic between husband and wife that this text espouses, we can also see in the charge given to the husbands in 3.7 that the stance and roles of the husbands within the household in general are carried over into this exhortation. Though in Peter's exhortations there may be a softening of the typically domineering temperament, the kyriarchal system is still in place and the roles the men have within the household are simply transferred into the religious communities. There is a feigned sense of the women being highly esteemed because they are exemplary in their work and behaviors, since all the while the men are still given the ultimate rule or the final word. For the women it is an example of tokenism. The rhetorical effect of the charge to the husbands in 1 Pet. 3.7 is the wink of acknowledging their ultimate control.

Margaret Y. MacDonald has noted that "the role of leaders as relatively well-to-do householders who act as masters of their wives, children, and slaves is inseparably linked with their authority in the church."[26] The same reality that the wives may have done all the hard work within the household including overseeing the work of the children and slaves, while the husband

26. MacDonald, *Pauline Churches*, 214.

had the ultimate authority, is then played out within the gatherings of the faith communities. The final authority in the household rests with the *paterfamilias*; the final authority within the *ekklesia* rests with men who were heads of their households, those who by "nature" or by experience have proven to be able to command such authority.

This connection is further supported by the fact that the author of Ephesians draws upon the husband and wife "unity" as the primary image of the church in relation to Christ. No matter how loving the husband-wife and Christ-church relationships may have been, they are clearly hierarchical and thus have one dominant member over the other in both situations. Given the socio-political context of both the authors and the recipients, it is understandable that the authors would draw upon the husband-wife relationship to help explain the kyriarchal relations of the church, Christ and God. Any of their alternatives would have been equally hierarchically determined, as this kind of worldview was part of the *habitus* at that time.[27]

One of the points of debate in the household code scholarship is that of determining which passages "count" as such material. 1 Peter presents an interesting twist in this debate. While Aristotle addresses three dyadic relation-ships — husband/wife, father/child, master/slave — the father/child dimension is conspicuously removed from the content in 1 Peter (along with the master role). The children do show up in 5.1-5, however. Just as the wives are "like-wise" exhorted to be submissive to their husbands and husbands are "likewise" encouraged to respect their wives, the young ones are "likewise" exhorted to submit themselves to the *presbuteroi*.[28]

The debate as to whether or not the section in 5.1-5 qualifies as household code material — and thus for some scholars means 1 Peter is legitimately included — serves to hide or deny the fact that a connection *can* be and is made between household roles and those of the gathered *ekklesia*. As MacDonald has noted, "Here one discovers evidence that roles in the patriarchal household are inseparably linked to ministry roles in the community and to the formation of offices."[29] While scholars do not agree as to whether the household code content is drawn upon for defining leadership roles within the church, they do agree that 5.1-6 *is* significant in this regard. The splitting of hairs over which texts specifically impact our understanding of leadership roles is itself an irrup-

---

27. We are not lacking in voices who would say that systemically and structurally this kyriarchal worldview dominates to this day.

28. I agree with most scholars that the "likewise" used in 3.7 is referring back to the initial exhortations to the slaves.

29. MacDonald, *Pauline Churches*, 216. See also, Bonnie Howe, *Because you Bear this Name*, 225.

tion worth noting. Why do some scholars reject this idea so assertively, one wonders? In the end, however, I agree with MacDonald that household and *ekklesia* are inseparably linked, thus the sacred space is structured and run in terms of the kyriarchal (imperial) roles and expectations.

Households in Empire

Schüssler Fiorenza has summarized the crux of the issue of the role of households in upholding Empire, suggesting that since the rules of the household, religious rites and ancestral customs all had political and economic implications, wives and slaves who chose not to worship the gods of the paterfamilias, "violate not only their household duties but also the laws of the state."[30] These conclusions are primarily drawn from Aristotle's ideas about households. What I would like to contribute to this discussion is an initial assessment of how this idea becomes manifest, an analysis that goes beyond the behaviors and roles within households. I suggest that what is needed is to address the various factors that make possible that these behaviors and these alone, which are conducive to the kyriarchal system, are accepted.[31]

For instance, Margaret MacDonald has noted how the use of the domestic code in 1 Peter has a subtle effect of invalidating any interest there may still have been to gravitate toward the ascetic lifestyle. While the household code may be specifically addressing relations between believing wives and non-believing husbands, failing to mention the Christian communal option of women living together, for instance, effectively erases this possibility from the

---

30. Schüssler Fiorenza, "The Praxis of Co-equal Discipleship," 241.

31. In the United States today, though there may be an individualistic worldview that esteems the self as first and foremost, the well-worn creed: "God, Country, Flag" is the motto our government would have us embody. As United States (non)citizens, we are to be obedient to and to serve "our" God, country and flag before all other masters or organizations. The resonance between Aristotle's view and that of the government of the United States is hard to miss. Both are based upon and thus perpetuate a kyriarchal worldview and socio-political structure, and both trade in the fears and insecurities of the populace. I am all too aware of my own context as I write these pages. In a time of "war on terror" that operates out of fear and the perpetual production of a state of fear within the people living within the borders of this country, I am struck by the daily advertisements for the armed forces and National Guard that I hear on the radio, which are usually followed by a recording of the National Anthem. These morning moments of patriotism are to me propaganda of the simplest and most effective kind. This parallel also brings to mind the effects of silence or denial for the sake of the honor of the military or for the greater cause, something we know is constantly at work today. "For example, the motto of the United States Marine Corps, 'Semper Fidelis' (Latin for always faithful), is further interpreted as 'faithful to my God, country, and the Corps.' It is a cherished and respected code used by marines with great pride. However, it has also been used as a shield of silence." T. S. Nelson, *For Love of Country: Confronting Rape and Sexual Harassment in the U.S. Military* (New York: Haworth Maltreatment and Trauma, 2002), 6.

collective consciousness.[32] It is a life lived in an orderly and fruitful patriarchal household that matters.[33]

Continuing with this train of thought, the general category "wives" gives the impression that all wives and their situations are the same, which is just as ridiculous today as it was then. Additionally, the other non-household members of the society are conspicuously not acknowledged in the letter. I am referring to the people who are most exploited by the economic structure, day-laborers in particular. We must remember that whether women were among the ranks of day-laborers, and thus attending to children simultaneously, or that they stayed at home to rear children, tending to all household matters, their labor was essential in all cases. Any such wives, widows and non-married young women who were members of these communities, already in a position of relative invisibility, would have the additional slap in the face that this letter engendered.

While it may at first seem to be an "innocent" mistake that only members of the household are acknowledged in this letter, it is also a symptomatic irruption of the underlying need to simultaneously affirm and control the people in these particular roles and the effectiveness of this approach. In choosing to elevate the roles of the household, the author makes an accommodation to Empire. Collusion with the exploitative system precludes seeking justice for those who are exploited *by* the system.

Within the context of the Roman Empire, one may ask about the citizenship of day-laborers or of any of the members of these faith communities. In fact, the opening lines of this letter raise this question for us when addressing the recipients as "chosen refugees." There is a curious tension between acknowledging the members of these communities as non-citizens and refugees at the outset of the letter, yet choosing to affirm a socio-political norm that exploits those particular people. It is not the *paroikoi* or *parepidemoi* (and their lifestyles and contributions to society) who are held up as exemplary members of the communities in this section of the letter. Now, the author turns his attention to those *in households* who were most essential for the maintenance of the kyriarchal socio-political structure that is an essential aspect of imperial rule and domination.

To put it another way, addressing these faith communities in rural areas but only noting the role of the household slaves and wives, with no mention of the realities/status of the wo/men laborers, elevates and valorizes the household

---

32. MacDonald, *Pauline Churches*, 216.

33. Given that most texts that might tell us something informative about women during this time were written by men from a man's perspective, we should not be surprised to see only pragmatic discussions of women and their roles. But it needs to be said that it is precisely such limited views of women then that have informed the structures and relationships of various institutions in the Western world today. The lack of representation then has become a lived reality for women today.

economic system and re-marginalizes the laborers and their realities. It is a form of collusion with the exploitative practices that prey upon those who are most vulnerable.

There is a curious piece of history about the Asia Minor region regarding the acceptability of Christianity that is relevant to this issue. According to the findings of Samuel Dickey, there were an unusual number of strikes or examples of "labor unrest" that occurred in the cities of Asia Minor in the second through the fifth centuries, events unparalleled elsewhere within Roman colonies at that time.[34] The elite and well-to-do peoples of these nether regions at first resisted Christianity, yet within 200 years they would be the people embracing it. Perhaps there were restless laborers claiming to be a part of this movement, making it less than appealing for those trying to stay in the good graces of Rome and its representatives to associate themselves with such a movement. This possibility would also explain the multiple exhortations to "do good" within this circular letter, and the striking parallel with the terminology associated with accusations made of "Christians."[35]

Only a transformation in the constitution of the movement/organization can account for such a drastic change in the population of this movement. Coincidence or not, it was not until the "household code" ethic had been introduced, which made Christianity adaptable for imperial goals and its adherents appear to be obedient citizens,[36] that the Asia Minor region began to embrace Christianity.

These things said, it seems that then as now the official institutions that are sanctioned are those that support the status quo and the roles and laborers outside of this system are overlooked, erased from the social discourse, and yet still exploited for their productivity. I am well aware of the debate regarding the "true" mission that Jesus led during his time on earth: was it a grassroots movement "for the people"? Was he merely claiming to be for those exploited by the system while spending all his time with the elite who benefited from that exploitation? Did he in fact envision his movement leading to a political coup? Was he more of a peripatetic gentle teacher and healer? and so on. It is worth pointing out, however, the potential interpretation that the movement changed from supporting "the people" to embracing the establishment of the ruling elite.

---

34. Samuel Dickey, "Some Economic and Social Conditions," 405.

35. See Chapter 3, "Emperor and Empire are Essential" section.

36. Of note is Goppelt's understanding of the use of *hypotagete*: "order yourselves," in 2.13. He read this command as a counter not to rebellion but to "the flight of emigration." Goppelt, *A Commentary of I Peter*, 168. They were to enlist themselves in the organizations of their society, as Epictetus notes in his *Dissertationes* that the "role of a Man" was to be a citizen of the world, which meant that one should bear in mind the proper character of a citizen (2.10.1) (Goppelt, 171).

Whatever the case, the institution of the household was deeply embedded in the societies of first-century Asia Minor. The well-run household (and the rearing of children) was the main contribution that wives, under the supervision of their husbands, could make to society that was productive and praise-worthy. It was a role defined by men and for the socio-political and economic benefit of men and the kyriarchal social structure. All that happened behind closed doors and beneath the outward appearance of orderliness was denied a presence or a voice within the socio-political discourse. Then as now, the focus was upon producing obedient citizens who conformed to certain socio-political ideals.

1 Peter's Haustafel *as Ambivalent Mimicry*

Having discussed some of the specific pieces of the *Haustafel* in 1 Peter and how those irruptions highlight, to some extent, the role of households in upholding Empire, I would now like to address the larger picture of the incorporation of this adapted socio-political construct within this letter.

For me, one of the most fascinating aspects of the inclusion of a version of the household code is how it plays upon the power of the metonymy of presence.[37] This presence is, in Homi Bhabha's words, one of the strategic objectives of colonial mimicry. In rearticulating an aspect of the colonial kyriarchal structural system of relations, the author of the letter invokes within his discourse the very institution he might ultimately wish to disavow.[38] By merely referring to a part of this imperial institution, without having to qualify the reference, the author confirms the power of this standard. In so doing, he simultaneously elicits the responses of fear and respect that are granted to imperial representatives, and claims for himself the attendant power and authority.

At the same time, the discourse of mimicry is "constructed around an ambivalence; in order to be effective, mimicry must continually produce its slippage, its excess, its difference."[39] The imitation can never be complete, but, in the face of a dominating imperial "other," the colonized seemingly have no other choice but to engage with the patterns and expectations of Empire. The author of 1 Peter makes the mimicry quite easy to recognize, as he includes striking Christological meaning in his adaptation. The idea of ambivalence within acts of mimicry — its "almost but not quite" nature — is what makes it difficult, if not impossible, to determine whether such rhetorical moves are subversive or collusionary.

37. Homi Bhabha, *The Location of Culture* (New York: Routledge, 1994), 89.
38. Ibid., 91.
39. Ibid., 86.

Symbolic Dominating Power of Author over Recipients

The two issues of power and authority keep resurfacing in this discussion, and it is to be expected. The inquisitive mind may ask how or why this letter was well received at the time and was passed along to the next generations. The answer has to do with the dynamics of authority — whose voice or opinion matters most — and power between groups of people. Power wielded in a kyriarchal structure of relations implies that a hierarchy is required and thus must be maintained for the relations to continue as they began.[40] Power is a function of relations, since authoritative language "never governs without the collaboration of those it governs."[41]

Balch notes that it is probably not a coincidence that all of the new testament letters that adopt the household code are written by someone from a Roman prison, to a community (or communities) experiencing tension with the Roman social order in general, and reflect a concern for how to respond to outsiders.[42] Letters from prison hold their own weighty authority.[43] Though we cannot know entirely how the location of the authors affected what was written or how the missive was received, we can appreciate that 1 Peter gains authority because it comes from someone who knows the consequences of having a "run in" with the ruling powers. The fact that Peter was in Rome, the central command of the Empire, adds another layer of experiential insight and importance to what he has to say. Having seen the grandeur of Rome and the power of its military, an extension of the power of the Caesar himself, Peter's exhortations to "do good" and to live in a way that invokes praise and not punishment must have held significant sway among his audience.

The discourse that is used in the letter draws upon the language of the colonizer in addition to the language of the faith tradition out of which the Christian movement developed. The power of the imperial language and the structures that it supports is due in part to the fact that it all goes without mention by so many scholars, or is noted in highly detached or spiritualized ways. I am convinced that the introduction of the household code in 1 Peter (as well as Colossians and Ephesians) was nothing of a surprise to those who read it, but was so much a part of the culture/society in which they lived that no one

---

40. Castelli, *Imitating Paul*.
41. Bourdieu, *Language and Symbolic Power*, 113.
42. Balch, *Let Wives be Submissive*, 80, n. 58.
43. There are many reasons for this pull or unique authority attributed to letters written from prison/jail. As a way of contextualizing this dynamic, one only needs to consider the respect that other writings from prison have received: Martin Luther King's famous "Letter from Birmingham Jail," Dietrich Bonhoeffer's writings and letters, even Hitler's *Mein Kampf* is the focus of interest in ways that his other "writings" of various forms are not.

thought twice about it. There is an all-pervasiveness to the Empire and its presence, such that accommodation to it requires no explanation.[44] The power and
authority associated with the Empire, in this metonymy of presence, is then
extended to the author of this letter, granting his exhortations and commands
authoritative status.

Cynthia Briggs Kittredge addresses the powerful and affective combination
of unity and obedience language in Pauline literature. Her insights can help us
to see a similar dynamic at work in 1 Peter between the commands to be obedient and to do good and the identity of the faith communities as chosen people
of God. Though the rhetoric and discourse of 1 Peter reflects the matters of the
household code and the need the recipients had to be winsome in their behavior,
this does not neutralize the fact that it is directly tied to Yahweh's calling for
them (1.1–2.12). In fact it makes it clear that God is monitoring them.

The obedience required in the socio-political dimension is here intimately
connected with their religious context and the deity that they worship. "The
conventional connotations of obedience language in the social contexts of the
patriarchal family and in the political context of ruling and being ruled *are not
transformed*" in Paul's writings, according to Kittredge.[45] I suggest the same can
be said within the letter of 1 Peter. The theological backing may not be explicit
at the end of Chapter 2, but there is no mistaking the imposition of the religious or theological justification onto the functioning imperial rule (2.13-17),
which is then reinforced by the familial realm of the household, itself now
inscribed in the religious realm. The household terminology contributes to the
possibility of such a circular path of theologically justified submission.

In analyzing power relations, we must look at, among other things, the
degree of rationalization required in order for the relations to be seen as obvious
and representing a larger truth.[46] For our purposes, the introductory chapters
of the letter serve as the rationalization for the commands. In the relationship
between the author and the recipients, an authorized act has been created and
received. It is something which is spoken by a person "legitimately licensed
to do so," in a legitimate situation with or according to the legitimate forms.[47]
The author has drawn upon "legitimate" symbolic universes, both the religious
and the imperial, to buttress his authority. In not only receiving but passing

---

44. Fernando Segovia, "Biblical Criticism and Postcolonial Studies," in *The Postcolonial Bible* (R.
S. Sugirtharajah, ed.; Sheffield: Sheffield Academic Press, 1998), 49–65.

45. Cynthia Briggs Kittredge, *Community and Authority: The Rhetoric of Obedience in the Pauline
Tradition* (Harvard Theological Studies 45; Harrisburg, Pa.: Trinity, 1998), 176. See also, Schüssler
Fiorenza, "Discipleship and Patriarchy," 148.

46. Castelli, *Imitating Paul*, 50.

47. Bourdieu, *Language and Symbolic Power*, 113. I address this matter in Chapter 2.

along the directives the author has created, the faith communities grant him power and respect. The kyriarchal power relation between the author and these communities that we see in the letter becomes realized in their lives.[48]

Adapted Household Code — Subversive or Collusionary?

Since in his adaptation of the household code, the author speaks on behalf of and to the members of these communities, and he does so with power and authority, perhaps the question should be how is this *not* a move of collusion with imperial ideology?

Speaking of the house churches in Rome, James Jeffers claims that the congregations associated with Clement and his understanding of how the churches were to relate to the Roman government "came to accept social distinctions among themselves as a basis for ordering their relationships. That is, through the influence of Roman ideology, they came to accept hierarchy as natural to Christianity."[49] Notice how simply he claims the influence of Roman ideology on the house churches in Rome. Certainly the influence of imperial ideology was present for and affected all groups of people, though to varying degrees.

Part of the power of imperial domination is that it often goes unnoticed or unquestioned. While some claim that taking the language of the colonizer and re-interpreting it for one's own cause is a move of subversion, I contend that it only helps to mask the extent of the control the colonizer has over the colonized. When the language that is "subverted" is violent and evokes images of war, destructive power and domination, then the colonizer, not the colonized, has won in the adaptation, and subversion quickly becomes collusion. For this situation of faith communities, the language of violence and war resonates more closely with a dominating presence's ideology than that of a liberating and loving God. What is intended to subvert actually reinforces and reinscribes the role of the colonizer.[50]

It also creates the need to maintain such a kyriarchal structure, otherwise the language used and the relationships that it creates no longer function in the way they did initially. Put positively, changing the structure or the paradigm from which the community is formed and gets its identity would require new language and ways of relating. But given the extent to which the *habitus* affects social norms, ways of behaving and relating to one another, and even the language that is official or legitimate, such changes would have to be very

---

48. Ibid., 37.

49. James S. Jeffers, *Conflict at Rome: Social Order and Hierarchy in Early Christianity* (Minneapolis: Fortress, 1991), 131.

50. Musa Dube, *Postcolonial Feminist*, 116.

intentional and carefully wrought. Neither of these things are what I see at work in the letter of 1 Peter.

Thus, this collusion with imperial ideology affects the language, power dynamics, and roles within these communities. It is almost irrelevant that this accommodation or adaptation was done for expediency and the survival of the Christian movement, because now it is safely tucked away within the canon of the Christian traditions ensuring its efficacy for thousands of years.

Canonizing Collusion

The language of the colonizer in the mouths and proclamations of the colonized is not a minor issue. Many scholars have pointed to the ways in which the Christian communities and the authors of the gospels adopted terms and labels from the imperial realm. In doing so, they make the language of Christus Victor, Savior, and King of Kings, for instance, "innocent" and valid. In this way, the church was a part of veiling the imperial impact and influence on the peoples and the regions that were dominated.

As Sarah Tanzer has noted, the household provided not just the initial meeting place for the church, but the conceptual foundation for "universal church" as well.[51] The appropriated household code then produces a certain kind of knowledge and defines the realm of behavior and of possibilities for the members of the faith communities. Because texts that embody elements of imperial ideology were canonized, the patterns of kyriarchal power relations and the expectation of ultimate obedience to the government become embodied in the structure, language and roles of the church.

In addition, the canonization and later transportation of this letter to various parts of the world serves to promulgate the underlying kyriarchal structure of the household code to these societies. While the extent to which these societies adapt the socio-political structure varies from place to place and over time, it is still relevant that this particular institutional and behavioral expectation is a part of the bible of the Western world. These texts may have inspired a significant amount of artistic expression over the centuries, but they have also been quite useful in colonization efforts and in justifying the suppression and oppression of myriad groups of people.[52] The imposition of such blatantly kyriarchal

51. Sarah Tanzer, "Ephesians," in *Searching the Scriptures* vol. 2, *A Feminist Commentary* (Elisabeth Schüssler Fiorenza, Ann Brock, and Shelly Matthews, eds; New York: Crossroad, 1993), 328–9. See also David Horrell, "Leadership Patterns," 335.

52. See Michael Prior, CM, *The Bible and Colonialism: A Moral Critique* (The Biblical Seminar 48; Sheffield: Sheffield Academic, 1999); R.S. Sugirtharajah, "Biblical Studies after the Empire: From a Colonial to a Postcolonial Mode of Interpretation," pp. 12–23 in *The Postcolonial Bible* (The Bible and

power structures on the communities gathered in the name of Christ contributed to the movement's ability to become the official religion of the Roman Empire. This is an important point for this discussion because of the role the ruling powers have on determining social roles and relations of power, as well as the language that is used to establish and control such behavior.

There are many details to which one can point to highlight a change that took place in the structure and definition of roles from the early movement and Pauline material to the second phase, as documented in Ephesians, Colossians and 1 Peter. I have addressed the Christological issue briefly already, in terms of the command to be silent and to embrace suffering. Schüssler Fiorenza has noted another poignant textual irruption in the move from "no longer male and female" to the employment of household roles to circumscribe obedience and relations among the members of the communities. If we understand Gal. 3.28 to be addressing the socially constructed relations of husbands and wives, masters and slaves, then it is making a claim that these relations do not exist within the body of Christ. So, the early radical denial of the relevance of social roles within the *ekklesia* is turned on its head as those very social roles define all relations within the *ekklesia*.[53]

While the adaptation of the *Haustafel* was imposed on the faith communities sometime around the end of the first century CE, the inclusion of 1 Peter in the canon ensures that its structure and role constructions become unconsciously upheld and embodied by future members of the *ekklesia*. The distance that many scholars would like us to believe exists between the influence of this text and matters within the church and society today is one that I cannot agree exists. It is precisely because of the presence in the Christian canon of texts such as 1 Peter, which reflect kyriarchal socio-cultural norms and power differential relations, that we still have the need for emancipatory movements within the church and Western societies today.

Postcolonialism, 1; R.S. Sugirtharajah, ed.; Sheffield: Sheffield Academic Press, 1999); Bhabha, *Location of Culture*, 102–22.

53. Schüssler Fiorenza, "The Praxis of Co-equal Discipleship," 227–8.

5

DAUGHTERS OF SARAH: FEAR-FULL SUBJECTS INDEED

> Inequalities in relationships, coupled with cultural values that embrace domination
> of the weaker by the stronger, creates the potential for violence.[1]

Introduction

The issue of constructing subjects within the context of first-century Asia
Minor taps into numerous socio-political dynamics of social acceptability
and sustainability of the nascent Christian movement, vertical and horizontal
power relations, matters of essentialism and representation, and even those of
mimicry and collusion.[2] The goal of this chapter is to address how 1 Peter
functions in "the discursive construction of the subject of woman,"[3] primarily
because having the power to name and define what a woman can know and do
is precisely the power to own/possess, control and dominate her.

Explaining the intimate relation between the creation of knowledge and the
construction of subjects is made simple by Rosemary Hennessy's idea that
what we do impacts what we can know; and what we know impacts what we
can do. The delineation of roles on a superficial level — in the public realm —
effectively serves to control all realms of subordinated peoples' lives. These
roles reflexively dictate what kinds of knowledge are possible or allowable
within the individual communities.

What Can She Know?

In this context, what a woman can know is determined by an analysis of what
is said to and about women. What is said to them — a set of commands or

---

1. Jacquelyn White, "Aggression and Gender," in *Encyclopedia of Women and Gender: Sex Similarities and Differences and the Impact of Society on Gender* (vol. 1, Judith Worell, ed.; San Diego: Academic Press, 2001), 93.
2. See Chapter 2 for clarification of how I use these terms.
3. Hennessy, *Materialist Feminism*, xiii.

"strong encouragements" — is reinforced by what is (or is not) said about them in the text and social fabric. Though Hennessy's assertion suggests that an analysis should begin with what women "do," I will begin with what women can "know" because of the extent to which women and their roles were confined and controlled by the kyriarchal society in which they found themselves.

The possibilities within a world are limited by, and according to, the concepts used to comprehend and domesticate that space or world.[4] In as much as men or kyriarchal representatives are defining and constructing the world, all aspects of it will reflect the interests and desires of those with the power to define and construct. After all, "knowledge is a construct that bears the marks of its constructors."[5] Women are, in fact, only able to know and be known in terms of the kyriarchal system and to participate corporately in terms of that system. While such restrictions may not be absolute,[6] in a system in which women are granted little if any power to change, and then those descriptions and prescriptions are themselves codified/canonized, they might as well be written on stone tablets.

I will first address the knowledge that 1 Peter constructs regarding women, knowledge created in terms of the commands addressed to them, i.e. what they are presumably allowed to do. This particular or specifically defined knowledge is reinforced by a brief comparison between this passage and the identity of the community as a whole. Then I will look at the implications or effects of this knowledge on the constructed subject who is dwelling in a colonized space.

Creating Knowledge in 1 Peter

An assessment of the creation of knowledge begins by addressing the power dynamics within and behind the text. The materiality of this knowledge is found in the subjects it constructs. These subjects are addressed by granting the importance of the content of ecclesial correspondence, naming the ideologies at work behind commands or prescriptions, acknowledging the various aspects of women's reality that are affected by such prescriptions, and sorting through how actions and behaviors are circumscribed by a text. These two pieces, the construction of knowledge and of subjects, are predicated upon an agreement

---

4.   This idea, which I have drawn upon from various scholars' work throughout this project, is also acknowledged indirectly by Ludwig Wittgenstein, "*The limits of my language* means the limits of my world." *Tractatus Logico-Philosophicus* (D. F. Pears and B. F. McGuinness, trans.; London: Routledge & Kegan Paul, 1975), 5.6 (italics original).

5.   Lorraine Code, *What Can She Know? Feminist Theory and the Construction of Knowledge* (Ithaca: Cornell University Press, 1991), 55.

6.   Ibid., 65.

with Nancy Hartsock's insight that the relations that define and circumscribe women's activity are embodied in and perpetuated by their communities.[7]

Knowledge from Submission

The first aspect of this passage that I will analyze is that of the nature of the submission that the wives are to have to their husbands. It is defined by fear. It is an injunction that resonates with the way the slaves are to relate to their masters, and the men are to relate to the imperial authorities. It is a fear marked by respect as much as a trembling before the person who is one's authority or superior. The way the wives live their lives is to be marked by holiness and fear (*ēn en fobō hagnēn anastrofēn*). This is also the same kind of behavior that marks priests before their god, an element of worship that is highly debated in terms of what kind of fear this is or to what extent a person is actually fearful, in today's terms, of the deity in question. From this perspective, the relationship between a worshipper and her god is not much different from that of a child to her parent, or, in the case of 1 Peter 3, a wife to her lord and husband.

While I appreciate the difficulty of naming the quality of this fear, it is the focus on requiring or failing to alleviate fear in the followers of Christ that I consider to be dangerous and self-defeating. An email conversation about the wrath of God with a male colleague from seminary shows my concern quite nicely. These are some of his thoughts: "Can't one have a loving relationship with a loving Creator who has the potential to wipe her life out or is that an oxymoron? (I might ask my daughter about that? Not that I'm God, but the principle might translate?)."[8] However one understands this fear/reverence alluded to in 1 Peter, it is clearly not devoid of mortal fear. As my colleague's comments indicate, when one sees her/his God as one just as capable of delivering a death blow as a loving embrace, the fear of disappointing this God creates a sense of vigilance and striving for perfection. This same dynamic is endemic to abusive relationships, wherein the person with less power is also dependent upon the other, who is her abuser. There is, understandably, a fear and constant vigilance that keeps her as close to "in line" as possible for fear of triggering the wrath of her partner or spouse.

---

7.   Nancy C. M. Hartsock, "Foucault on Power: A Theory for Women?" in *Feminism/Postmodernism*, (Linda J. Nicholson, ed.; New York: Routledge, 1990), 155.
8.   "And . . . I'm not sure, but if I was going to put my money on it . . . I'll choose fear of God (reverence that is) every time!" In all fairness to this friend, I believe that he truly does not have a difficulty embracing the (what I consider to be contradictory) ideas that his God could "wipe him out" and yet this God loves him utterly. He may define the fear that he has for his God as reverence, but there is no question that there is some mortal fear in the mix.

In terms of creating knowledge, then, what does this kind of submission, "accompanied by fear," allow a wife/woman to know? Ultimately, it is easier to say what these wives do not get to know, which is their own dreams and calling. They are not allowed to embody a position of subjectivity in their own life, but only for the furtherance of someone else's needs or agenda. They do know a mortal fear, one that keeps them sufficiently motivated to upholding their part of the kyriarchal structure. The proper behavior, marked by silence and a reverent and/or mortal fear, is an outward manifestation of the inner spirit.

Knowledge from a Quieted Spirit, Demure Dress
There is a strong connection between the clothes we wear and the role we inhabit or the personality we embody. In terms of roles, whether ecclesial or secular, our attire directly reflects what it is that we are empowered to do and indicates the realm of expertise with which we are supposedly conversant. I am aware that there is a great deal of scholarship on the issue of dress, in terms of gender roles and social conformity. Here again I can only direct the reader to other sources for a more thorough theoretical base on this matter.[9] An analysis of this irruption in the text of 1 Peter, however, highlights the fact that an outward appearance or orderliness is a reflection of a person's inner state. For the wives/women, this is most valuable when it is marked by a gentle and quiet spirit. The connection between dress (outward hyper-humility) and social control (inner docility or subjugation) of women in this passage is clear.

The only other places that attire is addressed directly, in new testament texts, is in 1 Timothy and 1 Corinthians 11, which are similarly connected with strong images of communal identity and behavioral control of women.[10] The result of these brief texts, in particular those of the post-Pauline tradition, along with a general social concern for women as property and a need to control women's

9. Judith Butler, *Gender Trouble: Feminism and the Subversion of Identity* (New York: Routledge, 1990). See also, Marjorie Garber, *Vested Interests: Cross-Dressing & Cultural Anxiety* (New York: Routledge, 1992) and Howard Eilberg-Schwartz and Wendy Doniger, eds, *Off with Her Head!: The Denial of Women's Identity in Myth, Religion, and Culture* (Berkeley: University of California, 1995).

10. For discussion on the role of veils — or hairstyles, as some understand the veiling issue — for women in the Corinthian discourse, see Jouette M Bassler, "1 Corinthians," in *Woman's Bible Commentary, with Apocrypha* (Carol A. Newsome and Sharon H. Ringe, eds; Louisville: Westminster John Knox, 1998), 411–19; Castelli, *Imitating Paul*; MacDonald, *Early Christian Women*; Dale Martin, *The Corinthian Body* (New Haven: Yale University, 1995); Margaret M. Mitchell, *Paul and the Rhetoric of Reconciliation: An Exegetical Investigation of the Language and Composition of 1 Corinthians* (Tübingen: J. C. B. Mohr, 1991); Jerome H. Neyrey, *Paul, In Other Words: A Cultural Reading of His Letters* (Louisville: Westminster/John Knox, 1990); David W. Odell-Scott, *A Post-Patriarchal Christology* (Atlanta: Scholars Press, 1992); Økland, *Women in Their Place*, esp. Chapters 4 and 6; Daniel Patte, *Paul's Faith and the Power of the Gospel: A Structural Introduction to the Pauline Letters* (Philadelphia: Fortress, 1983), esp. Chapter 8; Elisabeth Schüssler Fiorenza, *In Memory of Her*, esp. 226–36; and Wire, *The Corinthian Women Prophets*.

sexuality, is a heightened focus upon the clothing and outward adornment of women in certain Christian circles. The material reality of such a powerful combination is seen in the way pure or simple clothing has become a primary measure of Christian piety for *women*.

Modern readers of this passage tend to be either numb to this irruption, due to its familiarity, or appalled by its prudishness. It is because many devout Christians can and do read this call for overly simple dress for wives as justifiable and important that I draw attention to it. This call in 1 Peter 3 for simple dress that calls no attention to itself stands in stark contrast with the image of priests in their elaborate ornate robes. Not only does clothing make the human body "culturally visible," Kaja Silverman asserts that "clothing is a necessary condition of subjectivity — that in articulating the body, it simultaneously articulates the psyche."[11] The communities in this letter are associated with priesthood, as we see in 2.4-10, yet the wives, for having to be singled out, are not included in that priesthood and are relegated to the pews, condemned to sit there in muted attire until their labor is needed. This may be an "innocent" command given the socio-political dynamics that the members of these communities were facing, but the impression upon the wives' psyches, indelibly carved into future generations through the medium of the *habitus*, is one of silent, demure submission and subservience.

On the flip-side of this assertion, Freud himself made the claim that "the ego is first and foremost a body-ego; it is not merely a surface entity, but is itself the projection of a surface."[12] Though his phrasing implies a one-way relation between the external "body" and the internal ego or "self," he does appreciate the formative reciprocity at work between a person's interior and exterior worlds in the construction of subjectivity. Elizabeth Grosz brings in theories of gender and of space in her search to understand how a person's exteriority is psychically constructed, "and conversely, how the processes of social inscription of the body's surface construct for it a psychical interior."[13] The point is that what is happening to our bodies, in this case in terms of attire and what it communicates about a person, has an effect upon what a person internalizes about herself.

In many conservative circles today attire "provides a visual display of religiosity."[14] As Linda Boynton Arthur notes, for women within the Holdeman

---

11. Kaja Silverman, "Fragments of a Fashionable Discourse," in *Studies in Entertainment: Critical Approaches to Mass Culture* (Tania Modleski, ed.; Bloomington: Indiana University, 1986), 147.

12. Sigmund Freud, *The Standard Edition of the Complete Psychological Works of Sigmund Freud* (James Stratchey, trans.; 18 vols.; London: Hogarth, 1953–66), 9:26.

13. Elizabeth Grosz, "Bodies-Cities," in *Sexuality and Space* (Princeton Papers on Architecture; Beatriz Colomina, ed.; Princeton: Princeton University, 1992), 242.

14. Linda Boynton Arthur, "Clothing, Control, and Women's Agency: The Mitigation of Patriarchal

Mennonite community, "dress is a metaphor; it is interpreted as a visual symbol of the suppression of the self to the demands of the community."[15] These women struggle to define themselves within a restrictive circumscribed context within the twenty-first century. Their present-day reality is, by their own admission, directly connected to the commands seen here in 1 Peter. As people who identify with the "strangers" and "pilgrims" ascriptions in the first two chapters of this letter, they have adopted "plain" dress as indications of their commitment, non-conformity to worldly standards, and separateness. They also eschew displaying wealth through outer adornment out of a desire to be humble and modest, as this section of 1 Peter instructs.[16]

While Mennonite communities offer clear examples of the materiality of this passage, there are many faith communities that embody this admonition to varying degrees.[17] The issue here is not that modest clothing is a problem in itself, but that it has become a significant marker of godliness, which is often confused or collides with cultural norms of propriety. Given the connection between the inner person and prescribed clothing, how they inform and reflect one another, such requirements have the potential to squelch personality and spirit. Such expectations turn female members of the community into objects, reifying their role in social control.

Luce Irigaray speaks of the "dominant scopic economy" that women passively submit to or engage in today as objects to be admired or observed.[18] If this "dominant scopic economy" is the issue behind the directive in the text, we might applaud the author for wanting to "protect" the women in these faith communities from this objectivity. The situation remains, however, that prescribing extreme forms of attire on a daily basis is a textual symptomatic irruption indicating the need to control women. Whatever the motivation for it, what the text accomplishes is that women are repressed from self-expression through adornment entirely, all for the sake of social control and order. The desires or fears of males are here displaced onto the objects of their desires/

Power," in *Negotiating at the Margins: The Gendered Discourses of Power and Resistance* (Kathy Davis and Sue Fisher, eds; New Brunswick, New Jersey: Rutgers University, 1993), 66. She is speaking here in terms of Holdeman Mennonites, but also refers to scholarship on this topic in relation to the clothing of Hasidic Jews.

15. Ibid., 68.

16. Stephen Scott, *Why Do They Dress That Way?* (Intercourse, Pa.: Good Books, 1997), 4–17.

17. There is no question that my own attire was considerably less flattering or fitting for many years because of this same belief that not only did my attire reflect the purity of my "inner being" but that it also must not draw attention to me. My attire and I were both to be pure and demure. My own experiences aside, there is much to be said regarding clothing and various other religious traditions, whether regarding restrictive expectations (e.g. some branches of Judaism, Islam, Hinduism) or simply those that come from a sense of simplicity (e.g. Buddhism, Jainism).

18. Irigaray, *This Sex*, 28.

fears. In a move that we still hear of today, which names the woman's or victim's appearance as responsible for the treatment she receives, the author would have us believe that the issue is seemingly about a female's body, and thus the real issue is not addressed.

The wives are to know that a quiet submissive spirit is valuable to their god. Lest they forget, they also know to dress in a manner that will reflect, and perhaps at times remind them of, their inner gentle spirit. They are also, indirectly, informed that because they cannot don a priestly robe they are not able to be leaders of these communities. Their clothing tells them who they are and what they can and cannot do. They are to know the things that are focused upon forming a subjectivity that is conducive to sustaining others' visions and needs. This reality works to contain women's subjectivity within the spheres of kyriarchy and male privilege, where they know the tasks of maintaining and reproducing, rather than challenging or resisting, the social structures of domination, oppression and control.

Daughter of Sarah

> For this is also how the women of old who hoped in God once used to adorn themselves and were subordinate to their husbands; thus Sarah obeyed Abraham, calling him, "lord." You are her children when you do what is good and let nothing terrify you. 1 Pet. 3.5-6

> Coercing or leaving / Shutting down and punishing
> Running from rooms, defending / Withholding, justifying . . .
> Diagnosing, analyzing / Unsolicited advice
> Explaining and controlling, / Judging opining and meddling . . .
> This labeling / This pointing / this sensitive's unraveling
> This sting I've been ignoring / I feel it way down way down
> These versions of violence / Sometimes subtle sometimes clear
> And the ones that go unnoticed / Still leave their mark once disappeared.[19]

In this brief association between these wives and Sarah, the author creates what some see as a step toward the subject-hood of the women. From this perspective, the image "daughters of Sarah" parallels the "children of Abraham" communal identity. But in doing so it heightens our awareness that women were not, symbolically speaking, children of Abraham and that Sarah's role

---

19. Alanis Morissette, "Versions of Violence," from *Flavors of Entanglement*, 2008.

in the historiography of Israel is primarily that of child-bearer. The obedient wives in 1 Peter are related directly to Sarah not through faith or a covenant but in accordance with the proper deferential behavior that is here midrashically attributed to Sarah. In addition to creating a singular, essentialized image of "the faithful woman," it also raises the question, "What then does it mean to be Sarah's daughter?"[20]

Calling him "Lord"

Three stories are conflated in this brief comment about Sarah and her relationship with Abraham. In Gen. 12.11-20 we have the account of Sarah being taken into Pharaoh's house after the men in his court saw her, beheld her beauty and counseled him to procure her. Abraham did not resist him, rather, knowing how beautiful she was and that he might be harmed in order for other men to get to Sarah, he claimed that she was his sister in order to protect himself.[21] In Genesis 20, Abraham, again under the guise of being her brother and for the same reasons, handed Sarah over to the King of Gerar. In neither of these accounts is Sarah recorded as calling him lord/*kurios*/*adonai*.

She does call him lord, however, in Genesis 21, in a fit of laughter at the thought of Abraham giving her a son in their old age.[22] It is worth noting that the

20. I must acknowledge and thank Susan Hall, LMHC, for her insightful responses and suggestions that deepened and clarified the meaningfulness of this section.

21. This is not, of course, the only story in the biblical texts where the safety and well-being of the man is considered more important than that of the woman associated with him, or even that depicts how the former is 'bought' at the expense of the latter. See Judges 19 and Genesis 19 for two of the most notable examples of this in the Hebrew text; see also Phyllis Trible, *Texts of Terror: Literary-Feminist Readings of Biblical Narratives* (Philadelphia: Fortress, 1984). This is a practice that is still well attested today; and in particular within the realm of abusive marriages, where the husband feels justified in subjecting his wife to any kind of treatment, especially if it will lead to his own sexual gratification. A bill that would *remove the spousal exemption* from the state's rape law was before the Tennessee legislature ten years in a row before it was passed in 2005. Prior to its passage, a man could receive up to 15 years in prison for raping his wife, up to 60 years for a stranger or even "just" a girlfriend. While the distinction is now removed in the area of the penalty exacted, the action must still qualify as illegal, which is determined, in Tennessee, to be when he "uses a weapon, causes her serious bodily injury, or they are separated or divorcing." President Barak Obama declared October 2009 to be National Domestic Violence Awareness Month, though one wonders if this will be a yearly recognition. For a summary of rape legislation, including spousal rape, see: *http://open.salon.com/blog/ronp01/2009/10/29/the_law_of_spousal_rape_domestic_violence_awareness_month*, written October 29, 2009 (accessed July 20, 2010).

22. See, for instance, Jonathan Kirsch, *The Woman Who Laughed at God: The Untold History of the Jewish People* (New York: Viking, 2001), 7–9, where Kirsch claims that "the woman who laughed at God embodies one of the essential values of Judaism — the audacity, boldness, and daring that are summed up in the Yiddish word, 'chutzpah'" (9). As Elaine Phillips notes, the treatment of Sarah in the early Jewish and Christian traditions was determined by the agenda of the respective texts/sources/authors. Elaine Phillips, "Incredulity, Faith, and Textual Purposes: Post-biblical Responses to the Laughter of Abraham and Sarah," in *The Function of Scripture in Early Jewish and Christian Tradition* (JSNTSS 154; SSEJC 6; Sheffield: Sheffield Academic, 1998), 33. Most notably, according to the Aggadah (Genesis Rabbah, Leviticus Rabbah, and Megilloth), Sarah was highly praised and respected, she was a prophetess with

trajectory of Christian thought and theology on this matter has chosen to take the "lordship" aspect of this text and ignore Sarah's laughter, whereas many Judaic traditions have done just the opposite. What these three stories tell us, as we have them in the Hebrew bible, is that the two times Sarah *is* depicted as being obedient to her husband it is when she is being delivered into a dangerous situation in order to secure Abraham's safety.

The focus in interpretations of these two stories tends to be on Abraham, whether in terms of his choice to lie about his relation to Sarah or in terms of his clever way of working the system for his benefit and survival. Sarah is a pawn used for Abraham's survival in both instances. More to the point, Abraham's choice to deliver her over to the Pharaoh's or King's court confirms that Sarah is his possession. Much like the concubine in the Judges 19 story, Sarah is handed over to a more powerful male, without a word of protest from her recorded. All the while these encounters are her own fault — the victim is blamed — because she is so beautiful.

According to 1 Peter, Sarah is to be emulated for calling Abraham "lord" and for not being frightened by anything to which she was subjected. I see the use of Sarah in this particular way as a symptomatic irruption in the fabric of the text that indicates that the author is attempting to smooth over social disruptions. Re-interpreting Sarah as having called Abraham "lord" gives the author a shero, a model of obedience, which, when combined with the previous admonition to have a gentle and quiet spirit, is quite useful for controlling or containing the wives. She is depicted as being compliant with his will, no matter how frightened she might have been. In fact, Sarah is silent in the stories — like a lamb led to slaughter she was silent — just as these women are now to be silent.

It is not incidental to the passage that Sarah is claimed to have addressed Abraham as "lord." I refer here to a reflection from Frederick Douglass's *Narrative of the Life of Frederick Douglass*, where he comments upon his master. Note the connection between using a title that acknowledges the superiority of the other and one's disposition toward that person.

> He was a slaveholder without the ability to hold slaves. He found himself incapable of managing his slaves either by force, fear or fraud. We seldom called him "master"; we generally called him "Captain Auld," and were hardly disposed to title

greater powers than Abraham, *she* prayed to God for deliverance from Pharaoh, and at the news of her death the inhabitants of Hebron "closed their places of business out of respect for her memory and as a reward did not die before they participated 38 years later in the obsequies of Abraham (Gen. R. 58:7; 62:3)." Aaron Rothkoff, "Sarah," in *Encyclopedia Judaica* vol. 18 (Fred Skolnik, editor-in-chief, Michael Berenbaum, executive editor; Detroit: Macmillan Reference, 2007), 46–7.

him at all. . . . Our want of reverence for him must have perplexed him greatly. He wished to have us call him master, but lacked the firmness necessary to command us to do so.[23]

As Douglass so poignantly notes of the slave/master dynamic, the wife who willingly admits the "master" role or label of her husband is simultaneously admitting her dependence upon him and her fear/reverence and obedience toward him. These factors create a dynamic that perpetuates a (co-)dependent relationship at the expense of the slave's or wife's self-identity and worth.[24] The subjugated person is defined and controlled by this one-up/one-down relationship, and is simultaneously *needed* in order to maintain or justify the power-over role held by the master/lord. The author of 1 Peter is not-so-subtly implying that the wives need to get back in line with this familiar household role.

"Because of Sarah"
In both Genesis 12 and 20 the narrator notes that it was "because of Sarah" that things went well for Abram/Abraham, which some scholars take as a positive thing that she is given some credit in these events. As Gayle Rubin has noted, however, women have been and continue to be the conduits of exchanges or relations between men, exactly what we see happening to Sarah. She was not the direct benefactor of her own "circulation,"[25] but in her silent submission to the desires of her "lord" Sarah kept *him* safe. This bartering with Sarah puts her in a space in which we can expect her to be raped in some form. Instead of trotting out a list of the current global practices that are based primarily, if not solely, upon the circulation of women, I refer the interested reader to several sources on this matter. Sarah is not alone in her experience of trafficking and of frightful things.[26]

---

23. Frederick Douglass, *Narrative of the Life of Frederick Douglass, an American Slave, Written by Himself* (William L. Andrews and William S. McFeely, eds; New York: W.W. Norton & Company), 40.

24. As Susan Hall, LMHC, has noted, "Any psychologist worth her/his salt will tell you it is never appropriate for an adult to be dependent/obedient upon another adult unless there's some disability creating that dependence."

25. Gayle Rubin, "The Traffic of Women" in *Toward an Anthropology of Women* (Rayna R. Reiter, ed.; New York: Monthly Review Press, 1975), 174.

26. Subcommittee on Africa, Global Human Rights, and International Operations, "Germany's World Cup brothels: 40,000 women and children at risk of exploitation through trafficking: Hearing House of Representatives, One Hundred Ninth Congress, second session, May 4, 2006; United States, Congress, House, Committee on International Relations, Subcommittee on Africa, Global Human Rights, and International Operations," *http://www.internationalrelations.house.gov/archives/109/27330.PDF*; Julia O'Connell Davidson, *Children in the Global Sex Trade* (Malden, Mass.: Polity, 2005); Filomina Chioma Steady, ed., *Black Women, Globalization, and Economic Justice: Studies from Africa and the*

Interestingly enough, Sarah is depicted as responsible, due to her beauty, in both the text and the scholarship on this passage.[27] When the scholarship does not problematize this dynamic, it is merely reflecting what is "in the text" and as such belies the fact that many people today still believe that a woman "asks" for mistreatment any time she is not covering her body or hiding her beauty in any of its forms. When scholars have voiced the problem with Abraham trying to put the blame on Sarah, they have gone no farther than to note this problem in the text. This passage actually stands as a witness to the way blaming continues to this day; even those who see the problem with it are ill-equipped to redress it.

The voice of the author in 1 Peter looms overhead in this prescription for women to silently hope that their actions may win over their husbands, now read with the awareness of an allusion to Sarah's sexual abuse, followed by the example of not being frightened by terrifying things. What has been read for centuries as a clash of faith/religious traditions, between the supposedly newly converted wives and their still-pagan husbands, can be read with the insights we now have regarding sexual, emotional and physical violence and abuse in "committed" relationships.[28] That the author chose Sarah, as opposed to any of the other matriarchs of Israel, and chose to reinterpret her experiences in this manner, suggests that some form of physical and/or sexual abuse was also happening, and that the author of 1 Peter was trying to ignore the situation or to get the women to stop discussing it.[29]

African Diaspora (Rochester, Vt.: Schenkman Books, 2002); and Ursula Biemann, "Touring, Routing and Trafficking Female Geobodies: A Video Essay on the Topography of the Global Sex Trade," in *Mobilizing Place, Placing Mobility* (Ginette Verstraete and Tim Cresswell, eds; New York: Rodopi, 2002), 71–86.

27. Genesis 12.11-16: When he was about to enter Egypt, he said to his wife Sarai, "I know well that you are a woman beautiful in appearance; and when the Egyptians see you, they will say, 'This is his wife'; then they will kill me, but they will let you live. Say you are my sister, so that it may go well with me because of you, and that my life may be spared on your account." When Abram entered Egypt the Egyptians saw that the woman was very beautiful. When the officials of Pharaoh saw her, they praised her to Pharaoh. And the woman was taken into Pharaoh's house. And for her sake he dealt well with Abram.

28. I say "committed" in order to draw our attention away from violence perpetrated by strangers and to acknowledge that there is a spectrum of relationships that can be informed by these insights, not simply those that claim the married status.

29. I am confident that certain concepts have been interpreted and translated over the centuries in ways that have down-played their severity or seriousness, just as others have been heightened, due to the interests of the translators and those who controlled the translations. This term, *ptoēsis*, is a perfect example of such a concept. It is cited only twice in the LXX and Greek new testament combined, and is variously translated as "panic," "fear," "disaster," or "terror." (The other occurrence is in Prov. 3.25, "Do not fear the sudden terror that comes or the impulse of the wicked." The Greek and Hebrew are significantly different on this verse, which only adds to my fascination regarding what was being communicated and what was being covered over [or why things needed to change]. In any case, there is a sense the wise-one was referring to frightening things, due to the association with the wicked.) The Liddell and Scott lexicon suggests a more visceral understanding, "vehement emotion or excitement." While I will not try to make a definitive claim about the thrust of this term, I will suggest that the reader consider the terror or frightful aspect, in particular because the author of 1 Peter is addressing the dynamics between a wife and her abusive husband. Henry

It should not surprise us that one of the top ten myths about intimate violence against women today is that if she is patient and understanding her situation will get better.[30] The reality, according to research and testimonies within counseling settings, is that the longer a woman stays in such a situation, the more violent the abuse becomes.

Even I have a difficult time assenting to the likelihood that Sarah was raped in the ensuing days of her membership in the court concubinage, because I have been trained not to think of such possibilities. The mere acknowledgement by Abraham, however, that he had to relinquish his claim to her tells us that the Pharaoh of Egypt or King of Gerar would then seek to make such a claim over her for himself — in today's terms, non-consensual sex, that is rape.

In suggesting that these women endure their abuse, what does the author allow them to know? A woman/wife being abused by her partner does know physical and emotional pain, trauma, constant fear, helplessness, depression, anxiety, loss of self-esteem and a deeply rooted need to appease the man who has direct control over her.[31] A battered woman will learn to be helpless, will blame herself, and will feel extreme shame and humiliation.[32] In these situations, abuse of any form does not have to happen often in order to be a "constant, hidden, terrorizing factor."[33] As if these problems were not difficult enough, she is often isolated and silenced, both of which function as "weapons of subjugation."[34]

Silencing the Victim

As Andrea Dworkin, a survivor of partner abuse, has explained, "You become unable to use language because it stops meaning anything. . . . Once you lose language, your isolation is absolute."[35] When isolation is combined with a

George Liddell and Robert Scott, *A Greek-English Lexicon* (revised and augmented by Sir Henry Stuart Jones and Roderick McKenzie; New York: Oxford University, 1996).

30. Carol A. Grothues and Shelly L. Marmion, "Dismantling the Myths about Intimate Violence against Women," in *"Intimate" Violence against Women: When Spouses, Partners, or Lovers Attack* (Paula K. Lundberg-Love and Shelly L. Marmion, eds; Westport, Conn.: Praeger, 2006), 14.

31. Jean Giles-Sims, "The Aftermath of Partner Violence," in *Partner Violence: A Comprehensive Review of 20 Years of Research* (Jana L. Jasinski and Linda M. Williams, eds; Thousand Oaks: Sage, 1998), 44.

32. Margareta Hydén, *Woman Battering as Marital Act: The Construction of a Violent Marriage* (Oslo: Scandinavian University, 1994), 8–9.

33. Grothues and Marmion, "Dismantling the Myths," 10.

34. Eviatar Zerubavel, *The Elephant in the Room: Silence and Denial in Everyday Life* (New York: Oxford University, 2006), 41. In some ways isolation and silence are some of the most damaging things, because in isolation none of us can gain strength with which to resist. It is only in relationship and naming what has happened that we have a sense of self, out of which we may gain the fortitude to leave or fight back.

35. Andrea Dworkin, *Life and Death* (New York: Free Press, 1997), 53.

sense of powerlessness, it leads to hopelessness and desperation. A person experiencing such disconnection and isolation will do almost anything to overcome such feelings.[36] The victim, thus, becomes a willing participant in maintaining this place of isolation and desperation with her own silence — it becomes unsafe to speak because every word can and will be twisted and used against you.[37] Silence becomes a refuge of sorts even as it simultaneously damns one to isolation.

There are many factors that contribute to this silencing. The two most common means are by creating the illusion that the victim is responsible for her own abuse in some way and by threatening the life of the woman should she speak out about her situation. In the case of the former method, the victim often carries the guilt for what has been done *to* her. This response, taking on the shame that the *perpetrator* should be feeling, is referred to as "introjections," which in turn makes it incredibly difficult for the woman to report the abuse. This issue of blaming the victim, suggesting that something about her provoked the attack/maltreatment, is one reason so many women hate their beauty: they believe it caused their rape/abuse rather than making the rape/abuse about the men who inflict it. Instead of owning their own desires, males project the responsibility onto the females, and then proceed to control, constrain, circumscribe and dominate them.

As studies today indicate, simply the fear or anticipation of violence or abuse — whether from Abraham if she resists his idea or from those in the courts of the rulers — is enough to render Sarah mute and socially withdrawn. Regardless of how she was treated, the exchange itself is one of power and control between two men via Sarah, making any sexual encounter not one about love or sex, but power and marking territory.

We can call it coercion or manipulation, or more likely force, but in any case Sarah had no alternatives. The author of 1 Peter refers to Sarah's willingness to do what Abraham required of her as the trait worth emulating. The author would have us believe that her silent submission to abusive and manipulative treatment made her attractive to Abraham and is, according to 1 Peter, an attitude that is of great worth in God's perspective. If this were the case, then this god is

---

36. Jean Baker Miller and Irene Pierce Stiver, *The Healing Connection: How Women Form Relationships in Therapy and in Life* (Boston: Beacon, 1997), 72, 84.

37. I am reminded of the second item in the Miranda Rights read to a person taken into custody of a law enforcement office: "Anything you say can and will be used against you in a court of law." As is the case in so many circumstances in life, the very people who need protection, or who need to be believed and taken at their word, by a protector of any form — spouse, system of law, etc. — are in effect not able to be fully protected by that entity, due to the nature of the difficulty in conveying the problem to an entity that requires "facts." See, for instance, Robert F. Barsky, *Constructing a Productive Other: Discourse Theory and the Convention Refugee Hearing* (Philadelphia: John Benjamins, 1994).

also an abusive god. But the matter I am more interested in is that the author of 1 Peter found it appropriate to put such abusive and harmful intentions on God. The author of the letter is playing the card of all trump cards in this coercive or persuasive section of the text. Much like Abraham or the Levite,[38] the author of 1 Peter plays the role of the abusive husband in stating such expectations of the wives who would hear this letter read to them.

The silencing of women in such situations, keeping them from speaking out about any abusive treatment they have received, is not only a primary mode of control over them but also allows those around them to deny what is happening. It creates a secret, something appropriately referred to as "the elephant in the room." Various social cues teach us to keep such secrets or to "ignore" the elephant in the room.[39] In the case of an abused wife, it is the tenuous nature of her relationship with her husband and the fear of things becoming more intense that keep her silent. In 1 Peter we see a similar tenuousness, and their being urged to silently endure mistreatment serves to maintain the overall socio-political "peace."[40]

"Breaking the silence" is often used by therapists or in safety slogans in efforts to raise awareness about the extent of abusive relations in our culture today.[41] Speaking out gives the victim her personhood, allows her story to be heard and responded to, and helps to keep it from happening again. Airing a secret helps to remove the fear, shame and guilt, and brings the woman back into community from her space of isolation. Titles such as *Bearing Witness* and *Ending the Silence* give testimony to the need to put to words these abusive and harmful situations.[42] From this perspective, the feigning-calm, soothing voice of the author sends chills down the spine of a person in tune with these most basic dynamics associated with physical and sexual abuse.

Even if a person does not wish to see sexual abuse/rape in the backdrop of these commands in 1 Peter, it is worth noting that the emotional abuse that such limited roles and silence cause women is harmful in itself. Emotional abuse is considered the most common and harmful form of abuse, primarily because the scars created by emotional abuse remain with a person much longer

38. Or any number of other biblical characters, especially in the Hebrew bible, could be named here: David in his claim to Bathsheba, David's son Absalom in raping David's concubines as a signal that he had taken over his father's role and possessions.

39. Zerubavel, *The Elephant in the Room*, 21.

40. I have somewhat intentionally blurred the line between the women in the text of 1 Peter and women today in this last phrase. At a basic level, that comment applies to all relations within a kyriarchal system.

41. Giles-Sims, "The Aftermath of Partner Violence," 49.

42. Celia Morris, *Bearing Witness: Sexual Harassment and Beyond — Everywoman's Story* (New York: Little, Brown and Company, 1994); Ron Thorne-Finch, *Ending the Silence: The Origins and Treatment of Male Violence against Women* (Buffalo: University of Toronto, 1992).

than physical abuse.[43] Emotional abuse is also the most difficult to identify or prove, and is likely to be "the bedrock from which other forms of abuse, such as physical and sexual abuse, stem,"[44] and it becomes a part of the "grooming" process, also called the "set up." This process allows the perpetrator to create an emotional climate in/by which the transition of power, responsibility and guilt occurs: he takes the power and she takes the responsibility and guilt. This grooming is all on the emotional level before any kind of physical or sexual abuse even occurs.

The factors that create and sustain the abusive system all work without being seen explicitly; they function beneath the surface of everyday encounters. In reality, there is no aspect of a woman's life that is *not* affected by the abusive situation. Thus, its effects are all the more insidious for being unseen and unnamed.

Some scholars may think my suggestion regarding the connection between this text and abusive relations between husbands and wives is preposterous, and others may desire to silence this kind of suggestion altogether. Given the seriousness of these suggestions, reactions that would deny or disregard these connections would in themselves be symptomatic irruptions that should be read for what they disclose about the scholar, what it is that is being maintained by their reactions (protecting the bible?), and what the reaction tells us about the need to control information and the interpretation of the biblical texts.

Controlling Information
The power that allows the control of information, or of blocking access to it,[45] is also noted in Douglass's *Narrative* as an effective way to manage and control slaves. He sought an education on his own, out of the sight of his masters, precisely because it was something they did not want him to have.

> "Now," said [Mr. Auld] "if you teach that nigger (speaking of myself) how to read,
> there would be no keeping him. It would forever unfit him to be a slave. He would
> at once become unmanageable, and of no value to his master. As to himself, it

43. Brittney Nichols, "Violence against Women: The Extent of the Problem," in *"Intimate" Violence against Women: When Spouses, Partners, or Lovers Attack* (Paula K. Lundberg-Love and Shelly L. Marmion, eds; Westport, Conn.: Praeger, 2006), 7.
44. Susan Vas Dias, "Inner Silence: One of the Impacts of Emotional Abuse Upon the Developing Self," in *Psychodynamic Perspectives on Abuse: The Cost of Fear* (Una McCluskey and Carol-Ann Hooper, eds; Philadelphia: Jessica Kingsley, 2000), 159. See also, Nichols, "Violence against Women," 6; Grothues and Marmion, "Dismantling the Myths," 12.
45. Zerubavel, *The Elephant in the Room*, 39.

could do him no good, but a great deal of harm. It would make him discontented and unhappy."[46]

It seems to have been ubiquitously believed that slaves should not be allowed to learn to read or write, as this would give them a taste of all that they *could* be and accomplish. Being aware of the difference between their current state and the fulfillment of living a life of freedom would upset the already tenuous state of affairs between slaves and their masters. Douglass notes that "to make a contented slave, it is necessary to make a thoughtless one," and an obedient one.[47] Contentment in this case is merely being resigned to one's socio-political position, not having the will or the means to resist it. These passages from Douglass's *Narrative* help us to see the efficacious nature that controlling what a person knows and requiring her/his obedience has on a person.

So what is the material effect on women of the comparison to Sarah in 1 Pet. 3.1-6? What knowledge does this comparison serve to create and thus what does it allow females to do? As I see it, there are effects within the three primary realms of their lives. The first is the household and all that is a part of it: marriage, family, etc. The second is the socio-political realm, and the third has to do with their contributions to ministry or other religious/communal settings (or in contemporary Christian terms, their "call," whether in ordained, lay or volunteer positions). Because of importance of the house/home life for defining all aspects of a person's life and roles, the control that the husband/male has over his wife/partner has immense ramifications for her. This is not to say that a woman in this situation cannot function differently outside the home than she is forced to within it. I am simply suggesting that the dynamics in this central relationship strongly affect all areas of her life.

These women, these "daughters of Sarah," are highly gifted in myriad ways, yet those gifts are channeled toward the wants and needs of the patriarchal and kyriarchal power relations all around them. These women know the destructive effects of others' resistance to their own natural gifts and abilities; they know the frustration of not being heard, of being brushed aside, of being considered irrelevant or unimportant and of being devalued by various kinds of abusive relations. The consequences of such a simple phrase, "submit yourselves in silence," are far reaching and are anything but life-giving for the person who has been silenced. The subject that these women become outwardly, then, is one that is compliant and submissive, helpless and dependent, silent and demure, all characteristics that are helpful for maintaining the kyriarchal structure and

46. Douglass, *Narrative of the Life*, 29.
47. Ibid., 64, 66.

relations of power. One can see the damage this "simple" command creates, once it is codified and becomes absorbed into the *habitus* of the movement.

Colonized Daughters

What a person can know affects what she can do, a matter which is the focus of the next section of this chapter. As a bridge to that topic, I would like to tease out some of the implications of the knowledge that is created or that women are "allowed" by this text of 1 Peter, when written and received within a colonized space. For the wives, living in a colonized or occupied space compounds the limitations placed upon them in terms of the way that information is controlled and to what extent it is available to them. The dynamics of domination, control, fear, silencing and obedience take on new dimensions under the light of imperialism or colonization.

Written from the heart of the Empire by someone imprisoned yet who had an authoritative voice for these communities, the "daughters of Sarah" imagery reflects some of the concerns and structural needs of an imperial order. Matters of submission to the ruling powers and of populating an empire with obedient citizens are of utmost importance from the perspective of the ruler. Sarah, exemplary in her submissiveness to her husband, was (eventually) the vessel for the seed of Abraham, the nation of God's people. Her obedience to Abraham and courage when placed in terrifying situations are examples of behavior that are beneficial to the kyriarchal system of Empire. In addition, from a colonizer's perspective, a "gentle and quiet spirit" is much easier to control than an independent and strong-willed one.

The fact that this letter was written from prison gives it an appeal to and authority over the recipients that is stronger than that of correspondence written by a non-imprisoned person.[48] Pierre Bourdieu notes the "hidden correspondence" between the structure of the social space in which the communication is created and the structure of the overall social class in which this space is located.[49] In addition to the content of the letter, the author also communicates something of the imperial social structure and dominating nature, which he is experiencing viscerally as he writes. The letter, in a sense, embodies the imperial mindset and power dynamics so that the communities receiving it are affected by and embody them as well.

---

48. See Chapter 4, n. 43.

49. Bourdieu, *Language and Symbolic Power*, 40. Bhabha, *The Location of Culture*, discusses this phenomenon in terms of the resistant yet imitative response that a colonized people have toward an imperial power. In attempting to subvert or resist, a community mimics and reinscribes the very form they seek to undermine.

On a similar note, as Nancy Hartsock so poignantly stated,

> To the extent that either sexual relations or other power relations are structured by a dynamic of domination/submission, the other [relations within that community] as well will operate along those dimensions, and in consequence, the community as a whole will be structured by domination.[50]

It is clear that the sexual and household relations within these communities are based upon a dominant/submissive model. We could expect that all relations within these communities and their organizational structure to be marked by a dominant/submissive dynamic.

The effects of "power over" are many; of particular interest for this topic is the way it determines "the scope of the information others can access as well as what they pass on and thus promotes various forms of forced blindness, deafness, and muteness."[51] The women are being asked not to speak of some of the things they know and have experienced, in particular the truths that they most need to speak. Their muteness in relation to abusive situations not only allows those situations to continue, but teaches others not to see them as well. People then learn to "turn a blind eye" toward any injustice or abuse if speaking of it would upset the imperial stasis. This transfer of imperial relations and the knowledge it creates and prevents is no small matter.

It is no mere coincidence that the household code was drawn upon and adapted in this context, or that the general concepts behind the household code itself were as prevalent as they were. They address the most intimate and individual relationship between men and women and ensure that power remains within the hands of the men.[52] As Ann Oakley has noted, it is when women are embracing freedoms that we see men moving closer to women's power base in order to control and confine women.[53] Within the general context of the development of the Jesus movement, we can safely say that freedoms that women enjoyed in the beginning were being taken from them by texts such as this one.

Within the context of the discussion of what the women can know, we must also consider the elements of fear, silencing, and allusions to sexual (or other

---

50. Hartsock, *Money, Sex, and Power*, 155.

51. Zerubavel, *The Elephant in the Room*, 15.

52. Elisabeth Schüssler Fiorenza, "Introduction: Crossing Canonical Boundaries," in *Searching the Scriptures*, vol. 2, *A Feminist Commentary* (Elisabeth Schüssler Fiorenza, Ann Brock and Shelly Matthews, eds; New York: Crossroads, 1993), 7.

53. Though she is speaking of Ann Oakley's work in sociological studies, as she addressed the cyclical inequalities that maintained male supremacy within the field and within the findings of it, this claim has been affirmed time and again throughout the history of Western civilization (at least). Dale Spender, *For the Record: The Making and Meaning of Feminist Knowledge* (London: The Women's Press, 1985), 139.

forms of) abuse in this section of the letter. When men are socialized to use violence to maintain control, then there is every reason to think that violence is used within the household as well.[54] There is a logical connection between the societal norms and private interactions. The higher the man's need for power and control is, the higher the risk of violence or abuse.[55] This finding also suggests that a lack of control over one's life events is a higher risk factor than when the lack of control is in the husband/wife (partner) relationship.

In other words, in the atmosphere of general unrest in occupied regions of Asia Minor, we can expect men to have carried out aggressive, dominating or violent behaviors within the households. If one throws into the mix the added self-possession or self-confidence that many women gained through the early Christian gatherings, the independent spirit of women being subjects in their own lives and not just subjected to maintaining the lives of others, we can see how the reaction to such change might be the anger or frustration of the husbands/paterfamilia.

The women, these "daughters of Sarah," are to know their place and stay in line. They cannot be leaders, except in their willingness to lay down their lives for Empire. Most importantly for this discussion, they are not allowed to speak the truths that most need to be aired.

What Can She Do?

In light of the previous section, this question, "What can she do?" begins to sound like a search for solutions to the problem today instead of an inquiry regarding what activities were allowed a woman in these communities. In a sense, the two approaches to this question are intimately related. The kind of knowledge and circumscribed subjectivity this text engenders has been a part, consciously or not, of maintaining limited possibilities for women today. In spite of almost two thousand years in between, the options available to women and their representation are still significantly defined by these texts and the *habitus* that proffers them.

The commands in any of the letters retained by various Christian communities become performative utterances, in the sense that they create what they state. They are legitimized simply by being accepted and passed along, and

---

54. Glenda Kaufman Kantor and Jana L. Jasinski, "Dynamics and Risk Factors in Partner Violence," in *Partner Violence: A Comprehensive Review of 20 Years of Research* (Jana L. Jasinski and Linda M. Williams, eds; Thousand Oaks: Sage, 1998), 5.

55. Kantor and Jasinski, "Dynamics and Risk Factors," 5–6.

in so doing they take on the life or status of divine word.[56] The follower of Christ, then, will obey these commands and will embody the roles prescribed. Both the roles and the structure that need and maintain them are perpetuated by the faith communities that receive these texts. Members of these communities are compelled to behave according to the designations given to them. In other words, a woman will live into the name or role prescribed for her, she will live within the boundaries of appropriateness for the role, and so forth.

In terms of social control or social movement theory, this kind of interaction between the members and the authoritative voice of a leader is intended for accountability and to keep people in line, as much as it is to let members know what they cannot do.[57] Since the means through which these prescriptions are offered is a familiar socially normative expectation, however the form may be transformed in this instance, they take on the sense of being based upon natural or objective differences within the social, political and household realms. As Bourdieu reminds us, these are the most efficacious distinctions one can make.[58]

It is also important to note that these instances of accepting the authoritativeness of someone from outside their community, their submission to his commands, and the symbolic domination that these exchanges represent, are in themselves a form of complicity. The affectivity of the *habitus* upon the people in the community creates this ambiguity between willing and passive submission.[59] Perhaps we can talk about it in terms of being a hybridity of the two, or as an action that reflects the middle voice in some sense. Whatever the case, the women in these communities are just as wrapped up in conforming to, though perhaps at times not agreeing with, their socially predicated roles and expectations as any other member of society would have been.

The economic aspect of the households is never specifically addressed in any of the new testament texts,[60] which is part of the reason we can so easily forget that it is in the mix of relations that are effected by them. In the household code in 1 Peter, the peripheral, powerless and "otherness" status of the wives and slaves is centralized or elevated, yet it is done within the overarching power structure of the kyriarchal Empire. By avoiding addressing the economically

---

56. Bourdieu, *Language and Symbolic Power*, 42.
57. Ibid., 121; Benford, "Controlling Narratives," 53.
58. Bourdieu, *Language and Symbolic Power*, 120.
59. Ibid., 50–1, 114.
60. Certainly there are hints of the economic realities that the people dealt with, noted by the many references to money/economic issues in the teachings of Jesus and in the letter by James. But the direct acknowledgement of the household's role in sustaining and producing the socio-political reality is not addressed in any of the new testament texts.

sustaining aspect of the lives and production of the slaves and women within
the household, this aspect of their daily lives is taken for granted and is assumed
will remain the same. Granting honor and value within the social relations that
conform to the overall expectations,[61] the author ensures the maintenance of
this kyriarchal/patriarchal socio-political normative structure with all of its
attendant power relations.

From this perspective, this adaptation of the household code is read as a
symptom in the text that indicates the need to de-center or marginalize these
otherwise potentially powerful people. When that marginal space is elevated
and described as ordained by God, the consequence is that the so-honored people will not seek to change their location. As Toril Moi has so poignantly noted,
"The paradox of the position of women and the [slaves] is that they are at one
and the same time central and marginal(ized)."[62] The needs of the kyriarchal
structure are met and those meeting the needs are praised for their service. The
wives and slaves must remain in their subject positions in order to keep the
structure/order in place. Ironically, it is their relatively marginal location within
their socio-political identity that has created the sufferings that they are subject
to in the first place. Additionally, the master of the household is still in place as
the one with the final say, the man who is living into the three main roles of the
patriarch within a household. Upholding the status quo and behaving in proper
and non-disruptive ways are some of the things "she can do."

For these women immersed in their cultural norms, the line between household production and re-production is blurred. The acculturation of the household
order implicitly affirms, and thus circumscribes, women in their (re)productive
role. This claim may seem like a bit of a stretch, but their political reality was
structured to some extent by laws that favored the married state and encouraged
the rearing of children. There is no doubting that motherhood was an expectation
of married women. As Roland Boer has noted of Rebekah, one of the Mothers
of Israel, we can also say of the wives in these communities, which is that the
needs of the family and the state come together in their wombs.[63] So, while
the advice to be subject to their husbands may have been consciously about
the acceptability of the movement, the implicit messages reinscribe kyriarchal
roles and possibilities for the women in all areas of their lives.

According to the "seamless" narrative of kyriarchy, the grand narratives of
the faith communities only address the males and issues on the surface of social

---

61. See Barth Campbell, *Honor, Shame and the Rhetoric of 1 Peter* (Atlanta: Scholars, 1998).

62. Toril Moi, *Sexual/Textual Politics: Feminist Literary Theory* (2nd ed.; New York: Routledge,
2002), 170.

63. Roland Boer, *Marxist Criticism of the Bible* (New York: T & T Clark, 2003), 38–40.

interactions,[64] which is why the acknowledgement of wives and slaves is itself a symptomatic irruption in the narrative. Yet in the midst of it all, the aspects of life that are acknowledged or drawn upon are not those of the production and reproduction that sustains the system, their most important roles, but those of peaceable living instead of disruptive behaviors.

By focusing on the superficial level of "doing what is good and not being terrified of fearful things," the author overlooks the activities that sustain and maintain the household, which is certainly understandable due to space and the immediate need he is addressing. This oversight resonates with the need to separate "life from necessity," which is of course an ideological separation.[65] The realms that are superficially separated — that is, from the androcentric perspective — meet and are grounded in the lives and bodies of the women in these communities. For our purposes, then, we might ask, "What are the effects of this discursive separation on the construction of women?" These women, then, are talked about as subjects not in "life" matters, but only in the outwardly noted necessities. Though they are utterly essential, as reproducers, they are treated like vessels and pawns, possessed and used for the purposes of kyriarchal systems, structures and relations of power.

According to Jorunn Økland, we can see in the metaphors that Paul uses in his letters an attempt to create a sacred "sanctuary space" that is separate from the space in which usual events of household life take place. The metaphors helped to create rituals, boundaries, and "a meaning-full ordered territory, a different hierarchy and a different map of role models from outside the sanctuary space."[66] Later in the book, she notes that women's ritual dress and speech were also a part of creating this separate, *ekklesia*, space.

Økland's investigation of the use of gendered bodies and rituals in 1 Corinthians assumes that Paul is working with a purely performative social role of gender in contrast with our modern concept of *being* male or female.[67] The point, according to Økland, is that even though the presence of women is necessary for the creation of the "appropriately" constructed sacred space, women do not have a place or any representation within the hierarchy of the communities' structure.

Throughout this project I have been attempting to indicate how the metaphors used and the roles allowed for women in the letter of 1 Peter specifically

---

64. Mary O'Brien, *The Politics of Reproduction* (Boston: Routledge, 1981), 140–1.
65. Ibid., 141.
66. Økland, *Women in Their Place*, 4.
67. Thomas Walter Laquer, *Making Sex: Body and Gender from the Greeks to Freud* (Cambridge: Harvard University, 1990), 8.

exclude women from leadership positions, among other things. Whatever positive intentions Paul may have had regarding the roles of women in this movement, they were subverted by his successors. The introduction of the household code ordering and the subsequent overlapping with the roles within the household proper and the worshipping space meant a dissolution of the boundary between the daily life and the *ekklesia* space. The language used by the author of 1 Peter affectively gives women the roles of producers and maintainers of the population, sustainers of the means for economic production and survival, and beleaguered place holders for the kyriarchal structure of the household, *ekklesia* and Empire.

Granted, the author and the communities who received and embraced his writing felt a need to find a way to maintain the movement. Survival trumped any concept of seeking to change the social order. The premise of this project, however, is to attend to the materiality of these efforts, no matter how well-intentioned they may have been. Their attempts to sustain this movement do not allow for change, which is something that is inherent to human nature. Since what the women do matters a great deal, and their contributions and subjectivity are circumscribed within the household, I am led to ask: "Is a woman — and all she knows, signifies, and does — allowed to change within this movement?"

Conclusion: Subject as 1 Peter Constructs

The issue of constructing subjects taps into numerous socio-political dynamics of social acceptability and sustainability, vertical and horizontal power relations, essentialism and representation, and even mimicry and collusion. What we can do affects what we can know. What we can know is affected by the nature of the communities of which we are a part. The goal of this chapter has been to address how 1 Peter functions in "the discursive construction of the subject of woman,"[68] primarily because having the power to name and define what a woman can know and do is precisely the power to own/possess, control and dominate her. In order for women to (re)claim the role of self-possession, we must be able to see some of the ways they have been prevented from doing so.

The very nature of subject construction implies that there are counter-images simultaneously at work, ones that the dominant ideology needs to silence or eradicate. According to Carol Smart, each discourse constructs and thus brings into being its own version of "Woman" and in doing so proclaims that version

---

68. Hennessy, *Materialist Feminism and the Politics of Discourse* (New York: Routledge,1993), xiii.

to be "natural Woman."[69] In 1 Peter's household code, this construction of "wives," instead of "women" in general, implies that the wives represent a category to discuss and define while also inhabiting a subjective positioning within the early faith communities.[70] Given the nature of the household code — which only addresses women in terms of their married/maternal status — this focus upon "wives" is understandable. This essentialist focus becomes an issue, however, when we search for instructions, identity or even subject construction of the other women.

The women are to know their place and stay in line. They cannot be leaders, except in their willingness to lay down their lives for Empire. Most importantly for this discussion, they are not allowed to speak the truths that most need to be aired. But this also leads to a fascinating issue, which is why has this passage become determinative for *all* women, and not simply those in difficult circumstances? Why does this passage "legitimately" get to define all women? This is, in my opinion, one of the most startling material realities that this text has produced. It *is* only addressed to wives, initially, but is taken to be applicable for all females today within Christian communities. The ways this text is taught and applied today reinforce the kyriarchal perception of females that is present in the text. Women are (re)producers and sustainers of the family and of the State/Empire. These are their roles and it is only in these contexts that they are able to be seen or acknowledged. Focusing on the wives, who maintain the household realm, is the best way to steer a movement.

When the textual irruptions are interpreted in light of the wives' socio-political location, we see women constructed as silently submissive and subjugated wives, who are essential, as constructed, for the maintenance of Empire and the Christian *ekklesiai*. So it is only through a role in the kyriarchal system that the women are subjects in this Christian movement.[71] Their position is not one of freedom; rather, the author of 1 Peter limits the agency of women, circumscribing their activity within the household domain. It is not life-giving for the women, only for the kyriarchal society in which they live. Indirectly the letter prescribes the married status as the epitome of faithfulness for women, since only wives are addressed and none of the women can identify with the symbols attributed to the community as a whole. This self-sacrificial and child-bearing

69. Carol Smart, "Disruptive bodies and unruly sex: The regulation of reproduction and sexuality in the nineteenth century," in *Regulating Womanhood: Historical Essays on Marriage, Motherhood and Sexuality* (C. Smart, ed.; New York: Routledge, 1992), 7.

70. Ibid., 8.

71. Boer, *Marxist Criticism*, 38.

image of the socially constructed "woman" then remains in our consciousness and becomes our inheritance.

As Elisabeth Schüssler Fiorenza noted in the early 1980s, this adaptation of the Christian community to the ethos and *habitus* of the kyriarchal society in which they lived "open[ed] up the community to political co-optation by the Roman empire."[72] We can see how this is the case, since the household code and the knowledge it allows women to have and express creates and maintains obedient, submissive subjects.[73] As subjects of these kyriarchally determined Christian *ekklesiai*, they are good imperial subjects as well.

72. Schüssler Fiorenza, *Bread Not Stone*, 78.
73. Ibid., 78.

6

CONCLUSION

> The artist who invokes "inspiration" in order to avoid answerability has also
> misunderstood what is going on here. Inspiration that does not tend to the cares
> of this life is no inspiration at all; it is "possession."[1]

In this final chapter I will do three things. First, I will offer a précis of what was
discussed in Chapters 3–5; second, I will revisit the circumscribed symptomatic
subjectivity of women that I see 1 Peter constructing, what I am also calling
the materiality of the text in terms of the subject it constructs; and third, I will
offer some suggestions as to how the method developed here might be most
useful in moving forward with further engagements with biblical passages.

Précis of Findings

Chapters 3–5 address the rhetoric of the letter leading up to the household code,
the components of collusion with kyriarchal structures that are found within the
household code, and my understanding of the construction of women according
to this passage.

In Chapter 3, I choose to focus on two specific labels, "refugees and immigrants" and "royal priesthood and holy nation," and the command to "honor
the emperor," all in terms of their socio-political implications. The two labels,
as they are applied to the same group of people, stand in stark contrast to one
another, a seeming impossibility for one group to embrace. Though the first is
"purely" a socio-political label, perhaps meant to be re-interpreted with religious or spiritual overtones, the second is clearly drawing upon both realms of
terminology and structuration, the socio-political and the religious.

Furthermore, the socio-political implications of the label "refugees and
immigrants" is taken for granted and becomes a part of what is overlooked
within most subsequent malestream scholarship on it. Thus, this label itself

---

1. Bakhtin, *Art and Answerability*, 2.

has become an irruption, reminding the attentive reader of daily realities of the initial recipients that have long since been ignored within traditional interpretations. Not surprisingly, the victorious and privileged status of "royal priesthood and holy nation" has been gladly taken up, by pastors and biblical scholars alike, in the intervening millennia.

The general categories of priesthoods and nations evoke realms dominated by men and male terminology and imagery. There is no space for some "other" non-elite male within the ranks of these royal and holy leaders. This label remains a part of the *habitus* of the movement, and thus informs the structure of the community and the nature of the relationships within it. This is true, even in spite of the exhortation later in the letter for the elder and more spiritually mature men not to lord over the neophytes their privileged status.[2] These labels, then, added to the clearly kyriarchally driven exhortation to "honor the emperor," heighten the socio-political aspects of the rhetoric of this letter and create a natural preface for the inclusion of the adapted household code.

In Chapter 4 I focus upon the various symptomatic irruptions within the household code itself, specifically in terms of the call to silent suffering, the command regarding outward adornment and attire, and the new identity of "daughters of Sarah" ascribed to wives who do not fear the thing that terrifies them. Not only does the combination of these three commands produce a conveniently compliant imperial subject and heighten the distinction between "men" and "women," it also justifies the judgement of females' character by external appearances and gentle obedience and essentializes "women" in terms of a possession of the male head of the household. The fact that the passage is directed toward wives yet has become a common prescription for females in general is something of a curiosity, noteworthy for its effectiveness.

The command to be submissive to their husbands, in silence, and to never give up on the possibility that their actions might win over their husbands — from what to what is unclear — is also duly labeled a symptom or irruption. Since encouraging women to be submissive to their husbands was not a new idea, we are alerted to the fact that something was amiss for this cultural expectation to be deemed appropriate in this setting and was indeed necessary. In the vein of "he doth protesteth too much," the author is pulling in the reigns on active, powerful and influential wives/women. The image of wives that is constructed by: the reference to Sarah, the admonition to endure hardship, and the charge not to fear anything added to the submissively silent obedient model of Christ before his crucifiers, is the epitome of the idea that women are to serve

---

2. Schüssler Fiorenza, "1 Peter," 390–1.

the purposes and needs of men. From the perspective or belief that women are the possessions of men, any and all dominant/submissive dynamics are not only understandable but are necessary. It is frighteningly abusive, controlling, and belittling, and, according to counselors who specialize in relational and sexuality issues and domestic violence, it is "maladaptive in the highest degree to ask someone to forego their self-preservation instinct as this text is doing."[3]

The piece of this text prescribing plain clothing and simple adornment does not stand out in terms of topics discussed under household management, but it does become a symptomatic irruption within the context of this letter. The calling of the communities in general to be a royal priesthood and holy nation — supported by the reminder that they are now God's people, who, like living stones, come together to create the house of God and as God's people offer spiritual sacrifices (2.5) — evokes imagery of grandeur and holiness. Any roles of leadership that women might have had in these settings would have been marked by various forms of outward adornment and distinctive attire. Thus all the more do the glorious robes of these priestly people seem other-worldly in comparison to the demure and self-effacing clothing expectations imposed upon the wives.

The silence discussed in this section is to be directed toward their husbands; the adornment and attire is concerned with the character of the wives; the obedience and not-fearing are in terms of how wives are to relate to their husbands. Every aspect of what a woman/wife can know and who she can be is circumscribed by her relation to her husband, and this knowledge becomes the fabric of the constructed women, according to 1 Peter.

The admonition to the husbands to "show consideration for their wives, paying honor to them as the weaker sex," proves enlightening for this project, serving as a comparison to the silent submission that is expected of the wives. Regardless of how "egalitarian" or forward thinking the command to the husbands may have been at the time, the gap between being utterly submissive and showing consideration is a significant one. The cultural beliefs about "men" and "women" are thoroughly embedded within the commands, and are thus perpetuated by the text and materialized within the structures and relations of any movement that embraces them.

All of the symptomatic irruptions that I have discussed in this project point to the fact that the women have been vocal and influential, and the over-construction of women's silent subjectivity betrays a fear that the author might not be taken seriously. After all, it is deeply important that the women comply with proper and appropriate behavioral expectations. These textual

3. I refer here to an exchange with Susan Hall, LMHC.

irruptions, then, bear the mark of collusion with the kyriarchal structure of Empire, in particular in terms of the way they are all aimed at controlling the roles and influence of women. What is often taught today as (common sense) "proper and lady-like" behavior — quiet and submissive behavior, modest attire and being focused upon the male in one's life — is clearly supported by this kyriarchal text, and both requires and perpetuates the false belief that women are possessions of men.

These components of collusion aid in turning the households of God into the foundation of the Kingdom or Empire of God, which is just as hierarchically or kyriarchally structured as the Kingdoms and Empires on earth. This critique of the components of collusion then leads into my analysis in Chapter 5 of the construction of wives according to these same irruptions.

Drawing upon Hennessy's succinct description of the materiality of knowledge — what we know informs what we do; what we do informs what we know — I look at what this text allows women to know and, in light of this knowledge, to do. It seems that the essentialist view of women as producers and reproducers within the household defines the overall construction of women in 1 Peter. Not only are they confined to the roles allowed them within the household, but this realm becomes the primary, if not only, way for women to engage politically. Whereas her husband will have access, to some degree, to all realms of society, women and wives are circumscribed within the household, which is ultimately controlled by the male head of the household. All realms of society in which they choose to be involved will be similarly determined or defined in terms of being submissive to a male authority.

It is not simply that the household roles determine the parameters of what a woman can know and do, it is that the control over and silencing of women that is required to maintain this kyriarchal order constructs women to be utterly subservient, and willing to accept abuse and exploitation as a form of their own theologically justified self-sacrifice. These women know what it is to be afraid. They know that they belong to the man in their lives, and that the married and maternal state is their primary and necessary role. Thus, they are constrained to do not what is life-giving for themselves but must engage in maladaptive behavior, sacrificing themselves to *their* lord and master, the one to whom *they* belong: their husbands.

This concept stands in stark contrast to Paul's idea that followers of Christ belong to Christ, their lord. Now, we see females clearly belonging (again) to the men in their lives. By the end of the first century the males are clearly taking the mediating role between females and the deity within the Christian movement, which is a move that makes the males demi-gods. There is no question that this developed with the survival of the movement in mind; the question is, what kind of a movement did it then become? Given that these commands to wives (women) are part and parcel of the narrative that defines the Christian movement, and the role Christianity has had in developing the Western world and the norms of its societies, they reach into the "psychic depths" of all of us, "men" and "women."

Thus, the household code in 1 Peter stands within a stream of a particular worldview, one that has remained, in essence, the same for thousands of years. This domestic code, however transformed or "Christianized" for the particular situation of the house churches in Asia Minor, may not have been something new at the time, but it most certainly has not gone the way of other myths of the ancient world. No, it is one of many voices that affirm the subordination of women to men, this primary dynamic indicating that the whole of the system is shaped by a dominant/subordinate relation. The symptomatic irruptions in this text, irruptions that startle the reader or disrupt the flow of the narrative, have become materialized within the ecclesial, social, political and familial realms of the Western world today.

The real dilemma, in my opinion, is that, at the end of the day, women will do what they can to construct their own lives, to varying degrees, but they must do so within effectively circumscribed conditions and roles, for a woman cannot be defined *as woman*.[4] So it is *now* only through a role that upholds the kyriarchal system that women can participate in this Christian movement.[5] This is simply another layer of the fact that "normativity" is defined by male-centered realities, thus the view of women or construction of them as subjects is understood in terms of how they are "other" in relation to men and the components of malestream society.

Certainly, various denominational traditions today will attend to the specifics of passages such as this one in 1 Peter in many different ways. Thus, my intention has not been to prove that this particular passage is clearly materialized in all denominations, or even in some specifically named places. Rather, I am interested in noting how it *can* be materialized, and how a positivistic application of it will necessarily collude with imperialistic agendas.[6] Just as the kyriarchal rhetoric of the texts of the Christian movement helped it to survive initially, so too positivistic and compliant interpretations of these texts today embrace instead of challenge the imperialistic, circumscribing and kyriarchal

4.   Kathy Davis and Sue Fisher, "Power and the Female Subject," in *Negotiating at the Margins: The Gendered Discourses of Power and Resistance* (Kathy Davis and Sue Fisher, eds; New Brunswick, New Jersey: Rutgers University, 1993), 3.

5.   Boer, *Marxist Criticism of the Bible*, 38.

6.   Genevieve White, *Daughters of Sarah* (Columbus, Ga.: Brentwood Christian, 1991).

rhetoric of the texts, which ultimately makes them more appealing to those in power within our kyriarchally structured societies. We are left to wrestle with the implications of the nature of this canon that so consistently constructs women within very limited and controlled situations and roles. Additionally, we must deal with the reality that this text's aim — intentionally or not — is to create a normativity that is in fact the basis of harm to women.

Texts and their Subjects

The effects of patriarchy, as a social structure that presumes and perpetuates males as authoritative, permeate all relationships within that culture or society. Since males are authoritative in these cultures they are more powerful than females and thus, within a hierarchical framework, operate as if they are entitled to control/dominate anyone less powerful than themselves.[7] I would note that the issue in biblical texts or in our societies today is much more complicated than a simple male/female duality and inequality, thus the repeated use of "kyriarchy." There are multiple relations of oppression or exploitation simultaneously at work, including between various groups of marginalized peoples. As noted above, when the climate is marked by beliefs in certain members being authoritative or more valued than others, then all relationships take on this dynamic of ruler/ruled.

With the sense of entitlement to dominate and control others comes the added element of how to enforce or create such a dominant position. The use of aggression by the more powerful person to control the less powerful person(s), then, is not only acceptable, it is a normative aspect of relationships within a kyriarchal society.[8] By "aggression" I mean any action directed toward another person with the intent to do harm. It is worth noting, however, that people are often not aware of their own intentions, in particular when their socialization has taught them to behave in specific (often gendered) ways and to expect treatment or privileges accordingly. Thus it is possible to describe the actions or words of a person as aggressive even if she/he is not consciously seeking to harm the other person(s).

I am also wary of too easily applying the insights from psychological research of the twentieth century to texts from the first century CE or the sixth BCE. At the same time, there are aspects of these studies that are enlightening for any given society, especially a patriarchal Western one, regardless of its place in history. Given that the male/female gender divide, with its traditional

---

7.   Jacquelyn White, "Aggression and Gender," 82.
8.   Ibid., 83.

roles and expectations, is quite prevalent in biblical texts, and a large portion of biblical scholars acknowledge that the cultures or societies out of which the biblical texts have come can be designated "patriarchal" or "kyriarchal," I think it is appropriate to take into consideration how positions of domination are maintained or play out in these texts, not simply in terms of imperial relations but also within everyday relationships.

This kind of analysis could be quite productive when applied to certain texts in the new testament, the epistles in particular, given that their content was aimed at creating normative or appropriate behaviors and beliefs. Instead of reading letters such as 1 Peter positivistically or even simply raising questions of gender/sexism within the texts, I suggest that we look for elements of coercion, manipulation, and implied force, as well as manifestations of distrust of women, verbal aggression, and a sense of gratification in dominating women. All of these factors are documented in today's research on intimate relationships in particular and are manifestations of a man's need to dominate and control women. The intimate relationships become a lens through which to see the public exchanges more critically.

When we combine these pieces of "cultural norms governing the use of aggression as a tool of the more powerful to subdue the weaker" with the gender inequalities that exist in the texts of the bible, then we are looking at a "climate conducive to violence." In other words, we should be expecting or looking for violence in the relationships where males are dominating and controlling the females in their lives because violence is, according to Jacquelyn White, "inextricably bound to the social context of male domination and control."[9]

For example, a male is most at risk of harm or violence from another male, usually a stranger; a female, from her male partner. When I read with these thoughts in mind, I am struck by the ways biblical stories offer examples that confirm statistics drawn from relationships in the United States at the end of the twentieth century. In the stories alluded to in the 1 Peter passage, where Abraham barters Sarah for his own protection, Abraham suggests that he will be physically harmed by, that is receive violent treatment from, men who are strangers to him, because of Sarah, one of his possessions. We have no reason to question his judgement in the matter. Readers who "see his point," especially "for that culture and time," or are socialized to think that such an outcome is quite possible, indicate their own understanding of males seeking dominance over one another affected through female bodies.

Aggression as we see it playing out in this and other biblical texts is a

---

9. Ibid., 90.

positionality. Its purpose is to make the one being aggressive central, both in terms of importance and power. Aggression is neither foreign to the cultures out of which these texts come, nor to the texts themselves. This is an aspect of these scriptures that we would do well to attend to instead of ignoring for the sake of focusing on the positive points within them.

The Next Step

A text in non-biblical literature with a homogeneous and essentialized portrait of women or that mandates the silencing of them the way this passage of 1 Peter does can be easily noted and critiqued for its constrictive parameters for women. When it comes to a similar critique of texts in the Christian canon, however, the critique is not so easily heard, received, "allowed" or encouraged. The quality, or source, of the inspiration of scripture is deemed to be wholly Other than that of so-called secular texts. As I have suggested in various ways throughout this project, the claim that biblical texts or their interpretations are "God-inspired" has the power of performative speech: simply because it is in the bible, the content functions in people's lives. Thus, the application of them becomes materialized in our lives and in the structures of our society, along with the requisite silencing and marginalization of "others" that is required to sustain them.

As a woman who has embraced such silencing to my own detriment, taught it to the detriment of others, and who witnesses it every day in various forms all around me, I am reminded of how deeply affective these texts have been and that they continue to have a material reality today.

The battles that go on over women's reproductivity today are given solid grounding here in the scriptures, and the married, preferably maternal, state is therefore the most approved (ecclesiastically defined) role for women from the foundation of the ecclesiastical organization. As Rosemary Hennessy notes:

> If we acknowledge, for instance, that the discursive struggles over woman's repro-
> ductive body in the U.S. now have less to do with women's "choice" — or even
> with abortion per se — than with the maintenance of a social order in which the few
> still benefit from the work of many, where power and resources are distributed on
> the basis of wealth not human worth or need, and women are generally devalued,
> we can begin to make sense of the contest over abortion from the standpoint of
> those who are already most affected by the legislation of women's bodies — the
> thousands of poor women who are also disproportionately women of color.[10]

---

10. Hennessy, *Materialist Feminism*, xvi.

We should not be surprised to see women's reproductivity so closely associated with social order today, since it has been a focal concern since recorded history, both directly, as in the laws of a territory or anachronistically labeled "nation," and indirectly, as we see in this passage of 1 Peter. The question of the discursively constructed subject then applies to constructions within this new testament text as well as to the ways scholars, laity and the church have heeded or sought to deny the socio-political implications haunting its surface.

I look around me today and watch the battle over women's bodies, their presumably inherent right to do what they wish with their bodies in relation to other people, and their "right" to be able to have access to prophylactics. I see the government trying to decide how to handle social security in this country and hear vague resonances with commands and regulations recorded in the Hebrew bible and new testament. I see that orphans and widows are still, to this day, members of our society who are stigmatized for being who they are, not even for something they have done but for the circumstances of life. Further, to the extent that widows were dependent upon their former husbands for their needs, the issue of how they will survive is still very real and present in our society. The fact that "some things never change" drives me to look at how we handle these ongoing socio-cultural realities: have we improved upon the reactions and institutionalized responses of our forbears? Or are we simply repeating them, perhaps with our own style, but not in qualitatively or substantially different ways?

When irruptions in biblical texts are taken prescriptively or positivistically we end up reinscribing oppressive and exploitative relations within our socio-political structures. As Nancy Hartsock reminds us, the nature of the roles each person can have within a given social organization is determined by the nature of the overall ideology of the movement. If, however, we allow these texts to reveal to us the underside of kyriarchy, we might find a source of connection for those who are oppressed and, through their voices, the means to critique the social structure that creates their situation. The people who need empowerment would receive it and become the source of new knowledges and engaged power that will create a different world.[11]

It is my hope that in "taking seriously" the biblical texts in ways I have suggested in this project we can allow them to speak to us in ways that are not simply prescriptive — which is the understandable application when every word is believed to be "inspired" by God — but foremost and primarily as lenses that allow us to see the kyriarchal power relations, irruptions of the

---

11. Nancy Hartsock, "Foucault on Power," 4, 171.

struggle of women to liberate themselves and those around them from oppressive socio-political expectations and structures, and life-threatening (instead of life-giving) constructions of women in them. We must face these demons of possession before we can exorcise them and embrace lives of fullness, mutuality, and wholeness for all people.

BIBLIOGRAPHY

Aageson, James W. "1 Peter 2.11-3.7: Slaves, Wives and the Complexities
of Interpretation." In *A Feminist Companion to the Catholic Epistles
and Hebrews*, edited by A.-J. Levine and Maria Mayo Robbins, 34–49.
Cleveland: Pilgrim, 2004.

Achtemeier, Paul. "Newborn Babes and Living Stones: Literal and
Figurative in 1 Peter." In *To Touch the Text: Biblical and Related Studies
in Honor of Joseph A. Fitzmyer*, edited by Maurya P. Horgan and Paul J.
Kobelski, 207–36. New York: Crossroad, 1989.

— "Suffering Servant and Suffering Christ in 1 Peter." In *The Future of
Christology: Essays in Honor of Leander E. Keck*, edited by A. J. Malherbe
and Wayne A. Meeks, 176–88. Minneapolis: Fortress, 1993.

Alexander, M. Jacqui and Chandra Talpade Mohanty, eds. *Feminist
Genealogies, Colonial Legacies, Democratic Futures*. New York:
Routledge, 1997.

Alexander, M. Jacqui and Chandra Talpade Mohanty. "Introduction:
Genealogies, Legacies, Movements." In *Feminist Genealogies, Colonial
Legacies, Democratic Futures*, edited by M. Jacqui Alexander and Chandra
Talpade Mohanty, xiii–xlii. New York: Routledge, 1997.

Anderson, Herbert and Edward Foley. *Mighty Stories, Dangerous Rituals:
Weaving Together the Human and the Divine*. San Francisco: Jossey-Bass,
1998.

Applegate, Judith K. "The Co-Elect Woman of 1 Peter." In *A Feminist
Companion to the Catholic Epistles and Hebrews*, edited by A.-J. Levine
and Maria Mayo Robbins, 89–102. Cleveland: Pilgrim, 2004.

Aristotle. *Nicomachean Ethics*. Loeb Classical Library 73. English
translation by H. Rackham. Cambridge, Mass.: Harvard University, 1934.

— *Politics*, reprinted. Loeb Classical Library 264. Translation by
H. Rackham. Cambridge University, 1998. Original printing, 1932,
reprinted 1944.

Armour, Ellen. "Essentialism." In *Dictionary of Feminist Theologies*, edited
by Letty M. Russell and J. Shannon Clarkson, 88. Louisville: Westminster
John Knox, 1996.

Arthur, Linda Boynton. "Clothing, Control, and Women's Agency: The
Mitigation of Patriarchal Power." In *Negotiating at the Margins: The*

Gendered Discourses of Power and Resistance, edited by Kathy Davis and Sue Fisher, 66–84. New Brunswick, New Jersey: Rutgers University, 1993.

Ashcroft, Bill, Gareth Griffiths and Helen Tiffin. *Post-Colonial Studies: The Key Concepts*. New York: Routledge, 2002.

Bakhtin, Mikhail. *Art and Answerability: Early Philosophical Essays*, edited by Michael Holquist and Vadim Liapunov; translated and notes by Vadim Liapunov. Austin: University of Texas, 1990.

Balch, David. "Early Christian Criticism of Patriarchal Authority: 1 Peter 2:11-3:12." *Union Seminary Quarterly Review* 39 (1984): 161–73.

— "Household Codes." In *Greco-Roman Literature and the New Testament: Selected Forms and Genres*, edited by David Aune, 25–50. Society of Biblical Literature Sources for Biblical Study 21. Atlanta: Scholars, 1988.

— *Let Wives be Submissive: The Domestic Code in 1 Peter*. Society of Biblical Literature Monograph Series 26. Chico: Scholars Press, 1981.

Barsky, Robert F. *Constructing a Productive Other: Discourse Theory and the Convention Refugee Hearing*. Philadelphia: John Benjamins, 1994.

Bartholomew, Craig, ed. *A Royal Priesthood? The Use of the Bible Ethically and Politically: A Dialogue with Oliver O'Donovan*. Grand Rapids: Zondervan, 2002.

Bassler, Jouette M. "1 Corinthians." In *Woman's Bible Commentary, with Apocrypha*, edited by Carol A. Newsome and Sharon H. Ringe, 411–19. Louisville: Westminster John Knox, 1998.

Bauman-Martin, Betsy J. "Feminist Theologies of Suffering and Current Interpretations of 1 Peter 2.18-3.9." In *A Feminist Companion to the Catholic Epistles and Hebrews*, edited by A.-J. Levine and Maria Mayo Robbins, 63–81. Cleveland: Pilgrim, 2004.

— "Speaking Jewish: Postcolonial Aliens and Strangers in First Peter." In *Reading First Peter with New Eyes: Methodological Reassessments of the Letter of First Peter*, edited by Robert L. Webb and Betsy Bauman-Martin, 144–77. New York: T&T Clark, 2007.

Beare, Francis W. *The First Epistle of Peter: The Greek Text with Translation and Notes*. Oxford: B. Blackwell, 1947.

Bechtler, Steven Richard. *Following in His Steps: Suffering, Community and Christology in 1 Peter*. Atlanta: Scholars Press, 1998.

Benford, Robert D. "Controlling Narratives and Narratives as Control within Social Movements." In *Stories of Change: Narrative and Social Movements*, edited by Joseph E. Davis, 53–75. Albany: State University of New York, 2002.

Bhabha, Homi. *The Location of Culture*. New York: Routledge, 1994.

Biemann, Ursula. "Touring, Routing and Trafficking Female Geobodies: A Video Essay on the Topography of the Global Sex Trade." In *Mobilizing Place, Placing Mobility*, edited by Ginette Verstraete and Tim Cresswell, 71–86. New York: Rodopi, 2002.

Bird, Jennifer. "To What End? Revisiting the Gendered Space of 1 Cor. 11:2-16 from a Feminist Postcolonial Perspective." In *The Colonized Apostle: Paul and Postcolonial Studies.* Minneapolis: Fortress, forthcoming.

Bird, Phyllis. "The Place of Women in the Israelite Cultus." In *Women in the Hebrew Bible*, edited by Alice Bach, 3–21. NY: Routledge, 1999.

Boer, Roland. "Marx, Postcolonialism and the Bible." In *Postcolonial Biblical Criticism: Interdisciplinary Intersections*, edited by Fernando Segovia and Stephen Moore, 105–25. New York: T&T Clark, 2005.

— *Marxist Criticism of the Bible*. New York: Sheffield Academic, 2003.

Boring, Eugene. "Narrative Dynamics in First Peter: The Function of Narrative World." In *Reading First Peter with New Eyes: Methodological Reassessments of the Letter of First Peter*, edited by Robert L. Webb and Betsy Bauman-Martin, 7–40. T&T Clark: New York, 2007.

Botha, Jan. "Christians and Society in 1 Peter: Critical Solidarity." *Scriptura* 24 (1988): 27–37.

Bourdieu, Pierre. *Language and Symbolic Power*, edited by John B. Thompson; translated by Gino Raymond and Matthew Samson. Cambridge, Mass.: Harvard University, 1991.

— *Outline of a Theory of Practice*. Translated by Richard Nice. Cambridge: Cambridge University, 1977.

Bowersock, Glen Warren. *Martyrdom and Rome*. Cambridge: Cambridge University, 1995.

Brent, Allen. *Imperial Cult and the Development of Church Order*. Boston: Brill, 1999.

Brock, Daniel I. "Sojourner." In the *International Standard Bible Encyclopedia*, vol. 4, edited by Geoffrey Bromily, 561–4. Grand Rapids: Eerdmans, 1988.

Brown, Jeannine K. "Silent Wives, Verbal Believers: 1 Peter 3:1-6." *Word and World* 24, no. 4 (2004): 395–403.

Butler, Judith. *Gender Trouble: Feminism and the Subversion of Identity*. New York: Routledge, 1990.

Campbell, Barth L. *Honor, Shame and the Rhetoric of 1 Peter*. Atlanta: Scholars, 1998.

Cannon, George E. *The Use of Traditional Materials in Colossians*. Macon, Ga.: Mercer University, 1983.

Carter, Warren. "Going All the Way? Honoring the Emperor and Sacrificing Wives and Slaves in 1 Peter 2.13-3.6." In *A Feminist Companion to the Catholic Epistles and Hebrews*, edited by A.-J. Levine and Maria Mayo Robbins, 14–33. Cleveland: Pilgrim, 2004.

Cartwright, Michael G. "Radical Reform, Radical Catholicity: John Howard Yoder's Vision of the Faithful Church." In *The Royal Priesthood: Essays Ecclesiological and Ecumenical. John Howard Yoder*, edited by Michael G. Cartwright, 1–52. Grand Rapids: Eerdmans, 1994.

Castelli, Elizabeth A. *Imitating Paul: A Discourse of Power*. Louisville: Westminster John Knox, 1991.

Cicero. *De Senectute*, translated by William Armistead Falconer. Cambridge, Mass.: Harvard University, 1996.

Cixous, Hélène and Catherine Clément. *The Newly Born Woman*, translated by Betsy Wing. Minneapolis: University of Minnesota, 1986.

Coakley, John Wayland and Andrea Sterk, eds. *Readings in World Christian History.* Maryknoll, NY: Orbis, 2004.

Code, Lorraine. *What Can She Know? Feminist Theory and the Construction of Knowledge*. Ithaca: Cornell University, 1991.

Corley, Kathleen E. "1 Peter." In *Searching the Scriptures*, *Volume 2: A Feminist Commentary*, edited by Elisabeth Schüssler Fiorenza, Ann Brock and Shelly Matthews, 349–60. New York: Crossroad, 1994.

Countryman, L. William. "Patrons and Officers in Club and Church." In Society of Biblical Literature Seminar Papers #16, vol. 1, 135–44. Missoula: Scholars, 1977.

Crouch, James E. *The Origin and Intention of the Colossian* Haustafel. Forschungen zur Religion und Literatur des Alten und Neuen Testaments, 109. Göttingen: Vandenhoeck and Ruprecht, 1972.

Daly, Mary. *Beyond God the Father: Toward a Philosophy of Women's Liberation*. Boston: Beacon, 1973.

D'Angelo, Mary Rose. "Colossians." In *Searching the Scriptures*, vol. 2, *A Feminist Commentary*, edited by Elisabeth Schüssler Fiorenza, Ann Brock and Shelly Matthews, 313–24. New York: Crossroad, 1993.

Davidson, Julia O'Connell. *Children in the Global Sex Trade*. Malden, Mass.: Polity, 2005.

Davies, John H. *A Royal Priesthood: Literary and Intertextual Perspectives on an Image of Israel in Exodus 19.6. Journal for the Study of the Old Testament Supplemental Series* 395. London: Continuum, 2004.

Davis, Joseph E. "Narrative and Social Movements: The Power of Stories," In *Stories of Change: Narrative and Social Movements*, edited by Joseph E. Davis, 3–29. Albany: State University of New York, 2002.

Davis, Joseph E., ed., *Stories of Change: Narrative and Social Movements.* Albany: State University of New York, 2002.

Davis, Kathy and Sue Fisher. "Power and the Female Subject." In *Negotiating at the Margins: The Gendered Discourses of Power and Resistance*, edited by Kathy Davis and Sue Fisher, 3–20. New Brunswick, New Jersey: Rutgers University, 1993.

De La Torre, Miguel A. *Reading the Bible from the Margins.* Maryknoll: Orbis, 2002.

Dibelius, Martin. *An Die Kolosser, an die Epheser, an Philemon.* Handbuch zum Neuen Testament 12. Tübingen: J.C.B. Mohr, 1927.

Dickey, Samuel. "Some Economic and Social Conditions of Asia Minor Affecting the Expansion of Christianity." In *Studies in Early Christianity*, edited by Shirley Jackson Case, 393–416. New York: Century Co., 1928.

Dienst, Ferdinand. "Idealistic *Theologiegeschichte*: Ideology Critique and the Dating of Oracles of Salvation. Posing a Question Concerning the Monopoly of an Accepted Method." In *Studies in Isaiah*, edited by Wouter C. van Wyk, 53–78. Hercules, South Africa: NHW, 1981.

Dionysius, of Halicarnassus. *Roman Histories*, edited by Earnest Cary and Edward Spelman. Cambridge, Mass.: Harvard University, 1950.

Douglass, Frederick. *Narrative of the Life of Frederick Douglass, an American Slave, Written by Himself*, edited by William L. Andrews and William S. McFeely. New York: W.W. Norton & Company, 1997.

Downing, F. Gerald. "Pliny's Prosecutions of Christians: Revelation and 1 Peter." *Journal for the Study of the New Testament* 34 (1988): 105–23.

Dube, Musa W. *Postcolonial Feminist Interpretation of the Bible.* St. Louis: Chalice, 2000.

Dubis, Mark. *Messianic Woes in First Peter: Suffering and Eschatology in 1 Peter 4:12-19.* Studies in Biblical Literature 33. New York: Peter Lang, 2002.

— "Research on 1 Peter: A Survey of Scholarly Literature Since 1985." *Currents in Biblical Scholarship* 4, no. 2 (2006): 199–239.

Dworkin, Andrea. *Life and Death.* New York: Free Press, 1997.

Eagleton, Terry. *Ideology: An Introduction.* New York: Verso, 1991.

Eilberg-Schwartz, Howard and Wendy Doniger, eds. *Off with Her Head!: The Denial of Women's Identity in Myth, Religion, and Culture.* Berkeley: University of California, 1995.

Eisenstein, Zillah. *The Color of Gender: Reimaging Democracy.* Berkeley: University of California, 1994.

Elliott, John H. *1 Peter: A New Translation with Introduction and Commentary.* Anchor Bible 37B. New York: Doubleday, 2000.

— *The Elect and the Holy: An Exegetical Examination of I Peter 2:4-10 and the Phrase* basileion hierateuma. Leiden: Brill, 1966.

— *A Home for the Homeless: A Social-Scientific Criticism of 1 Peter, Its Situation and Strategy, With a New Introduction.* Minneapolis: Fortress, 1981.

— "Ministry and Church Order in the New Testament: A Tradio-Historical Analysis (1 Pt 5, 1-5 & plls.)." *Catholic Biblical Quarterly* 32: 367–91.

— "The Rehabilitation of an Exegetical Step-Child: 1 Peter in Recent Research." *Journal of Biblical Literature* 95, no. 2 (1976): 243–54.

— *What is Social-Scientific Criticism?* Minneapolis: Fortress, 1993.

Falk, Pesach Eliyahu. *'oz vəhadar levushah: Modesty, as Adornment for Life: Halachos and Attitudes Concerning Tznius of Dress and Conduct.* Nanuet, NY: Feldheim, 1998.

Fears, J. Rufus. Princeps a Diis Electus*: The Divine Election of the Emperor as a Political Concept at Rome.* Rome: American Academy in Rome, 1977.

Feldmeier, Reinhard. *Die Christen als Fremde: Die Metapher der Fremde in der antiken Welt, im Urchristentum und im 1. Petrusbrief.* Wissenschaftliche Untersuchungen zum Neuen Testament 64. Tübingen: Mohr-Siebeck, 1992.

Foucault, Michel. *Power/Knowledge: Selected Interviews and Other Writings, 1972–1977*, translated by Collin Gordon, et al. New York: Pantheon, 1980.

Frank, Tenney. *An Economic History of Rome.* Baltimore: John's Hopkins, 1927.

Freud, Sigmund. *The Standard Edition of the Complete Psychological Works of Sigmund Freud*, translated by James Stratchey. Vol. 9. London: Hogarth, 1953–66.

Friesen, Stephen J. *Twice Neokoros: Ephesus, Asia and the Cult of the Flavian Imperial Family.* New York: Brill, 1993.

Garber, Marjorie. *Vested Interests: Cross-Dressing and Cultural Anxiety.* New York: Routledge, 1992.

Giles-Sims, Jean. "The Aftermath of Partner Violence." In *Partner Violence: A Comprehensive Review of 20 Years of Research*, edited by Jana L. Jasinski and Linda M. Williams, 44–72. Thousand Oaks: Sage, 1998.

Glancy, Jennifer. *Slavery in Early Christianity.* Oxford: Oxford University, 2002.

Glenny, W. Edward. "The Israelite imagery of 1 Peter 2." In *Dispensationalism, Israel and the Church*, edited by Draig A. Blaising and Darrell L. Bock, 156–87. Grand Rapids: Zondervan, 1992.

Goppelt, Leonhard. *A Commentary on I Peter*, translated by John E. Alsup.
Grand Rapids: Eerdmans, 1993.

Gross, Carl D. "Are the Wives of I Peter 3.7 Christians?" *Journal of the
Study of the New Testament* 35 (1989): 89–96.

Grosz, Elizabeth. "Bodies-Cities." In *Sexuality and Space*, edited by
Beatriz Colomina, Jennifer Bloomer, et al., 241–53. Princeton Papers on
Architecture 1. Princeton: Princeton Architectural Press, 1992.

Grothues, Carol A. and Shelly L. Marmion. "Dismantling the Myths about
Intimate Violence against Women." In *"Intimate" Violence against Women:
When Spouses, Partners, or Lovers Attack*, edited by Paula K. Lundberg-
Love and Shelly L. Marmion, 9–14. Westport, Conn.: Praeger, 2006.

Grudem, "Wives Like Sarah, and the Husbands Who Honor Them: 1 Peter
3:1-7." In *Recovering Biblical Manhood and Womanhood: A Response to
Evangelical Feminists*, edited by John Piper and Wayne Grudem, 194–208.
Wheaton: Crossway Books, 1991.

Harnack, Adolf von. *Die Chronologie der altchristlichen Litteratur bis
Irenaus*, 2nd ed. Vol. 1. Leipzig: Hinrichs, 1897.

Hartsock, Nancy C. M. "Foucault on Power: A Theory for Women?" In
Feminism/Postmodernism, edited by Linda J. Nicholson, 157–75. New
York: Routledge, 1990.

— *Money, Sex and Power: Toward a Feminist Historical Materialism*.
Boston: Northeastern University, 1985.

Hawley, Richard. "The Dynamics of Beauty in Classical Greece." In
*Changing Bodies, Changing Meanings: Studies on the Human Body in
Antiquity*, edited by Dominic Montserrat, 37–54. New York: Routledge,
1998.

Hennessy, Rosemary. *Materialist Feminism and the Politics of Discourse*.
New York: Routledge, 1993.

Hill, David. "On Suffering and Baptism in 1 Peter." *Novum Testamentum* 18
(1976): 181–9.

Horrell, David. "Between Conformity and Resistance: Beyond the Balch-
Elliott Debate Towards a Postcolonial Reading of First Peter." In *Reading
First Peter with New Eyes: Methodological Reassessments of the Letter of
First Peter*, edited by Robert L. Webb and Betsy Bauman-Martin, 111–43.
T&T Clark: New York, 2007.

— "Leadership Patterns and the Development of Ideology in Early
Christianity." *Sociology of Religion* 58, no. 4 (1997): 323–41.

Howe, Bonnie. *Because You Bear This Name: Conceptual Metaphor and the
Moral Meaning of 1 Peter*. Biblical Interpretation Series 81. Boston: Brill,
2006.

Hydén, Margareta. *Woman Battering as Marital Act: The Construction of a Violent Marriage*. Oslo: Scandinavian University, 1994.

Irigaray, Luce. *This Sex Which is Not One*. Translated by Catherine Porter with Carolyn Burke. Ithaca: Cornell University, 1985.

James, Steven. "Divine Justice and Retributive Duty of Civil Government." *Trinity Journal* 6, no. 2 (1985): 199–210.

Jameson, Frederic. *The Political Unconscious: Narrative as a Socially Symbolic Act*. Ithaca, NY: Cornell University, 1981.

Jasinski, Jana L. and Linda M. Williams. *Partner Violence: A Comprehensive Review of 20 Years of Research*. Thousand Oaks: Sage, 1998.

Jeffers, James S. *Conflict at Rome: Social Order and Hierarchy in Early Christianity*. Minneapolis: Fortress, 1991.

Johnson, E. Elizabeth. "Colossians." In *Women's Bible Commentary, Expanded Edition with Apocrypha*, edited by Carol A. Newsom and Sharon Ringe, 437–9. Louisville: Westminster John Knox, 1998.

— "Ephesians." In *Women's Bible Commentary, Expanded Edition with Apocrypha*, edited by Carol A. Newsom and Sharon Ringe, 428–32. Louisville: Westminster John Knox, 1998.

Johnson, Elizabeth A. *She Who Is: The Mystery of God in Feminist Theological Discourse*. New York: Crossroad, 1998.

Josephus. *Against Apion*. In *The Works of Josephus: Complete and Unabridged*, translated by William Whiston, 773–812. Peabody, Mass.: Hendrickson, 1987.

Kantor, Glenda Kaufman and Jana L. Jasinski. "Dynamics and Risk Factors in Partner Violence." In *Partner Violence: A Comprehensive Review of 20 Years of Research*, edited by Jana L. Jasinski and Linda M. Williams, 1–43. Thousand Oaks: Sage, 1998.

Keohane, Nannerl O., Michelle Z. Rosaldo, Barbara C. Gelpi, eds. *Feminist Theory: A Critique of Ideology*. Chicago: University of Chicago, 1982.

Kiley, Mark. "Like Sara: The Tale of Terror Behind 1 Peter 3:6." *Journal of Biblical Literature* 106 (1987): 689–92.

Kim, Jean K. "Uncovering her Nakedness: An Inter(con)textual Reading of Revelation 17 from a Postcolonial Feminist Perspective." *Journal for the Study of the New Testament* 73 (1999): 61–81.

— *Woman and Nation: An Intercontextual Reading of the Gospel of John from a Postcolonial Feminist Perspective*. Boston, Brill, 2004.

Kirsch, Jonathan. *The Woman Who Laughed at God: The Untold History of the Jewish People*. New York: Viking, 2001.

Kittredge, Cynthia Briggs. *Community and Authority: The Rhetoric of*

Obedience in the Pauline Tradition. Harvard Theological Studies 45.
Harrisburg, Pa.: Trinity, 1998.

Knox, John. "Pliny and 1 Peter: A Note on 1 Pet 4:14-16 and 3:15." *Journal
of Biblical Literature* 72, no. 3 (1953): 187–9.

Knox-Little, William J. *The Christian Home: Its Foundations and Duties*.
London: Longmans, Green & Co., 1895.

Krentz, Edgar. "Order in the 'House' of God: The *Haustafel* in 1 Peter
2:11-3:12." In *Common Life in the Early Church: Essays Honoring
Graydon Snyder*, edited by Julian Victor Hills and Richard B. Gardner,
279–85. Harrisburg, Pa.: Trinity, 1998.

Kroeger, Catherine Clark. "Toward a Pastoral Understanding of 1 Peter 3.1-6
and Related Texts." In *A Feminist Companion to the Catholic Epistles
and Hebrews*, edited by A.-J. Levine and Maria Mayo Robbins, 82–8.
Cleveland: Pilgrim, 2004.

Kwok, Pui Lan. *Postcolonial Imagination and Feminist Theology*.
Louisville: Westminster John Knox, 2005.

Lakoff, George and Mark Johnson, *The Metaphors We Live By*. Chicago:
University of Chicago, 1980.

Laquer, Walter Thomas. *Making Sex: Body and Gender from the Greeks to
Freud*. Cambridge: Harvard University, 1990.

Laub, Franz. *Die Begegnung des frühen Christentums mit der antiken
Sklaverei*. Stuttgart: Katholisches Bibelwerk, 1982.

Liddell, Henry George and Robert Scott. *A Greek-English Lexicon*, revised
and augmented by Sir Henry Stuart Jones and Roderick McKenzie. New
York: Oxford University, 1996.

Lohmeyer, Ernst. *Die Briefe an die Kolosser und an Philemon*. Göttingen:
Vandenhoeck & Ruprecht, 1961.

Lohse, Eduard. *Märtyer und Gottesknecht; Untersuchungen zur
urchristlichen Verkündigung vom Sühntod Jesu Christi*. Göttingen,
Vandenhoeck & Ruprecht, 1955.

Loomba, Ania. *Colonialism/Postcolonialism*. New York: Routledge,
2002.

Lührmann, Dieter. "Neutestamentliche Haustafeln und antike Ökonomie."
New Testament Studies 28 (1980).

— "Wo man nicht mehr Sklave oder Freier ist. Überlegungen zur Struktur
frühchristlicher Gemeinden." *Wort und Dienst* 13 (1975): 53–83.

Luz, Ulrich. *Matthew in History: Interpretation, Influence, and Effects*.
Minneapolis: Fortress, 1994.

MacDonald, Dennis Ronald. *The Legend and the Apostle: The Battle for
Paul in Story and Canon*. Philadelphia: Westminster, 1983.

MacDonald, Margaret Y. *Early Christian Women and Pagan Opinion: The Power of the Hysterical Woman*. Cambridge, UK: Cambridge University Press, 1996.
— "Early Christian Women Married to Unbelievers." *Studies in Religion* 19 (1990): 221–34.
— *The Pauline Churches: A Socio-Historical Study of Institutionalization in the Pauline and Deutero-Pauline Letters*. New York: Cambridge University Press, 1988.
MacIntyre, Alasdair C. *After Virtue: A Study in Moral Theory*. Notre Dame: Notre Dame University, 1981.
Malherbe, Abraham. *Moral Exhortation: A Greco-Roman Sourcebook*. Philadelphia: Westminster, 1986.
Marchal, Joseph A. *Hierarchy, Unity and Imitation: A Feminist Rhetorical Analysis of Power Dynamics in Paul's Letter to the Philippians*. Academia Biblica 24. Atlanta: Society of Biblical Literature, 2006.
— *The Politics of Heaven: Women, Gender and Empire in the Study of Paul*. Minneapolis: Fortress, 2008.
Martin, Clarice J. "The *Haustafeln* (Household Codes) in African American Biblical Interpretation: 'Free Slaves' and 'Subordinate Women.'" In *Stony the Road We Trod: African American Biblical Interpretation*, edited by Cain Hope Felder, 206–31. Minneapolis: Fortress, 1991.
Martin, Dale. *The Corinthian Body*. New Haven: Yale University, 1995.
Martin, Troy W. *Metaphor and Composition in 1 Peter*. Society of Biblical Literature Dissertation Series 131. Atlanta: Scholars Press, 1992.
— "The Rehabilitation of a Rhetorical Step-Child: First Peter and Classical Rhetorical Criticism." In *Reading First Peter with New Eyes: Methodological Reassessments of the Letter of First Peter*, edited by Robert L. Webb and Betsy Bauman-Martin, 41–71. T&T Clark: New York, 2007.
Mauch, T. M. "Sojourner." In *Interpreter's Dictionary of the Bible*, vol. 4, edited by George Arthur Buttrick, et al., 337–9. New York: Abingdon, 1962.
McDermott, Patrice. *Politics and Scholarship: Feminist Academic Journals and the Production of Knowledge*. Chicago: University of Illinois, 1994.
McGuire, Ann. "Equality and Subordination in Christ: Displacing the Powers of the Household Code in Colossians." In *Religion and Economic Ethics*. Annual Publication of the College Theology Society, 31, edited by Joseph Gower, 65–85. Lanham, Md.: University Press of America, 1990.
Michaels, J. Ramsey. "St. Peter's Passion: The Passion Narrative in 1 Peter." *Word and World* 24, no. 4 (2004): 387–94.
Millar, Fergus. *The Emperor in the Roman World (31 BC–AD 337)*. London: Duckworth, 1992.

Millauer, Helmut. *Leiden als Gnade: eine traditionsgeschichtliche Untersuchung zur Leidenstheologie des ersten Petrusbriefes*. Bern: Herbert Lang, 1976.

Miller, Jean Baker and Irene Pierce Stiver. *The Healing Connection: How Women Form Relationships in Therapy and in Life*. Boston: Beacon, 1997.

Misset-van de Weg, Magda. "Een vrouwenspiegel, 1 Petrus 3, 1-6." In *Proeven van Vrouwenstudies Theologi*, vol. 4, edited by A.-M. Kort, et al., 145–82. IIMO Research Publication 44. Zoetermeer: Meinema, 1996.

— "Sarah Imagery in 1 Peter." In *A Feminist Companion to the Catholic Epistles and Hebrews*, edited by A.-J. Levine and Maria Mayo Robbins, 50–62. Cleveland: Pilgrim, 2004.

Mitchell, Margaret M. *Paul and the Rhetoric of Reconciliation: An Exegetical Investigation of the Language and Composition of 1 Corinthians*. Tübingen: J. C. B. Mohr, 1991.

Moi, Toril. *Sexual/Textual Politics: Feminist Literary Theory*. 2nd ed. New York: Routledge, 2002.

Moore, Stephen D. *Empire and Apocalypse: Postcolonialism and the New Testament*. Sheffield: Sheffield Phoenix Press, 2006.

Morris, Celia. *Bearing Witness: Sexual Harassment and Beyond — Everywoman's Story*. New York: Little, Brown and Company, 1994.

Müller, Karlheinz. "Die Haustafel des Kolosserbriefes und das antike Frauenthema: Eine kritische Rückschau auf alte Ergebnisse." In *Die Frau im Urchristentum*, edited by G. Dautzenberg, et al., 263–319. Freiburg: Herder, 1983.

Murphy-O'Connor, Jerome. *Paul the Letter-Writer: His World, His Options, His Skills*. Collegeville, Minn.: Liturgical, 1995.

Needham, Anuradha Dingwaney. *Using the Master's Tools: Resistance and the Literature of the African and South-Asian Diasporas*. New York: St. Martin's, 2000.

Nelson, T. S. *For Love of Country: Confronting Rape and Sexual Harassment in the U.S. Military*. New York: Haworth Maltreatment and Trauma, 2002.

Neyrey, Jerome H. *Paul, In Other Words: A Cultural Reading of His Letters*. Louisville: Westminster/John Knox, 1990.

Nichols, Brittney. "Violence against Women: The Extent of the Problem." In *"Intimate" Violence against Women: When Spouses, Partners, or Lovers Attack*, edited by Paula K. Lundberg-Love and Shelly L. Marmion, 1–8. Westport, Conn.: Praeger, 2006.

Nicholson, Linda J., ed. *Feminism/Postmodernism*. New York: Routledge, 1990.

O'Brien, Mary. *The Politics of Reproduction*. Boston: Routledge, 1981.

O'Brien, Peter T. "Letters, Letter Forms." In *Dictionary of Paul and His Letters*, edited by Gerald F. Hawthorne, Ralph P. Martin, and Daniel G. Reid, 550–3. Downers Grove, Ill.: InterVarsity, 1993.

Odell-Scott, David W. *A Post-Patriarchal Christology*. Atlanta: Scholars Press, 1992.

Økland, Jorunn. *Women in Their Place: Paul and the Corinthian Discourse of Gender and Sanctuary Space*. *Journal for the Study of the New Testament*, Supplement Series 269. New York: T&T Clark, 2004.

Osiek, Carolyn. "The Bride of Christ (5:22–23): A Problematic Wedding." *Biblical Theology Bulletin* 32, no. 1 (2002): 29–39.

Osiek, Carolyn, Margaret Y. MacDonald with Janet H. Tulloch. *A Woman's Place: House Churches in Earliest Christianity*. Minneapolis: Fortress, 2006.

Pateman, Carole. "Introduction." In *Feminist Challenges: Social and Political Theory*, edited by Carole Pateman and Elizabeth Gross, 1–13. Boston: Northeastern University, 1981.

Patte, Daniel. *Paul's Faith and the Power of the Gospel: A Structural Introduction to the Pauline Letters*. Philadelphia: Fortress, 1983.

Pearson, Sharon Clark. *The Christological and Rhetorical Properties of 1 Peter*. Studies in Bible and Early Christianity 45. Lewiston, NY: Edwin Mellon, 2001.

Perdelwitz, Richard. *Die Mysterienreligion und das Problem des I. Petrusbriefes: Ein literarischer und religionsgeschichtlicher Versuch*. Religionsgeschichtliche und Vorarbeiten 11, no. 3; Giessen: Töpelmann, 1911.

Phillips, Elaine. "Incredulity, Faith, and Textual Purposes: Post-biblical Responses to the Laughter of Abraham and Sarah." In *The Function of Scripture in Early Jewish and Christian Tradition. Journal for the Study of the New Testament* Supplement Series 154. Studies in Scripture in Early Judaism and Christianity 6, edited by Craig A. Evans and James A. Sanders, 22–33. Sheffield: Sheffield Academic, 1998.

Philo. *Apology for the Jews*. In *The Works of Philo: Complete and Unabridged, in one volume*. Translated by C. D. Yonge, 742–6. Peabody, Mass.: Hendrickson, 2000.

Pomeroy, Sarah B. *Xenophon, Oeconomicus: A Social and Historical Commentary*. New York: Oxford University, 1994.

Price, S. R. F. *Rituals and Power: The Roman imperial cult in Asia Minor*. 1984; repr. Cambridge: Cambridge University Press, 1998.

Prior, Michael, CM. *The Bible and Colonialism: A Moral Critique*. The Biblical Seminar 48. Sheffield: Sheffield Academic, 1999.

Pryor, John W. "First Peter and the New Covenant (II)." *Reformed Theological Review* 45, no. 1: 1–4; 45, no. 2: 44–51.

Ramsay, W. M. "The Church and the Empire in the First Century, III: The First Epistle Attributed to St. Peter." *Expositor* 4, no. 8 (1893): 282–96.

Rengstorf, Karl Heinrich. "Die neutestamentlichen Mahnungen an die Frau, sich dem Manne unterzuordnen." In *Verbum Dei manet in aeternum: Eine Festschrift für Otto Schmitz zu seinem siebzigsten Geburtstaf am 16. Juni 1953*, edited by Werner Foerster and Otto Schmitz, 131–45. Witten: Luther-Verlag, 1953.

Richardson, Robert L., Jr. "From 'Subjection to Authority' to 'Mutual Submission': The Ethic of Subordination in 1 Peter." *Faith and Mission* 4 (1987): 70–80.

Ringe, Sharon. "1-2 Peter, Jude." In *Global Bible Commentary*, edited by Daniel Patte, Teresa Okure, et al., 545–52. Nashville: Abingdon, 2004.

Rostovtzeff, Michael Ivanovitch. *The Social and Economic History of the Roman Empire*. New York: Oxford, 1926.

Rothkoff, Aaron. "Sarah." In *Encyclopedia Judaica*. Vol. 18, editor-in-chief, Fred Skolnik, executive editor, Michael Berenbaum, 46–7. Detroit: Macmillan Reference, 2007.

Rubin, Gayle. "The Traffic of Women" In *Toward an Anthropology of Women*, edited by Rayna R. Reiter, 157–210. New York: Monthly Review Press, 1975.

Said, Edward. *Culture and Imperialism.* New York: Vintage, 1994.
— *Orientalism.* New York: Vintage, 1994.

Sampley, J. Paul. *'And the Two Shall Become One Flesh': A Study of Traditions in Ephesians 5:21-33*. Society for New Testament Studies, Manuscript Series 16. Cambridge: Cambridge University, 1971.

Schertz, Mary H. "Nonretaliation and the Haustafeln in 1 Peter." In *The Love of Enemy and Nonretaliation in the New Testament*, edited by W. H. Swartley, 258–86. Louisville: Westminster John Knox, 1992.

Schnarch, David Morris. *Passionate Marriage: Love, Sex and Intimacy in Emotionally Committed Relationships*. New York: H. Holt, 1998.

Schottroff, Luise. *Feminist Interpretation: The Bible in Women's Perspective*. Minneapolis: Fortress, 1998.

Schroeder, David. *Die Haustafeln des Neuen Testaments*. Hamburg Dissertation, 1959.

Schüssler Fiorenza, Elisabeth. "1 Peter." In *A Postcolonial Commentary on the New Testament Writings*, edited by Fernando F. Segovia and R. S. Sugirtharajah, 380–403. Sheffield: Sheffield Academic, 2007.

— *Bread Not Stone: The Challenge of Feminist Biblical Interpretation.* Boston: Beacon, 1984.

— "Discipleship and Patriarchy: Early Christian Ethos and Christian Ethics in a Feminist Theological Perspective." *Annual of the Society of Christian Ethics* 2, no. 1 (1982): 131–72.

— *In Memory of Her: A Feminist Theological Reconstruction of Christian Origins.* New York: Crossroads, 1992.

— "Introduction: Crossing Canonical Boundaries." In *Searching the Scriptures, Volume 2: A Feminist Commentary*, edited by Elisabeth Schüssler Fiorenza, Ann Brock and Shelly Matthews, 1–14. New York: Crossroad, 1993.

— "The Praxis of Co-equal Discipleship." In *Paul and Empire: Religion and Power in Roman Imperial Society*, edited by Richard Horsley, 224–42. Harrisburg, Pa.: Trinity, 1997.

— *Rhetoric and Ethic: The Politics of Biblical Studies.* Minneapolis: Fortress, 1999.

Schüssler Fiorenza, Elisabeth, Ann Brock and Shelly Matthews, eds. *Searching the Scriptures, Volume 2: A Feminist Commentary.* New York: Crossroad, 1993.

Scott, James C. *Domination and the Arts of Resistance: Hidden Transcripts.* New Haven: Yale University, 1990.

Scott, Stephen. *Why Do They Dress That Way?* People's Place Book 7. Intercourse, Pa.: Good Books, 1997.

Sedgwick, Peter. "Essentialism." In *Cultural Theory: The Key Concepts*, edited by Andrew Edgar and Peter Sedgwick, 131–2. New York: Routledge, 2002.

Segovia, Fernando. "Biblical Criticism and Postcolonial Studies: Toward a Postcolonial Optic." In *The Postcolonial Bible*, edited by R. S. Sugirtharajah, 49–65. Sheffield: Sheffield, 1998.

Segovia, Fernando F. *Decolonizing Biblical Studies: A View from the Margins.* Maryknoll, NY: Orbis, 2004.

Segovia, Fernando and R. S. Sugirtharajah, eds. *A Postcolonial Commentary on the New Testament Writings.* Sheffield: Sheffield Press, 2007.

Segovia, Fernando and Stephen Moore, eds. *Postcolonial Biblical Criticism: Interdisciplinary Intersections.* New York: T&T Clark, 2005.

Seland, Torrey. *Strangers in the Light: Philonic Perspectives on Christian Identity in 1 Peter.* Boston: Brill, 2005.

Selwyn, Edward Gordon. *The First Epistle of Saint Peter: The Greek Text with Introduction, Notes and Essays.* London: Macmillan, 1946.

Sharpe, Jenny. "The Unspeakable Limits of Rape: Colonial Violence and

Counter-Insurgency." In *Colonial Discourse and Post-Colonial Theory: A Reader*, edited by Patrick Williams and Laura Chrisman, 221–43. New York: Columbia University, 1994.

Shivanandan, Mary. "Feminism and Marriage: A Reflection on Ephesians 5:21-33." *Diakonia* 29, no. 1 (1996): 5–22.

Silverman, Kaja. "Fragments of a Fashionable Discourse." In *Studies in Entertainment: Critical Approaches to Mass Culture*, edited by Tania Modleski, 139–52. Bloomington: Indiana University, 1986.

Slaughter, James. "Peter's Instructions to Husbands in 1 Peter 3:7." In *Integrity of Heart, Skillfulness of Hands*, edited by Charles H. Dyer, Roy B. Zuck and Donald K. Campbell, 175–85. Grand Rapids: Baker Book House, 1994.

— "Sarah as a Model for Christian Wives (1 Pet. 3:5-6)." *Bibliotheca Sacra* 153 (1996): 357–65.

— "The Submission of Wives (1 Pet 3:1a) in the Context of 1 Peter." *Bibliotheca Sacra* 153 (1996): 63–74.

— "Winning Unbelieving Husbands to Christ (1 Peter 3:1b-4)." *Bibliotheca Sacra* 153 (1996): 199–211.

Sleeper, C. Freedman. "Political Responsibility According to I Peter." *Novum Testamentum* 10 (1968): 270–89.

Sly, Dorothy I. "1 Peter 3:6b in the Light of Philo and Josephus." *Journal of Biblical Literature* 110 (1991): 126–9.

Smart, Carol. "Disruptive Bodies and Unruly Sex: The Regulation of Reproduction and Sexuality in the Nineteenth Century." In *Regulating Womanhood: Historical Essays on Marriage, Motherhood and Sexuality*, edited by Carol Smart, 7–32. New York: Routledge, 1992.

Spencer, John R. "Sojourner." In *Anchor Bible Dictionary*, vol. 6, editor-in-chief David Noel Freedman, 103–4. New York: Doubleday, 1992.

Spender, Dale. *For the Record: The Making and Meaning of Feminist Knowledge*. London: The Women's Press, 1985.

Spivak, Gayatri Chakrovorty. "Can the Subaltern Speak?" In *Colonial Discourse and Post-Colonial Theory: A Reader*, edited by Patrick Williams and Laura Chrisman, 66–111. New York: Columbia University, 1994.

— *A Critique of Postcolonial Reason: Toward a History of the Vanishing Present*. Cambridge, Mass.: Harvard University, 1999.

Stanton, Elizabeth Cady. "Epistles of Peter and John." In *The Woman's Bible*, edited by Elizabeth Cady Stanton, 174–5. Seattle: Coalition Task Force on Women and Religion, 1974.

Steady, Filomina Chioma, ed. *Black Women, Globalization, and Economic Justice: Studies from Africa and the African Diaspora*. Rochester, Vt.: Schenkman Books, 2002.

Subcommittee on Africa, Global Human Rights, and International
    Operations. "Germany's World Cup brothels: 40,000 women and children
    at risk of exploitation through trafficking." No pages. Online: *http://www.
    internationalrelations.house.gov/archives/109/27330.PDF*.
Sugirtharajah, R. S. "Biblical Studies after the Empire: From a Colonial to a
    Postcolonial Mode of Interpretation." In *The Postcolonial Bible. The Bible
    and Postcolonialism*, 1, edited by R.S. Sugirtharajah, 12–23. Sheffield:
    Sheffield Academic Press, 1999.
— "Postcolonial and Biblical Interpretation: The Next Phase." In *A
    Postcolonial Commentary on the New Testament Writings*, edited by
    Fernando F. Segovia and R. S. Sugirtharajah, 455–66. Sheffield: Sheffield
    Press, 2007.
— *The Postcolonial Bible*. Sheffield: Sheffield Academic Press, 1998.
Talbert, Charles. "Once Again: The Plan of 1 Peter." In *Perspectives on
    First Peter*. National Association of Baptist Professors in Religion,
    Special Study Series 9, edited by Charles Talbert, 141–51. Macon: Mercer
    University, 1986.
— ed. *Perspectives on First Peter*. National Association of Baptist Professors
    in Religion, Special Study Series 9. Macon: Mercer University, 1986.
Tanzer, Sarah. "Ephesians." In *Searching the Scriptures, Volume 2: A
    Feminist Commentary*, edited by Elisabeth Schüssler Fiorenza, Ann Brock,
    and Shelly Matthews, 328–9. New York: Crossroad, 1993.
Theissen, Gerd. *The Social Setting of Pauline Christianity: Essays on
    Corinth*. Philadelphia: Fortress, 1982.
Thistlethwaite, Susan Brooks. "Every Two Minutes: Battered Women and
    Feminist Interpretation." In *Feminist Interpretation of the Bible*, edited by
    Letty M. Russell, 96–107. Philadelphia: Westminster, 1985.
Thompson, James W. "The Rhetoric of 1 Peter." *Restoration Quarterly* 36
    (1994): 237–50.
Thorne-Finch, Ron. *Ending the Silence: The Origins and Treatment of Male
    Violence against Women*. Buffalo: University of Toronto, 1992.
Thraede, Klaus. "Zum historischen Hintergrund der 'Haustafeln' des NT."
    In *Pietas: Festschrift für Bernhard Kötting*, edited by Ernst Dassmann und
    K. Suso Frank, 359–68. *Jahrbuch für Antike und Christentum*, 8. Münster:
    Aschendorff, 1980.
Thurén, Lauri. "Jeremiah 27 and Civil Obedience in 1 Peter." In *Zwischen
    den Reichen: Neues Testament und Römische Herrschaft: Vorträge auf der
    Ersten Konferenz der European Association for Biblical Studies*, edited
    by Michael Labahn and Jrgen Zangenberb, 215–28. Tübingen: A. Francke
    Verlag, 2002.

— *The Rhetorical Strategy of 1 Peter with Special Regard to Ambiguous Expressions*. Åbo: Åbo Academy Press, 1990.

Torrance, Thomas Forsyth. *Royal Priesthood*. Edinburgh: Oliver and Boyd, 1955.

Trible, Phyllis. *Texts of Terror: Literary-Feminist Readings of Biblical Narratives*. Philadelphia: Fortress, 1984.

Vas Dias, Susan. "Inner Silence: One of the Impacts of Emotional Abuse Upon the Developing Self." In *Psychodynamic Perspectives on Abuse: The Cost of Fear*, edited by Una McCluskey and Carol-Ann Hooper, 159–71. Philadelphia: Jessica Kingsley, 2000.

Volf, Miroslav. "Soft Difference: Theological Reflections on the Relation Between Church and Culture in 1 Peter." *Ex auditu* 10 (1994): 15–30.

Walker, William O. "The 'Theology of Women's Place' and the 'Paulinist' Tradition." *Semeia* 28 (1983): 101–12.

Wallace-Hadrill, Andrew. "Patronage in Roman Society: From Republic to Empire." In *Patronage in Ancient Society*, edited by Andrew Wallace-Hadrill, 63–87. New York: Routledge, 1989.

Warden, Duane. "Imperial Persecution and the Dating of 1 Peter and Revelation." *Journal of the Evangelical Theological Society* 34 (1991): 203–12.

Webb, Robert L. "Intertexture and Rhetorical Strategy in First Peter's Apocalyptic Discourse: A Study in Sociorhetorical Interpretation." In *Reading First Peter with New Eyes: Methodological Reassessments of the Letter of First Peter*, edited by Webb, Robert L. and Betsy Bauman-Martin, 72–110. T&T Clark: New York, 2007.

Webb, Robert L. and Betsy Bauman-Martin, eds. *Reading First Peter with New Eyes: Methodological Reassessments of the Letter of First Peter*. T&T Clark: New York, 2007.

Weidinger, Karl. *Die Haustafeln, ein Stück urchristlicher Paranaese*. Untersuchen Neuen Testament 14. Leipzig: J. C. Heinrich, 1928.

Wengst, Klaus. *Pax Romana and the Peace of Christ*. Translated by John Bowden. London: SCM Press, 1987.

Wheelwright, Philip. *Metaphor & Reality*. Bloomington, Ill.: Indiana University, 1962. Repr. Eugene, Ore.: Wipf and Stock, 1997.

White, Genevieve. *Daughters of Sarah*. Columbus, Ga.: Brentwood Christian, 1991.

White, Jacquelyn. "Aggression and Gender." In *Encyclopedia of Women and Gender: Sex Similarities and Differences and the Impact of Society on Gender*. Vol. 1, editor-in-chief Judith Worell, 81–93. San Diego: Academic Press, 2001.

Windisch, Hans. *Die katholischen Briefe*, revised by Herbert Preisker. Tübingen: J. C. B. Mohr, 1951.

Winter, Bruce. *Seek the Welfare of the City: Christians as Benefactors and Citizens*. Grand Rapids: Eerdmans, 1994.

Wire, Antoinette Clark. *The Corinthian Women Prophets: A Reconstruction through Paul's Rhetoric*. Minneapolis: Fortress, 1990.

Wittgenstein, Ludwig. *Tractatus Logico-Philosophicus*, translated by D. F. Pears and B. F. McGuinness. London: Routledge & Kegan Paul, 1975.

Xenophon. *Memorabilia; Oeconomicus*. Loeb Classical Library 168, translated by E. C. Marchant and O. J. Todd. Cambridge, Mass.: Harvard University, 1992.

Zerubavel, Eviatar. *The Elephant in the Room: Silence and Denial in Everyday Life*. New York: Oxford University, 2006.

INDEX OF ANCIENT SOURCES

Index of Modern Authors